PROGRAMMING
IN
COMMON
LISP

PROGRAMMING IN COMMON LISP

RODNEY A. BROOKS
Massachusetts Institute of Technology

John Wiley & Sons
New York   Chichester
Brisbane   Toronto   Singapore

Library of Congress Cataloging in Publication Data:

Brooks, Rodney Allen.
 Programming in Common LISP.

 Includes indexes.
 1. LISP (Computer program language)   I. Title.
QA76.73.L23B76   1985   001.64'24   85-9587
ISBN 0-471-81888-7

Printed in the United States of America

10 9 8 7 6 5 4 3 2 1

TO NUI

PREFACE

Lisp is the second oldest computer language still in everyday use (the oldest is Fortran). Other computer languages were aimed primarily at solving numeric problems—for instance, adding up debits and credits in business applications, simulating loads and stresses in engineering, counting events in physics experiments, solving differential equations for ballistics tables, and compiling statistics for the census bureau.

Lisp was designed to make it possible to compute with abstract symbols rather than with numbers. The earliest applications were in writing programs that could prove theorems. This soon extended to programs that could do symbolic algebra.[1]

Lisp soon become the major language for work in artificial intelligence. It is used for programs for such diverse tasks as understanding textual natural language, spoken language, computer vision, medical diagnosis (and more generally "expert systems"), automatic programming, program verification proof systems, symbolic algebra systems (e.g., REDUCE and MACSYMA), planning systems, and robot control systems.

In addition, Lisp recently has become a popular language in which to write compilers for other languages, VLSI design systems, mechanical CAD systems, and animation graphics. Originally, Lisp was used only on general-purpose computers, but now special-purpose "Lisp machines" have become common.

LISP DIALECTS

Unlike Pascal or Fortran, there has been no solid language definition for Lisp. In fact, there are more incompatible dialects of Lisp than there are machine architectures on which Lisp runs. Happily, that situation is now changing.

---

[1] As an example of the difference between numeric and symbolic algebra consider the problem of finding the derivative of $f(x) = x^2 + 3x + 4$. A numeric program could find the derivative at any particular point; for example, at $x = 1.5$ the derivative is 6.0, but a symbolic differentiation program would decide that the derivative was $2x + 3$.

Lisp was first developed at MIT in 1959. On an early IBM machine, Lisp 1.5 was the first "public" Lisp system. Thereafter, reasonably compatible versions of Lisp 1.5 were implemented on a variety of machines. Two distinct dialects, modifications, and improvements on the original arose over the next few years.

BBN-Lisp was first implemented on the PDP-1 and then on the SDS-940, and eventually grew into Interlisp on the PDP-10 (an immediate precursor to the DEC-20). More recently, there have been implementations of Interlisp for the VAX and a line of personal Lisp machines made by Xerox.

Meanwhile, at MIT a new implementation of Lisp was begun for the PDP-6 (a direct precursor of the PDP-10). It became known as Maclisp and runs on DEC-20s today. An early version of Maclisp went to Stanford and became Lisp 1.6. That split off again in two directions: UCI-Lisp at the University of California at Irvine and Standard Lisp at the University of Utah. Maclisp development continued independently at MIT, inspiring a host of descendent and reasonably compatible dialects. The major one was Lisp Machine Lisp, a large extension of the language for personal Lisp machines designed and built at MIT. Two manufacturing companies sprang up for Lisp machines and two subdialects developed. In addition, Franz Lisp was developed for the VAX (under UNIX) at Berkeley, and Nil, another descendant of Maclisp, was developed for the VAX (under VMS) at MIT. All the descendants of Maclisp were now slightly or grossly mutually incompatible. Finally, in 1981 a Common Lisp committee was formed to try to bring order to the chaos of the Maclisp world. They have recently defined a version of Lisp that all the current Maclisp descendant groups have agreed to work toward.

This new Lisp is called Common Lisp. There is a manual and language specification called *Common Lisp: The Language* by Guy L. Steele (see appendix 3). Common Lisp is being adopted by a large number of government and industrial organizations as the implementation language for their artificial intelligence systems. Many companies (including Lisp machine companies) now offer Common Lisp for their computers. It is available on some personal computers, and despite the popularity of PROLOG in Japan, there are implementations of Common Lisp available from Japanese organizations too.

Common Lisp has two key virtues:

- Many of the inconsistencies and illogical conventions in earlier Lisp dialects have been removed or rationalized. Common Lisp is a very "clean" dialect of Lisp.
- The existence of a complete specification of the language and a published manual ensures that programs will be *transportable*. Programs written in Common Lisp and debugged on one manufacturer's machine should run on another manufacturer's machine without change.

GOOD PROGRAMMING AND COMMON LISP

This book is about writing good programs in Lisp. The dialect chosen to illustrate both Lisp and good Lisp is Common Lisp.

The theme of what is said throughout the book applies to most dialects of Lisp. There may be some small variations in details for other dialects. The details of these variations are given for Maclisp and for Franz Lisp in Appendix 1.

The book is divided into 12 chapters and five major sections.

- Chapters 1, 2, 3, and 4 introduce the fundamentals of Lisp. With just these techniques it is possible to write quite complex artifical intelligence programs. By the time we reach the end of chapter 4, for instance, we will be able to write a system to store and retrieve facts about family-member relationships and a natural language understanding system to let us query and update our family database in English.

- Chapter 5 deals with principles of good programming style and introduces Lisp debugging techniques. Good Lisp style is harder to develop than good style in other languages. Lisp does provide a much richer set of debugging tools, however.

- Chapters 6 and 7 round out the basic elements of Lisp, including input and output and using functions as data objects. Many practicing Lisp programmers will be surprised to learn that there is much more to Lisp than is covered up to this point.

- Chapters 8, 9, and 10 discuss how Lisp works on a real machine and thus motivate the usefulness and power of Lisp macros. Lisp macros are explained at some length and examples are given of how to exploit their power in order to embed other languages in Lisp.

- Chapters 11 and 12 round out the discussion of programming in Common Lisp in two ways. First, very advanced features of Lisp are introduced, including nonlocal exits and multiple-valued functions. Second, some of the more "traditional" parts of Lisp (such as the "program" feature) are introduced for the first time. These parts of Lisp are anachronisms and are included only to help the reader to understand existing Lisp programs written in the baroque style of bygone days. They are included in the official Common Lisp language definition so that old programs can run unchanged in Common Lisp.

The chapters are designed to be read from page 1 through to the last page in the order in which they are numbered. The whole book makes a fast-paced course for a single quarter for enthusiastic undergraduate or graduate students with previous programming experience in a modern computer language. The same material also could be spread over a full semester at a more leisurely pace.

The book was developed from a set of notes prepared at Stanford University to teach CS-122 (formerly CS-102) *Programming in Lisp*.

Throughout the book you will see the road sign that heads this paragraph. It indicates that the following paragraphs describe aspects of Common Lisp that may differ from other Lisps. Refer to the corresponding section of Appendix 1 for details.

Most sections have quick exercises associated with them, many of which can be done without a computer, although you might find it interesting to check your answers on a machine and explore any misunderstandings. At the end of each chapter are more substantial problem sets that require the writing and debugging of Lisp programs. These problems require the synthesis of concepts introduced throughout the chapter. Solutions are presented in Appendix 2.

While the book introduces Common Lisp and shows how to write efficient and beautiful programs in Common Lisp, it does not completely specify the language. After all, the Common Lisp manual is a much thicker book than this one. Once the contents of this book are mastered, however, a Lisp programmer will have no trouble in using the manual to find the exact details of obscure nooks and crannies of the language.

ACKNOWLEDGMENTS

This book grew out of course notes for an introductory Lisp course at Stanford University. Many students in that course gave advice and provided criticisms that led to the writing of this book. Additional encouragement was provided by Bill Scherlis and Dick Gabriel. Atul Bajpai, Steve Gordon, Sathya Narayanan, Eric Benson, and Dan Weinreb read early drafts, and their comments have significantly improved the presentation. Matt Mason and Wade Henessey have taught courses from a draft of this book and have provided valuable feedback. Ana Haunga and Claudia Smith provided valuable help in manuscript preparation. Throughout it all, Nui has been patient beyond belief and has provided much encouragement. This book is dedicated to her.

CONTENTS

1

ESSENTIAL LISP

The essential elements of Lisp are few and fit into a uniform and regular structure. This chapter introduces almost all of the major conceptual ideas in Lisp. The rest of the book builds on these concepts (literally and figuratively), and also explains the blemishes in the regular structure introduced here.

The two major components of Lisp are a list-based representation of data and an interpreter, or evaluator, that treats some lists as programs.

1.1 WHAT DOES LISP LOOK LIKE?

A few examples of some Lisp statements follow. The Lisp system types a prompt "eval> "[1] to the user, who responds by typing a Lisp statement. The Lisp system responds in turn by "evaluating" the statement and printing the result on the line below.

```
eval> (+ 2 3)
5

eval> (+ 2 (* 3 4))
14

eval> (CAR '(A B C))
A

eval> (CDR '(A B C))
(B C)

eval> (CONS 'A '(B C))
(A B C)

eval> (CONS '+ '(2 3))
(+ 2 3)

eval> (CAR (CONS '+ '(2 3)))
+

eval> (CDR (CONS '+ '(2 3)))
(2 3)
```

---

[1]Different Lisp systems will use different prompts; none is standard. We will use "eval> " as our prompt throughout the book.

```
eval> (CAR (CDR '(+ 2 3))
2

eval> (CAR (CDR '(A (B C) D)))
(B C)

eval> (CAR (CAR (CDR '(A (B C) D))))
B

eval> (CONS 'FRUIT
            (CDR (SUBST 'BANANA
                        'ARROW
                        '(TIME FLIES LIKE AN ARROW))))
(FRUIT FLIES LIKE AN BANANA)
```

The foregoing examples illustrate two of the key properties of Lisp:

- Lisp provides an interactive system in which the user types an expression and Lisp *interprets* it (or *evaluates* it) and prints out the result. Thus, large programs can be built and tested incrementally, and at each stage of testing the full power of Lisp is available to examine the state of the program and data structures. Rather than go through another edit–compile–link–run cycle to test a bug hypothesis, the user can test it directly by typing Lisp statements to the interpreter.

- Lisp programs and data have the same form. An often-touted consequence of this is that Lisp programs can modify themselves. A more important result is that it is very simple to write embedded languages in Lisp. For a particular application, a user often can very quickly write a language (i.e., a translator from the language into Lisp) that is in some way well suited to the problem being solved.

Other key properties of Lisp are

- Lisp systems manage storage allocation for the user by providing a dynamic heap of storage that is allocated for data storage as needed, and then "garbage collected" (i.e., reclaimed) in a manner invisible to the user when no longer needed. The user is freed from worrying *a priori* about how much storage will be needed for a particular procedure over all possible inputs.

- Most Lisp systems include a compiler that compiles programs written in Lisp into efficient machine code. Thus, user programs can be run efficiently. In addition, a user-written embedded language can be compiled into machine code essentially for free; it need only translate user language programs into Lisp.

■ Lisp functions (equivalent to subroutines or procedures in other languages) are data objects that can be passed as parameters to other functions. This makes it possible to write extensible control structures in user programs that are very difficult to duplicate in more traditional languages.

1.2 CONSES AND ATOMS

Every Lisp object, whether a program or data, is either a *cons* or an *atom*.

Atoms are objects that are atomic, or indivisible, in nature.[2] Numbers— for example, 3, 5.7, and -2—are atoms. Symbols also are atoms. Roughly, a *symbol* is something that can be typed as a string of characters, excluding spaces and parentheses and including characters that make it invalid as a number. For example, A, CAR, B12, and NIL are all symbols as well as atoms. Symbols in Lisp play the roles of both reserved words and variables in other languages. They also play a deeper role, providing uniquely identifiable objects for reference.

There is a special symbol (and hence atom) in Lisp of pervasive importance —NIL. We will see it on almost every page of this book.

A cons is an ordered *conjunction* of two other Lisp objects; each of them might be another cons or an atom. A cons is represented in a computer as a pair of storage elements, each of which can contain a reference to (i.e., the address of, or a pointer to) another Lisp object. We often refer to conses as cons cells, and will illustrate their internal representation as boxes with two compartments. For instance,

If a compartment is a reference to an atom, we will write the printed representation of the atom directly in the compartment. If it is a reference to another cons cell, we will draw an arrow to a picture of that cons cell.

The function CONS is used to construct a cons. A Lisp function, named by a symbol, takes arguments, does some computation, and returns a result.[3] For instance, (CONS 'B 'NIL) gives two arguments, B and NIL, to the function CONS, which constructs a cons of the atoms B and NIL. We can illustrate it as

---

[2]This is not strictly true in Lisp, as we will see later, but it was true in early Lisps. The same thing happened in physics, so we should not be too embarrassed by this nomenclature.

[3]Lisp functions play the roles of both built-in operators and user-defined procedures or subroutines of other languages. Built-in Lisp functions are referred to as *predefined functions*.

We can illustrate the result of (CONS 'A 'B) as

The two parts of a cons are accessible by the functions CAR and CDR. For example,

```
eval> (CAR (CONS 'A 'B))
A

eval> (CDR (CONS 'A 'B))
B

eval> (CAR (CDR (CONS '2 (CONS 'BAD 'NIL))))
BAD
```

Function CAR accesses the left compartment of a cons cell and CDR accesses the right. The box notation representation of the cons cells constructed in the foregoing third example is

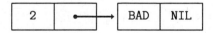

Lisp systems do not display cons cells to the user in this box notation. Rather, they list the contents in a linear character string using parentheses to delimit cons cells.[4]

The printed representation of a cons starts with a left parenthesis and ends with a right parenthesis. Atoms never contain parentheses, and so the distinction is clear.

If a cons is made up of an atom and NIL, the atom is simply printed between the parentheses. The cons constructed with (CONS 'B 'NIL) prints as (B). If a cons is made up of an atom and another cons, the atom is printed following

---

[4]Rumor has it that the true origin of the name Lisp is *Lots of Insidious Silly Parentheses*.

the left parenthesis, and then a space; then the inner cons is printed without its surrounding parentheses. Consider the following examples:

```
eval> (CONS 'B 'NIL)
(B)

eval> (CONS '4 'NIL)
(4)

eval> (CONS 'B (CONS '4 'NIL))
(B 4)

eval> (CONS '2 (CONS 'BAD 'NIL))
(2 BAD)
```

If the first component of a cons is not an atom, it must be a cons itself and so it is printed as such. Thus, in the first example that follows, the cons cell is printed by first printing a left parenthesis. Then the CAR is printed. Since it is not an atom, it must be printed as a cons. So a left parenthesis is printed followed by its CAR, which is B, and so on as in the first example just given.

```
eval> (CONS (CONS 'B 'NIL) (CONS '4 'NIL))
((B) 4)

eval> (CONS (CONS 'B 'NIL) 'NIL)
((B))

eval> (CONS 'A (CONS (CONS 'B (CONS 'C 'NIL)) (CONS 'D 'NIL)))
(A (B C) D)
```

There is one more case to consider: cons cells whose CDRs are atoms other than NIL. They are printed as a left parenthesis, their CAR, a space, a period, a space, and then their CDR. If the cons is the CDR of another cons, the parentheses are omitted. For example,

```
eval> (CONS 'A 'B)
(A . B)

eval> (CONS 'A (CONS 'B (CONS 'C 'D)))
(A B C . D)
```

```
eval> (CONS (CONS 'A 'B) (CONS 'C 'NIL))
((A . B) C)
```

Cons cells with a non-NIL atom as their CDR are often referred to as *dotted pairs* (since their printed representation separates their components with a period, or "dot").

Lisp is happy to read in such expressions and to construct internal representations. In fact, we can view every cons cell as a dotted pair, even when the CDR references NIL or another cons cell. This consistency is reflected in the fact that all of (A . (B . (C . NIL))), (A . (B . (C))), and (A B C) produce the same internal representation when read by Lisp. However, the last one is the only representation printed out because some choice must be made and that is the easiest representation for humans to read. They all are translated into the following internal structure:

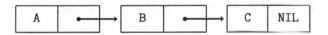

As a final example of box notation, consider that the list constructed by

```
eval> (CONS 'A (CONS (CONS 'B (CONS 'C 'NIL)) (CONS 'D 'NIL))
(A (B C) D)
```

is represented internally as

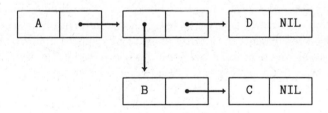

EXERCISES

E1.2.1 For each of the following Lisp expressions, draw the box notation for the cons structures it creates, and write down the printed representation.

```
(CONS 'THE (CONS 'CAT (CONS 'SAT 'NIL)))
(CONS 'A (CONS 'B (CONS '3 'D)))
(CONS (CONS 'A (CONS 'B 'NIL)) (CONS 'C (CONS 'D 'NIL)))
(CONS 'NIL 'NIL)
```

E1.2.2 Draw the box notation for each of the following printed representations of cons cells:

```
(THE BIG DOG)
(THE (BIG DOG))
((THE (BIG DOG)) BIT HIM)
```

1.3 LISTS

Atoms and cons cells provide the building blocks from which Lisp objects are built. A Lisp programmer often uses a slightly different view of Lisp objects, considering them as atoms and *lists*. The name Lisp is derived from *list processor*.

The user's view of a list is that of a series of cons cells, linked by their CDRs, and having CARs that are the *elements* of the list. Thus, the list (A (B C) D), which is represented as

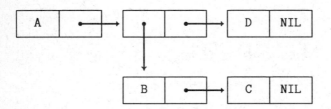

is a list of three elements: A, (B C), and D. The printed representation of cons cells makes explicit the view of them as lists. A list is printed as a left parenthesis, followed by the elements of the list separated by spaces, followed by a right parenthesis. The elements of a list are sometimes referred to as *top-level* elements of the list. Thus (B C) is a top-level element of the list (A (B C) D), while C is an element of (B C).

Now consider

```
eval> (CDR '(A B C))
(B C)
```

```
eval> (CDR (CDR '(A B C))
(C)
```

```
eval> (CDR (CDR (CDR '(A B C)))
NIL
```

The *length* of a list is the number of top-level elements in the list. This also is the number of times CDR must be applied to it to get to the end of the list (i.e., the NIL in the CDR of final cons). From the foregoing example, it might seem that () would be a more logical printed representation for NIL—that is, the *empty list*. It is only a historical accident that the empty list is a symbol. In fact, in most Lisps typing in () is indistinguishable from typing in NIL.

Recall that a series of cons cells linked by their CDRs need not terminate in NIL. Any atom could be the last CDR—for example, in the list (A B C . D). Lists that terminate with NIL are sometimes called *proper lists*, while others are sometimes called *improper lists*.

The Lisp function LIST makes the construction of proper lists of any given length easier than using a series of calls to the function CONS. It takes any number of arguments and returns a list of them. Examine the following:

```
eval> (LIST 'A 'B '3 'D)
(A B 3 D)

eval> (CONS 'A (CONS 'B (CONS '3 (CONS 'D 'NIL))))
(A B 3 D)

eval> (LIST 'A (LIST 'B 'C) 'D)
(A (B C) D)

eval> (LIST 'A)
(A)

eval> (LIST 'B 'NIL)
(B NIL)

eval> (LIST)
NIL
```

The predefined functions CAR and CDR can be applied to any list, but not to atoms other than NIL. Both functions return NIL itself when applied to NIL.[5]

Function CAR extracts the first element of a list, while CDR extracts the rest of a list. For instance,

---

[5] In some Lisp dialects, CAR or CDR applied to NIL causes an error. This is usually terribly inconvenient. It requires extra testing of lists to make sure they are not empty before applying one of these functions.

```
eval> (CAR '(A B C))
A

eval> (CDR '(A B C))
(B C)

eval> (CAR (CDR '(A B C))
B

eval> (CAR (CDR (CAR (CDR '(A (B C) D)))))
C
```

EXERCISES

E1.3.1 Write down the results of typing the following expressions to Lisp.

```
(LIST 'BIG 'CAT 'SAT)
(CONS 'THE (LIST 'BIG 'CAT 'SAT))
(LIST 'ALL (LIST 'GOOD 'PEOPLE) 'SHOULD (LIST 'GO 'AHEAD))
```

E1.3.2 Write down the results of typing the following expressions to Lisp.

```
(CAR (CDR '(A B C D))
(CAR (CDR (CAR '((A B) C D))))
(CDR (CAR (CDR '(A (B C) D))))
```

1.4 THE LISP EVALUATION RULE

Lisp objects often are referred to as *s-expressions*, for "symbolic expressions."

Lisp computes by *evaluating* s-expressions input to it. We will call the piece of the Lisp system that does this the *evaluation procedure*.[6]

Some Lisp atoms evaluate to themselves; numbers and NIL are examples. Thus, the value of the s-expression "3" is 3.

Symbols (the other type of atom we have talked about) have changeable values. Values of symbols can be set with the Lisp function SET. Then the symbol evaluates to that value until SET is applied again. For example,

---

[6]Other programming languages compute by compiling and running programs. (Later we will see that it is possible to compile the evaluation of s-expressions into efficient machine code and to run that code within a Lisp evaluation environment.)

```
eval> (SET 'A '(X Y))
(X Y)

eval> A
(X Y)
```

Notice that the symbol NIL always has NIL as its value. It cannot be changed with SET, or in any other way for that matter.

A list to be evaluated must have a symbol as its CAR—that is, its first element. Furthermore, the symbol must have a functional value associated with it. We have already seen a few such symbols—for example, CAR, CDR, CONS, +, and *. The rest of the elements of the list are treated as arguments to the function.

All the arguments are evaluated by applying the evaluation procedure itself to the s-expressions in each of the argument positions. The results are then handed to the function associated with the symbol in the functional position of the s-expression. The value that it returns is the value of the original s-expression.

The evaluation procedure is thus a *recursive* procedure, one that might call itself during its own execution. The evaluation procedure eventually "bottoms out" when it gets to numbers or symbols, both of which can be evaluated without reinvoking the full procedure.

In the first example that follows, the function is "+". Its two arguments are numbers that evaluate to themselves. The following result occurs:

```
eval> (+ 2 4)
6

eval> (+ (+ 3 4) 5)
12

eval> (+ (CAR (LIST 2 3)) 4)
6

eval> (+ (CAR (CDR (LIST 2 3))) 4)
7
```

In the second example, the first argument is another list, (+ 3 4), and it must be evaluated by the evaluation procedure before passing the result—namely 7—on to "+". The third and fourth examples have even more deeply nested structures and the evaluation procedure must evaluate each deeper level before completing the evaluation of the top level.

1.5 QUOTE: **THE EVALUATION BLOCKER**

There are some exceptions to the uniform evaluation scheme. If the symbol in the functional position is one of a small set of *special forms*, the usual evaluation rule is replaced by a special one for that symbol *before* the arguments are evaluated.

The simplest special form is "QUOTE". Some examples of expressions involving it are

```
eval> (QUOTE A)
A

eval> (QUOTE (X Y))
(X Y)

eval> (CONS 3 (QUOTE (X Y)))
(3 X Y)

eval> (CONS 3 (QUOTE (PLUS 5 6)))
(3 PLUS 5 6)
```

Thus, QUOTE appears to be a function that takes one argument. However, it is a special form, and so the expression in its "argument" position is not evaluated by the evaluation procedure. Instead, as with all special forms, a form whose CAR is the symbol QUOTE is treated specially by the evaluation procedure. In the case of QUOTE, the *subform* that appears to be in the argument position of a QUOTE expression is used as the value of the complete expression, without any evaluation. Thus, the value of the s-expression (QUOTE (X Y)) is the s-expression (X Y). Similarly, the value of the s-expression (QUOTE (+ 5 6)) is the s-expression (+ 5 6).

We have seen QUOTE already in a disguised form. The single character "'" provides a shorthand for typing in a QUOTE expression. For example,

```
'(A B 'C D)
```

is read by Lisp just as if it were

```
(QUOTE (A B (QUOTE C) D))
```

and

```
''A
```

is read just as if it were

```
(QUOTE (QUOTE A))
```

Thus, the result of typing these expressions to Lisp is

```
eval> '(A B 'C D)
(A B (QUOTE C) D)

eval> ''A
(QUOTE A)
```

Notice that in each of these examples the first QUOTE formed by reading the first quote character is not printed in the value of the expressions, because as usual the read expressions are handed to the evaluation procedure, which treats them as special forms and returns their first subforms.

The single quote character shorthand makes it easier to type in constant expressions, so the examples at the beginning of this section become

```
eval> 'A
A

eval> '(X Y)
(X Y)

eval> (CONS 3 '(X Y))
(3 X Y)

eval> (CONS 3 '(+ 5 6))
(3 + 5 6)
```

Recall that numbers evaluate to themselves. This made it unnecessary to quote them in the foregoing examples. Of course, it wouldn't hurt to quote them because the result of evaluating the QUOTE form would be just the number itself. For example,

```
eval> (+ 3 4)
7
```

```
eval> (+ (QUOTE 3) (QUOTE 4))
7


eval> (+ '3 '4)
7
```

The uniform evaluation scheme of Lisp makes for an elegant and wonderfully simple language. However, were it not for the special forms that are exceptions to the scheme, Lisp would not be very useful. For instance, if it were not for QUOTE disrupting the work of the evaluator, we would be able only to refer to numbers and NIL and lists made from them.

Now that we understand QUOTE, we can look at some more complex examples using SET. For example,

```
eval> (SET 'A '(X Y))
(X Y)


eval> (CAR A)
X


eval> (SET 'B '3)
3


eval> (SET 'Y 'A)
A


eval> Y
A


eval> (SET 'Z A)
(X Y)


eval> A
(X Y)
```

Notice that the value of A is the list (X Y). The value of Y is the value of the s-expression 'A or (QUOTE A), which is the symbol A itself. The value of symbol Z, on the other hand, is the value of the s-expression A, which is the Value of the symbol A—namely, (X Y).

Another special form is SETQ. On the surface, it looks very similar to SET. However, SETQ is a special form whereas SET is just an ordinary Lisp function. We will see the deeper consequences of this distinction in later chapters.

The first subform of a SETQ expression (i.e., the expression that is in the same position as is usually occupied by the first argument to a function) must be a symbol whose value is to be set. The second subform is handed to the usual Lisp evaluation procedure and its value becomes the new value of the symbol. Thus,

```
eval> (SETQ A '(A B))
(A B)

eval> (SETQ B 'X)
X

eval> (SET B 'Y)
Y

eval> B
X

eval> X
Y
```

EXERCISES

Assume that each set of the following s-expressions is typed to Lisp. What will be the value of the last expression in each case?

E1.5.1

```
(SETQ A '(U V W))
(SET (CAR (CDR A)) 'B)
(CONS V A)
```

E1.5.2

```
(SETQ A '(U V W))
'(SETQ A '(X Y Z))
A
```

E1.5.3

```
(SETQ A 'A)
(SETQ B 'A)
(LIST A B 'B)
```

E1.5.4

```
(LIST (LIST 'A 'B) '(LIST 'A 'B))
```

1.6 EVAL: **THE EVALUATOR ITSELF**

The Lisp evaluator is a function callable directly by users. Its name is EVAL. It is an ordinary function, and so the normal evaluation rule applies to an expression headed by it. For instance, when the expression (EVAL (LIST 'LIST ''A ''B)) is evaluated, the s-expression in the argument position for EVAL—that is (LIST 'LIST ''A ''B)—is first evaluated with a result of (LIST (QUOTE A) (QUOTE B)). This expression is handed to the explicit call to the EVAL function, which evaluates it to be (A B).

Some further examples are

```
eval> (SETQ A (LIST '+ 5 6))
(+ 5 6)

eval> (CONS A '(IS THE ANSWER))
((+ 5 6) IS THE ANSWER)

eval> (CONS (EVAL A) '(IS THE ANSWER))
(11 IS THE ANSWER)
```

1.7 **USER-DEFINED FUNCTIONS**

In Lisp, users can define their own functions whose use is syntactically indistinguishable from predefined Lisp functions. Consider the following:

```
eval> (DEFUN SQUARE (X) (* X X))
SQUARE

eval> (SQUARE 5)
25

eval> (DEFUN THIRD (LIST) (CAR (CDR (CDR LIST))))
THIRD
```

```
eval> (THIRD '(A B C D E))
C

eval> (THIRD (THIRD '(A (B C) (D E F) (G H I J))))
F

eval> (DEFUN CYLINDER-VOLUME (LENGTH RADIUS)
            (* LENGTH (* 3.14159265 (SQUARE RADIUS))))
CYLINDER-VOLUME

eval> (CYLINDER-VOLUME 2.5 2.0)
31.4159265
```

The special form DEFUN is used to define new functions. A function definition takes the general form:

(DEFUN function-name argument-list body)

Notice that this is a special form, so the subforms are not evaluated as arguments.

The *function-name* must be a symbol and can be any symbol other than NIL (once again we see the special nature of NIL). After the function is defined, it can be invoked by using this name as the first element of a list to be evaluated. For instance, the first example defines the function SQUARE, which then can be used like a predefined Lisp function, such as, say, *.

The *argument-list* is a list of symbols (excluding NIL again) that will be given the arguments that the evaluation procedure hands to the function as their values. These arguments will be the results of evaluating the subforms that follow the name of a function in an expression to be evaluated. For instance, after defining SQUARE, and upon being given the s-expressions (SQUARE 5), the Lisp evaluation procedure temporarily gives the symbol X, which was the single member of SQUARE's argument list, the value 5. When the body of SQUARE is evaluated (the body is (* X X)), it is then equivalent to evaluating (* '5 '5). In the last example illustrated, the symbol LENGTH is given 2.5 as a temporary value, and RADIUS is given 2.0, during the evaluation of the body of CYLINDER-VOLUME given the two arguments 2.5 and 2.0. Notice that we used floating-point numbers in this example. Lisp can handle integers, floating-point numbers, and others uniformly without the need for declarations.

The number of symbols in the argument list is the number of arguments the function must be handed by the Lisp evaluation procedure. Thus, for the moment, we will only define functions that require a fixed number of arguments (whereas LIST, +, *, etc., can take an arbitrary number of arguments).

The *body* is an s-expression that will be evaluated whenever the function is called. It is evaluated after the symbols (or variables) in the argument list have been bound to the arguments that were passed to the function. The value returned from evaluating the *body* is returned as the value of the function.

EXERCISES

What will be the result of each of the following sets of s-expressions typed to Lisp?

E1.7.1

```
(DEFUN DOUBLE (X) (* 2 X))
(DOUBLE 2.3)
```

E1.7.2

```
(DEFUN TIMES-SQUARE (X Y) (* X Y Y))
(TIMES-SQUARE 4 3)
```

E1.7.3

```
(DEFUN TIMES-CUBE (X Y) (* X Y Y Y))
(DEFUN CUBE-TIMES (X Y) (TIMES-CUBE Y X))
(CUBE-TIMES 3 2)
```

1.8 VARIABLES AND REFERENCE

The symbols in the argument list of a function (the variables that get bound to the function's arguments) are only bound temporarily to the arguments given to a function. The variable only has the value while the body of the function is being evaluated. For example,

```
eval> (SETQ X 3)
3

eval> (SQUARE 4)
16

eval> X
3
```

Within a function, all variable references (i.e., symbols whose value must be computed) should be to variables named in the argument list of the function definition. For instance, LENGTH and RADIUS are the variables of the function CYLINDER-VOLUME. No reference should be made to other variables—for example, X within the body of CYLINDER-VOLUME. Many Lisps do in fact allow outside references but the rules on when and what can be referenced vary from dialect to dialect.

Most introductory texts discuss this issue at great length and use outside references as part of their programming technique. It is not often good programming practice, even in a Lisp dialect that allows it. Generally, the techniques are not necessary and lead to many unnecessary complications. They make programs more difficult to debug and understand. We will not use such references, except in one particular limited way that will be discussed in chapter 2.

1.9 PREDICATES

Predicates are functions that are used to test for the truth of some assertion about one or more Lisp objects. For instance, the Lisp function ATOM tests whether or not an object is an atom. Thus, (ATOM '3), (ATOM 'NIL), and (ATOM 'X) each return an indication of true and (ATOM '(X Y)) returns an indication of false.

There are many predicates in Common Lisp. For instance, CONSP tests whether its argument is a cons, LISTP whether its argument is a list (i.e. a cons or NIL), NUMBERP whether its argument is a number, and ZEROP whether its argument is zero. These particular predicates go along with a loose convention in Lisp that predicate names end with the letter P.

How are falsehood and truth represented in Lisp? Our old friend NIL represents false, and anything else represents true! Most predicates return the symbol T for truth, but that is simply a matter of convenience. Some examples of predicates in action are

```
eval> (ATOM '3)        eval> (CONSP '3)        eval> (LISTP '3)
T                      NIL                     NIL

eval> (ATOM 'X)        eval> (CONSP 'X)        eval> (LISTP 'X)
T                      NIL                     NIL

eval> (ATOM 'NIL)      eval> (CONSP 'NIL)      eval> (LISTP 'NIL)
T                      NIL                     T

eval> (ATOM '(X Y))    eval> (CONSP '(X Y))    eval> (LISTP '(X Y))
NIL                    T                       T
```

```
eval> (NUMBERP '3)      eval> (NUMBERP '2.3)    eval> (NUMBERP 'X)
T                       T                       NIL

eval> (ZEROP '3)        eval> (ZEROP '0)        eval> (ZEROP '-1)
NIL                     T                       NIL

eval> (NULL '(X Y))     eval> (NULL 'NIL)       eval> (NULL 'X)
NIL                     T                       NIL

eval> (NOT '(X Y))      eval> (NOT 'NIL)        eval> (NOT 'X)
NIL                     T                       NIL
```

The predicate NULL tests whether its argument is NIL. It returns T if it is and NIL for all other arguments. The predicate NULL usually is used to test for an empty list.

Now compare NULL to the logical operator NOT. From the previous examples, it seems that NOT is identical in operation to NULL. This is correct. It returns the same result on every argument as would NULL. However, the intended "meaning" of NOT is different. It is logical inversion. Given truth, it returns falsehood; given falsehood, it returns truth. One *could* use NULL and NOT interchangeably in Lisp programs, but one *shouldn't* as a matter of style. Instead, the use of NULL or NOT should be chosen to reflect the semantics of the intended computation: NULL when testing for an empty list and NOT when inverting the sense of some logical test. This makes the intent of the program clear when the original writer, or someone different, reads it at a later time.

Given the predefined Lisp function ATOM, we could define CONSP ourselves:

```
(DEFUN CONSP (OBJECT) (NOT (ATOM OBJECT)))
```

Not all predicates take a single argument. Some *compare* two arguments. In particular, predicates < (*less than*) and > (*greater than*) compare two numbers and return T if they satisfy the tested relation. Thus,

```
eval> (< 3 4)           eval> (> 3 4)
T                       NIL

eval> (< 3.4 2)         eval> (> 3.4 2)
NIL                     T

eval> (< 5 5)           eval> (> 5 5)
NIL                     NIL
```

A further note about T: The symbol T has a special place in Lisp similar to, but not as extensive, as NIL. The value of T is always itself, T. Furthermore, it cannot be used in an argument list for a function. Whenever T appears in a program, it is definite that it will evaluate to T.

EXERCISES

E1.9.1 Evaluate each of the following s-expressions:
a. (ZEROP '3)
b. (ZEROP 3)
c. (ATOM 3)
d. (NULL '(A B))
e. (NUMBERP '(A B))
f. (CONSP '(A B))
g. (LISTP '(A B))
h. (CONSP 'NIL)

E1.9.2 Evaluate each of the following s-expressions:
a. (NOT (NULL 'NIL))
b. (NOT (NULL 3))
c. (NOT (ATOM '(A B)))
d. (NOT (ATOM 'A))
e. (NOT (NULL '(A B)))
f. (NOT (ZEROP 3.3))
g. (NOT (ZEROP 0.0)
h. (NOT (NUMBERP 'B))

1.10 IF: **A CONDITIONAL FORM**

Predicates provide the ability to test the truth or falsity of a condition. The special form IF provides the ability to change the behavior of a program conditional on the outcome of such a predicate. IF has the general form:

(IF *test-form then-clause else-clause*)

When an IF form is evaluated, not all of its subforms are evaluated. First, the *test-form* is evaluated. If it is non-NIL, the *then-clause* is evaluated and the result of that form is the result of the IF form. If the *test-form* evaluates to NIL, the *test-clause* is skipped and the *else-clause* is evaluated in its place, providing the value for the IF form. Consider the following examples:

```
eval> (IF (ATOM 'X) 'YES 'NO)
YES

eval> (IF (ATOM '(X Y)) 'YES 'NO)
NO

eval> (* 5 (IF (NULL (CDR '(X))) 0 (+ 11 12)))
0

eval> (* 5 (IF (NULL (CDR '(X Y))) 0 (+ 11 12)))
115
```

In the third example, the form (+ 11 12) does not get evaluated as it does in the fourth example.

Now we can write some more interesting programs. Consider this function definition:

```
(DEFUN LENGTH (LIST)
       (IF (NULL LIST)
           0
           (+ 1 (LENGTH (CDR LIST))))))
```

The function LENGTH computes the length of a list by seeing how many times CDR must be applied to it until the list is empty. For example (in the following first example, recall that typing "()" is identical in effect to typing "NIL"):

```
eval> (LENGTH '())
0

eval> (LENGTH '(A))
1

eval> (LENGTH '(B A))
2

eval> (LENGTH '(C B A))
3

eval> (LENGTH '((A B C D E F) G H (I J) K))
5
```

```
eval> (LENGTH (CAR '((A B C D E F) G H (I J) K)))
6
```

The function LENGTH has been defined *recursively*; it calls itself on a smaller list each time, until finally its argument is the empty list.

As it happens, there is a predefined Lisp function called LENGTH, that computes the length of a list.[7]

Notice that in our definition of LENGTH we typed the code broken into lines and indented according to the structure of the intended computation. This is extremely important in making programs readable by people. The Lisp system ignores new lines and indentation and would be just as happy with

```
(DEFUN LENGTH (LIST) (IF (NULL LIST) 0 (+ 1
(LENGTH (CDR LIST)))))
```

but this is very difficult for us to read. Many text editors are able to help in automatically indenting Lisp programs as they are typed in. Even with an editor that doesn't provide such assistance, it is extremely important to get into the habit of structuring your programs textually as you type them. It soon becomes second nature and the payoff in ease of debugging is enormous.

SUMMARY

Lisp programs and data are both represented as lists, made up of atoms and conses. Atoms include numbers and symbols. Symbols have alterable values. Numbers are their own values. Lists are evaluated by applying the functional value of their first element to the individual evaluations of the rest of the list's elements. The functions we have seen appear in Table 1-1.

All functions return a value. Functions CONS and LIST construct lists by making new conses. CAR and CDR can access the components of a cons. There are functions for arithmetic operations and functions that test the type of other properties of data objects. The latter are all predicates and return NIL for false and anything else (but often T) for true.

The Lisp evaluation procedure is directly available to the user as the function EVAL.

---

[7] It does it a little more efficiently than our example here; we will see how to match its performance later.

Table 1-1

Function	Args	Description
CONS	2	add another element at the head of a list
CAR	1	first element of list
CDR	1	rest of a list after first element
+	$0 \Rightarrow \infty$	add two or more numbers
*	$0 \Rightarrow \infty$	multiply two or more numbers
LIST	$0 \Rightarrow \infty$	construct a list from the arguments
SET	2	set the first arg to the second
EVAL	1	the Lisp evaluation procedure
LENGTH	1	count elements in a list
ATOM	1	test for an atom
CONSP	1	test for a cons cell
LISTP	1	test for a list
NUMBERP	1	test for a number
ZEROP	1	test whether a number is zero
NULL	1	test for NIL
NOT	1	invert logical value
<	2	test for first argument less than second
>	2	test for first argument greater than second

The usual evaluation of an expression is suspended for special forms. Some special forms are shown in Table 1-2. Since the elements following the symbol for a special form are not evaluated, we say that special forms have *subforms* rather than *arguments*.

Table 1-2

Special Form	Subforms	Description
QUOTE	1	returns its subform
SETQ	2	set the first subform to value of second
IF	3	conditionally evaluate consequent or alternate form
DEFUN	3	define a function

Special form QUOTE simply blocks evaluation of s-expressions so that they can be used as data objects.

Function SET and special form SETQ can set the value of a symbol. The latter, as a special form, does not let its first subform be evaluated.

User-defined Lisp functions are indistinguishable from predefined functions.

PROBLEMS

P1.1 Write a function DOT-PRODUCT that takes two lists, each of three numbers, and produces the dot product of the vectors that they represent. For example,

```
eval> (DOT-PRODUCT '(1.2 2.4 -0.3) '(0.0 4.5 3.8))
-0.6
```

P1.2 Write a function COUNT-NUMBERS that counts the number of numbers that occur in a list. It should work like this:

```
eval> (COUNT-NUMBERS '(A 2.3 B 5 4.53 C D))
3

eval> (COUNT-NUMBERS '(NO NUMBERS IN THIS LIST!))
0
```

P1.3 Write a function LONGER-LISTP that takes two lists as arguments and returns T if the first list is longer than the second and NIL otherwise.

P1.4 Write a function SAME-LENGTH that takes a list as its argument and creates a new list of the same length, whose elements are all T.

P1.5 Write a function NEW-LIST that takes a number as its argument and constructs a list of that length containing all Ts.

2

STANDARD
LIST
OPERATIONS

Chapter 1 discussed how to construct lists from individual elements (using CONS and LIST), how to take them apart a piece at a time (using CAR and CDR), and how to find their length (using LENGTH). In this chapter, we look at the standard list manipulating functions to do more interesting operations, while extending our understanding of how lists are represented.

2.1 APPENDING TWO LISTS

Suppose that we have two lists: (A B C) and (D E F). How can we put them together to form the list (A B C D E F)? The APPEND function is a predefined Lisp function of two or more arguments that allows us to do this.

Suppose that we have already done the following:

```
(SETQ SUBJECT1 '(THE COW))
(SETQ SUBJECT2 '(THE QUICK BROWN FOX))
(SETQ PREDICATE1 '(JUMPED OVER THE MOON))
(SETQ PREDICATE2 '(JUMPED OVER THE LAZY DOG))
```

Then the APPEND function will work in the following way:

```
eval> (APPEND '(A B C) '(D E F))
(A B C D E F)


eval> (APPEND SUBJECT1 PREDICATE2)
(THE COW JUMPED OVER THE LAZY DOG)


eval> (APPEND SUBJECT2 PREDICATE1)
(THE QUICK BROWN FOX JUMPED OVER THE MOON)
```

If APPEND is given more than two arguments, it appends them in left-to-right order.

Although APPEND comes predefined in Lisp, it turns out that we already knew enough Lisp to write it ourselves. The key observation is that appending (A B C) to (D E F) is the same as appending (B C) to (D E F) and then consing A onto the front of the result. This suggests the following definition for a two-argument version of APPEND:

```
(DEFUN APPEND (X Y)
    (CONS (CAR X)
          (APPEND (CDR X) Y)))
```

But this is not quite correct because every time APPEND is called it will call itself again, leading to an infinite recursion. Sometime we must stop CDRing down X. When? Well, when X is empty, (APPEND X Y) should simply evaluate to the value of Y because X contributes nothing to the result. This suggests the following (correct) definition:

```
(DEFUN APPEND (X Y)
      (IF (NULL X) Y
          (CONS (CAR X) (APPEND (CDR X) Y))))
```

Let us now consider more carefully what goes on inside the machine when APPEND is executed. Consider the following Lisp-level operations on lists:

```
eval> (SETQ X '(R S T))
(R S T)


eval> (SETQ Y '(U V W))
(U V W)


eval> (SETQ A (APPEND X Y))
(R S T U V W)


eval> (SETQ B (APPEND X Y))
(R S T U V W)
```

Given the earlier definition of APPEND, the internal representations of X, Y, A, and B now look like:

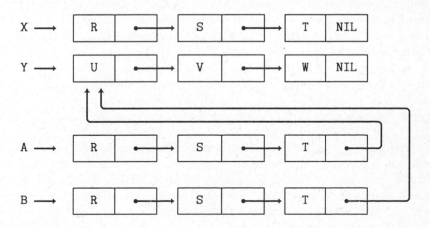

The values of A and B share some structure, or memory locations, with the value of Y. This is exactly what happens with the built-in version of APPEND. Later in this chapter, we will see how operations on the value of Y can affect the values of A and B.

EXERCISES

E2.1.1   What is the result of typing each of the following s-expressions to Lisp?
a. (APPEND '(A A A) '(A A))
b. (APPEND '(A A A) 'NIL)
c. (APPEND '(A (B C)) '(B C))
d. (APPEND 'NIL '(ADDS NOTHING))

E2.1.2   Draw the box notation representations of the values of A, B, and C after the following expressions have been typed to Lisp.

```
(SETQ A '(U (V W) X))
(SETQ B (APPEND A 'NIL))
(SETQ C (APPEND A (CAR (CDR A))))
```

2.2 RECURSIVE FUNCTIONS AND DEBUGGING

The definitions that we have used for function APPEND and function LENGTH are examples of the simplest form of *recursive* functions in Lisp. A function is recursive if it uses itself in its own definition.

In each case, the function checks whether a particular of its arguments is the empty list. If so, it returns a value that requires no computation. If the argument is not the empty list, the function calls itself on the CDR of the list, which is clearly a shorter list. It augments the result of itself applied to the shorter list through a simple computation, thus taking into account the contribution of the CAR of the argument being CDRed down.

We will see other forms of recursive functions later in this chapter.

An extremely useful debugging tool for recursive and other functions is the *trace* facility. It is invoked by calling the TRACE special form with one or more arguments (or subforms), each of which should be the name of a function to be traced.

As TRACE is a special form, the Lisp evaluation procedure does not evaluate the subforms in its argument positions. A typical use might be in debugging the APPEND function that we developed earlier; typing (TRACE APPEND) will cause the function APPEND to be traced. Thereafter, whenever the Lisp evaluation procedure applies so-named functions to arguments, two messages are printed on the console.[1] The first is on entry to the function when the function name and a list of arguments being passed to it are printed. As the function is exited, the value returned by the function is printed. The following demonstrates:

```
eval> (APPEND '(A B C) '(D E F))
(A B C D E F)

eval> (TRACE APPEND)
(APPEND)

eval> (APPEND '(A B C) '(D E F))

(1 ENTER APPEND ((A B C) (D E F)))
  (2 ENTER APPEND ((B C) (D E F)))
    (3 ENTER APPEND ((C) (D E F)))
      (4 ENTER APPEND (NIL (D E F)))
      (4 EXIT APPEND (D E F))
    (3 EXIT APPEND (C D E F))
  (2 EXIT APPEND (B C D E F))
(1 EXIT APPEND (A B C D E F)) (A B C D E F)
```

Notice that the entrance and exit messages are not necessarily printed contiguously as other traced functions might be called from within an invocation of the function (in this case, recursive calls of the function itself). So they easily can be matched up visually because the trace facility indents the messages according to the depth of tracing at which they occurred and numbers them by the recursion level for each particular function.

Other features of the trace facility are

- TRACE with no subforms returns a list of all currently traced functions.
- UNTRACE, another special form, with one or more subforms turns off tracing for each function whose name appears as a subform. Thus, a typical use might be (UNTRACE APPEND).
- UNTRACE with no subforms switches off tracing for all currently traced functions.

When writing Lisp functions, it usually is not very much fun typing them directly to the Lisp system, especially when you make mistakes. The Lisp function

---

[1] The format of the printed messages varies between Common Lisp implementations, but the information conveyed by all of them is the same.

LOAD reads in a file of s-expressions (typically function definitions and setting of data variables), evaluating each expression one by one.

The function LOAD takes one argument: the name of a file to be loaded. It should be represented as a *string*[2]—that is, as a string of characters enclosed in double quotes. For instance, (LOAD "foo.lisp") will look for a file named "foo.lisp" on your directory and load it if it is there, returning T as a result. If the file does not exist or it is unreadable, Lisp will signal an error.

The exact details about what strings correspond to which files on disk are operating system dependent, and thus are not part of the Common Lisp definition. Your particular Common Lisp implementation will assume certain defaults about which disk area should be searched for a file and whether a default file extension (on operating systems where that makes sense) should be used.

EXERCISES

E2.2.1 Create a file with a definition of function called MY-APPEND in it, following our earlier description of APPEND. Load in your file and try out the trace facility to see its behavior.

E2.2.2 Speculate on why it might be *dangerous* to use the function name APPEND instead of MY-APPEND in the previous definition.

2.3 REVERSING A LIST

Later, we often will find it convenient to reverse a list using the supplied Lisp function REVERSE. It takes a single argument that should be a proper list (i.e., NIL or a list whose last top-level cons has NIL as its CDR). It produces a new list that contains the same top-level elements as the original list, but in reverse order. For example,

```
eval> (REVERSE '(A B C))
(C B A)

eval> (REVERSE '(A (B C) (D E) F G))
(G F (D E) (B C) A)
```

---

[2] A string is another type of Lisp atom. We have already seen numbers and symbols. Strings will be examined further in chapter 12.

For now, REVERSE provides another simple example for studying recursion.

Suppose that we try to apply the same sort of reasoning to develop REVERSE as we used to develop the APPEND function. The reverse of the list (A B C) is the list made up the reverse of (B C) appended to the list (A). This definition can be applied recursively until we get down to the simple case of the empty list (i.e., NIL or ()). The reverse of the empty list is simply the empty list. This gives us the following definition:

```
(DEFUN REVERSE (LST)
    (IF (NULL LST)
        'NIL
        (APPEND (REVERSE (CDR LST))
                (CONS (CAR LST) 'NIL))))
```

This definition is correct in that it does indeed return the reverse of a list given to it as an argument. However, it is not very efficient because after each recursive call to REVERSE the constructed result is handed to another recursive function APPEND that decomposes it into a series of CARs and CDRs. We can see this by using the trace facility:

```
eval> (TRACE REVERSE APPEND)
(REVERSE APPEND)

eval> (REVERSE '(A B C))

(1 ENTER REVERSE ((A B C)))
   (2 ENTER REVERSE ((B C)))
      (3 ENTER REVERSE ((C)))
         (4 ENTER REVERSE (NIL))
         (4 EXIT REVERSE NIL)
         (1 ENTER APPEND (NIL (C)))
         (1 EXIT APPEND (C))
      (3 EXIT REVERSE (C))
      (1 ENTER APPEND ((C) (B)))
         (2 ENTER APPEND (NIL (B)))
         (2 EXIT APPEND (B))
      (1 EXIT APPEND (C B))
   (2 EXIT REVERSE (C B))
   (1 ENTER APPEND ((C B) (A)))
      (2 ENTER APPEND ((B) (A)))
         (3 ENTER APPEND (NIL (A)))
         (3 EXIT APPEND (A))
      (2 EXIT APPEND (B A))
```

```
     (1 EXIT APPEND (C B A))
   (1 EXIT REVERSE (C B A)) (C B A)
```

We can try a different decomposition of the problem. To reverse the list (A B C), we should put A at the end of the new list and then put B (the start of the rest of the list to be reversed) in front of A in the reversed list. This formulation suggests the following definition for REVERSE:

```
(DEFUN REVERSE (LST)
    (REVERSE-AUX LST 'NIL))

(DEFUN REVERSE-AUX (REM SOFAR)
    (IF (NULL REM)
        SOFAR
        (REVERSE-AUX (CDR REM) (CONS (CAR REM) SOFAR))))
```

Clearly, the crux of the definition is the introduction of an auxiliary function REVERSE-AUX. It takes two arguments. The first is the part of the original list that remains to be reversed. The second is the part of the reversed list so far constructed. If there is no more of the original list, all that has been constructed is returned. Otherwise, the first remaining element of the original list is removed and added to the head of the reversed list, and the rest of the original list is reversed. Tracing the functions should illuminate their behavior.

```
eval> (TRACE REVERSE REVERSE-AUX)
(REVERSE REVERSE-AUX)

eval> (REVERSE '(A B C))

(1 ENTER REVERSE ((A B C)))
  (1 ENTER REVERSE-AUX ((A B C) NIL))
    (2 ENTER REVERSE-AUX ((B C) (A)))
     (3 ENTER REVERSE-AUX ((C) (B A)))
        (4 ENTER REVERSE-AUX (NIL (C B A)))
        (4 EXIT REVERSE-AUX (C B A))
      (3 EXIT REVERSE-AUX (C B A))
    (2 EXIT REVERSE-AUX (C B A))
  (1 EXIT REVERSE-AUX (C B A))
(1 EXIT REVERSE (C B A)) (C B A)
```

Compare the foregoing trace to that shown earlier for APPEND. In REVERSE-AUX, the construction of the result happens as the recursion proceeds deeper, and nothing is done during the exit phase. On the other hand, APPEND does no construction on the way down through recursive levels and does all construction as it exits from each recursion.

EXERCISES

E2.3.1 Evaluate the following s-expressions:
a. (REVERSE '(A B C D))
b. (REVERSE '(A (B C) (D E)))
c. (REVERSE '((A (B C)) D ((E F G) H)))

2.4 GLOBAL VARIABLES

Now that we have seen user-defined functions calling each other, we can expand on our rules for variable reference. The techniques given in this section also are useful for providing monitoring of running functions to help with debugging.

Variables can be either *global* or *local*.

 Global variables may be referenced in any function. They must be declared using the special form DEFVAR. It takes the form:

$$(\text{DEFVAR } variable \ initial\text{-}value)$$

and optionally gives the variable an initial value. The variable form is not evaluated and should be a symbol. The *initial-value* form is evaluated and can be omitted.

Local variables may only be referenced in the function in which they are introduced. They can be introduced by appearing in a function's argument list, or they can be introduced explicitly by the control structures of chapter 3. A function may only refer to its own local variables or to global variables. A function may not refer to local variables of other functions, even those functions that might call it.[3] Two different functions may have local variables with the same name, but they are different variables.

A popular convention, and one used in this book, is to make the appearance of global and local variables different by enclosing the former in asterisks. Thus, *COUNT* might be used as a global variable while COUNT would be used as a local variable. Although the Common Lisp language definition does not make this a

---

[3]The latter is allowed in the many Lisp interpreters, but few Lisp compilers. Common Lisp presents a consistent picture by outlawing such references in both the interpreter and compiler.

requirement, this convention is rigidly adhered to throughout the definitions of predefined Common Lisp functions that refer to global parameters. We will see examples of this in chapter 6.

Global variables serve two main purposes. First, they can be used to provide global information to functions called deep within a program without extra parameters having to be passed from function to function along the way. Second, they can provide handles into a global database, where many functions can update the data using SET or SETQ.

As an example, we will write a new version of CONS that keeps a count of how many times it has been called. Since consing is often an expensive operation in Lisp, such execution monitoring might be of extremely practical value in evaluating different algorithms for solving a particular computational problem.

We first need one additional tool. Special form PROGN provides a way of explicitly sequencing Lisp statements to be evaluated. This capability is only useful when some of the statements have side effects on the values of either global or local variables. The general form of PROGN is

$$(\text{PROGN } \textit{form-1 form-2} \dots \textit{form-n})$$

The subforms are evaluated sequentially and the value of the last is returned as the value of the PROGN form.

Now we can define our function COUNT-CONS, which seems to act just like ordinary CONS in that it returns a fresh cons cell with the function's two arguments filling the CAR and CDR. Notice, however, that this function also increments the global variable *COUNT* by one every time.

```
(DEFVAR *COUNT* 0)

(DEFUN COUNT-CONS (X Y)
    (PROGN (SETQ *COUNT* (+ 1 *COUNT*))
           (CONS X Y)))
```

In this function, there is one global variable referenced, *COUNT*, and two local variables referenced, X and Y. As an example, let's try our earlier definition for APPEND, but this time let's use the "cons counting" function:

```
(DEFUN COUNT-APPEND (X Y)
    (IF (NULL X)
        Y
        (COUNT-CONS (CAR X)
                    (COUNT-APPEND (CDR X) Y))))
```

Now let's see how many times CONS is called on typical operations:

```
eval> (SETQ *COUNT* 0)
0

eval> (COUNT-APPEND '(A B C) '(D E F))
(A B C D E F)

eval> *COUNT*
3

eval> (SETQ *COUNT* 0)
0

eval> (COUNT-APPEND '(A B) '(C D E F))
(A B C D E F)

eval> *COUNT*
2
```

EXERCISES

E2.4.1 Type the definitions for COUNT-CONS and COUNT-APPEND into a file and reproduce the results shown in the section. Then write a new function REPORT-APPEND that takes two argument lists and tells how many cons cells were used in appending them. Do not use any global variables other than *COUNT*.

2.5 EQ: **IDENTICAL EQUALITY**

We have seen that there appear to be at least two sorts of equalness in Lisp: identity of the internal Lisp objects and identical printed representations. In fact, there are a number of shades of equality in Lisp, and corresponding predicates to test for those different shades.

The function EQ is a predicate that compares two Lisp objects and tells whether they are the *same* object—that is, whether they occupy the same storage locations in the machine. EQ returns T if the same object is given as both its arguments.

Two cons cells are EQ if and only if they are the same cons cell. Thus, the following occurs:

```
eval> (SETQ C '(F 2.3))
(F 2.3)

eval> (SETQ D '(F 2.3))
(F 2.3)

eval> (EQ C D)
NIL

eval> (EQ C C)
T

eval> (EQ D (CAR (LIST D C)))
T
```

A symbol is always EQ to itself. This is true because internally a symbol occupies a unique piece of storage. Numbers with the same value are not usually EQ because Lisp does not bother to ensure that every instance of, say, 3.14 occupies the same piece of storage.[4] Therefore, it could be the case that (EQ 3.14 3.14) returns either NIL or T; the Common Lisp definition does not define what the result should be so it may vary between implementations.

Using the foregoing example, the following might happen:

```
eval> (EQ (CAR C) (CAR D))
T

eval> (EQ (CAR (CDR C)) (CAR (CDR D)))
NIL

eval> (EQ (CAR (CDR C)) (CAR (CDR C)))
T
```

Now consider again the earlier example of two lists with shared tails. We can use EQ to detect their shared component.

```
eval> (SETQ X '(R S T))
(R S T)
```

---

[4]Accidentally, small integers in one particular Lisp, Maclisp, are in fact EQ. Thus, (EQ 3 3) is always T while (EQ 2001 2001) is NIL. Similar things for various size integers occur in some other Lisps also.

```
eval> (SETQ Y '(U V W))
(U V W)


eval> (SETQ A (APPEND X Y))
(R S T U V W)


eval> (SETQ B (APPEND X Y))
(R S T U V W)


eval> (EQ A B)
NIL


eval> (EQ (CDR (CDR A)) (CDR (CDR B)))
NIL


eval> (EQ (CDR (CDR (CDR A))) (CDR (CDR (CDR B))))
T
```

Since APPEND essentially copies its first argument and joins it onto its second argument, the values of A and B share just the last three top-level cons cells making the list (U V W). Thus, it is not until we CDR down to the fourth top-level cons cells of the two lists is EQ comparing the *same* cons cells. Refer to the box notation diagram on page 29 and count off the CDRs to see this. Notice, however, that since the CARs of all the cons cells in the two lists are symbols, they will be EQ even among the first three elements of the lists. Thus, for instance,

```
eval> (EQ (CAR A) (CAR B))
T


eval> (EQ (CAR (CDR (CDR A))) (CAR (CDR (CDR B))))
T
```

EXERCISES

E2.5.1 Evaluate the following s-expressions if the result is well defined by Common Lisp.
a. (EQ 'A 'A)
b. (EQ '(A B) (LIST 'A 'B))
c. (EQ 2 3)
d. (EQ 2 2)
e. (PROGN (SETQ *LIST* (LIST 'A 'B))

```
          (SETQ *BIG* (LIST 'C *LIST*))
          (EQL *LIST* (CAR (CDR *BIG*))))
```
f. (EQ 2.3 (+ 1.1 1.2))
g. (EQ '(A B (C D)) '(A B (C D)))
h. (EQ 3 3.0)

2.6 EQL: AN INTERMEDIATE EQUALITY TESTER

The Common Lisp predicate EQL is a slightly weaker[5] version of EQ. It compares two Lisp objects and returns T if they are numbers of the same *type* with the same value, or if they are the same Lisp object. Thus, it is like EQ but it is also able to test for numbers that have the same internal representation.

We have seen a few different sorts of Lisp objects: cons cells, numbers, and symbols. In fact, Common Lisp has many more *data types* than that. There are strings, arrays, and a large number of more specialized number types.

There are only two types of numbers likely to be used in most programs: FIXNUMs and SINGLE-FLOATs. These usually correspond to the standard single-precision fixed-point and floating-point arithmetic available on the machine on which your particular version of Common Lisp is running. Common Lisp also includes arbitrarily large integers, three other precisions of floating–point numbers, complex numbers, and rationals. We will not consider them in this book.

Numbers of type FIXNUM correspond to integers in most other computer languages, while those of type SINGLE-FLOAT correspond to real numbers in other languages. In Common Lisp, FIXNUMs are printed without a decimal point, while SINGLE-FLOATs have either a decimal point or an exponent field included. Thus, 3, -257, and 65578 are all examples of FIXNUMs while 3.0, -3E27, and 3.141559265 are all examples of SINGLE-FLOATs.

Given a Lisp object, it can be easily tested to see if it is of a given type using the two argument predicate TYPEP. Its first argument is an object to be tested and its second argument is a symbol that is the name of the type being tested for. If the first argument is an instance of the tested type, T is returned; otherwise, NIL is the result. Some of the types that might be tested for include ATOM, SYMBOL, CONS, NUMBER, STRING and, of course, FIXNUM and SINGLE-FLOAT. Clearly, types are not mutually exclusive because any symbol is also an atom. Thus for instance, the following can happen:

---

[5]We say that EQL is weaker than EQ because (EQ X Y) returning true implies that (EQL X Y) will also return true, and in addition EQL does not discriminate between certain objects that EQ does.

```
eval> (TYPEP 'ZTESCH 'SYMBOL)
T


eval> (TYPEP '3 'SYMBOL)
NIL


eval> (TYPEP 'ZTESCH 'NUMBER)
NIL


eval> (TYPEP '3 'NUMBER)
T


eval> (TYPEP 'ZTESCH 'ATOM)
T


eval> (TYPEP '3 'ATOM)
T


eval> (TYPEP -3.57 'FIXNUM)
NIL


eval> (TYPEP -3.57 'SINGLE-FLOAT)
T
```

Like NUMBERP and ATOM, there are some additional predicates that check for specific types. In particular, SYMBOLP checks for a symbol and STRINGP checks for a string.

Given these definitions of *type* and what it means for two numbers to have the same type, the EQL predicate has the following behavior:

```
eval> (EQL 'A 'A)
T


eval> (EQL 2 2)
T


eval> (EQL 2.2 (+ 0.7 1.5))
T


eval> (EQL 2 2.0)
NIL
```

To be sure we understand `EQL`, we can write our our own limited version of it that works for `FIXNUM`s and `SINGLE-FLOAT`s. We will ignore the other types of numbers in this example.

The function must determine whether its two arguments are numbers of the same type and then must see if they have the same value. That can be done by checking whether their difference is zero; we already know about the predicate `ZEROP`, which checks for zeros. The difference of two numbers can be computed with the function "-", which subtracts its second argument from its first. If the arguments are not numbers, then `EQ` can be used to check whether they are the same Lisp object. Consider the following definition:

```
(DEFUN EQL (A B)
    (IF (TYPEP A 'FIXNUM)
        (IF (TYPEP B 'FIXNUM)
            (ZEROP (- A B))
            'NIL)
        (IF (TYPEP A 'SINGLE-FLOAT)
            (IF (TYPEP B 'SINGLE-FLOAT)
                (ZEROP (- A B))
                'NIL)
            (EQ A B))))
```

The function may look a little unsymmetrical at first glance. If argument A does not have type `FIXNUM`, argument B never gets checked to see whether it has type `FIXNUM`. If the latter were the case, the result of `EQL` ought to be `NIL`. But that will be the result, whether because the `SINGLE-FLOAT` test for A succeeds while it fails for B, or if A is not a `SINGLE-FLOAT` then A and B will be compared with `EQ`, which must return `NIL` if B is a `FIXNUM` and A is not. A similar argument explains why the tests for whether A and B have type `SINGLE-FLOAT` also seem unsymmetric.

EXERCISES

E2.6.1 Evaluate the following s-expressions if the result is well defined by Common Lisp.

a. `(EQL 'A 'A)`
b. `(EQL '(A B) (LIST 'A 'B))`
c. `(EQL 2 3)`
d. `(EQL 2 2)`
e. `(PROGN (SETQ *LIST* (LIST 'A 'B))`
         `(SETQ *BIG* (LIST 'C *LIST*))`
         `(EQL *LIST* (CAR (CDR *BIG*))))`
f. `(EQL 2.3 (+ 1.1 1.2))`

g. (EQL '(A B (C D)) '(A B (C D))
h. (EQL 3 3.0)

2.7 EQUAL: **EQUALNESS OF LISP OBJECTS**

The function EQUAL is a predicate to test whether two Lisp objects look the same—that is, to test whether two objects would be printed the same by Lisp. Notice the differences between EQ, EQL, and EQUAL:

```
eval> (SETQ X '(R S T))
(R S T)

eval> (SETQ Y '(U V W))
(U V W)

eval> (EQ (APPEND X Y) (APPEND X Y))
NIL

eval> (EQL (APPEND X Y) (APPEND X Y))
NIL

eval> (EQUAL (APPEND X Y) (APPEND X Y))
T

eval> (EQ 4.5 (+ 1.2 3.3))
NIL

eval> (EQL 4.5 (+ 1.2 3.3))
T

eval> (EQUAL 4.5 (+ 1.2 3.3))
T
```

Predicate EQUAL is even weaker than EQL in the sense that any two objects that are EQL are certainly also EQUAL, and in addition EQUAL does not distinguish between all pairs of objects distinguished by EQL. However, EQUAL is very useful because it lets us compare lists built at different times during a computation.

Can we write EQUAL ourselves? Yes! It is quite easy using EQL.

We first need to break up EQUAL into a two cases. For two Lisp objects to be EQUAL, they must be both cons cells or both atoms.

If they are both atoms, they should be EQL, since otherwise they will not print the same. If the two objects to be compared are cons cells, they will have the same printed representation if their CARs have the same representation and their CDRs have the same representation.

We can put these pieces together into the following definition of EQUAL:

```
(DEFUN EQUAL (X Y)
    (IF (ATOM X)
        (EQL X Y)
        (IF (ATOM Y)
            'NIL
            (IF (EQUAL (CAR X) (CAR Y))
                (EQUAL (CDR X) (CDR Y))
                'NIL))))
```

If X is an atom, there is no need to check specifically whether Y is an atom or a cons cell. In the latter case, EQL will dispose of it, and in the first case, EQL is the right test to apply anyway. If X is not an atom, it must be a cons cell, so X cannot possibly be equal to Y unless that also is a cons cell. This is the point of the (ATOM Y) test. Now it is known that both X and Y are cons cells, and so equality of both their CARs and CDRs can be tested. Note that if the first of those two tests fails, there is no point in carrying out the second. If the first succeeds, whatever is the result of comparing the CDRs is the outcome for the original equality test.

Notice that T does not appear explicitly in this definition of EQUAL, whereas NIL does. How can the function ever return T?

The following is a trace:

```
eval> (TRACE EQUAL EQL ATOM)
(EQUAL EQL ATOM)

eval> (EQUAL '(F 2.3) '(F 2.3))

(1 ENTER EQUAL ((F 2.3) (F 2.3)))
   (1 ENTER ATOM ((F 2.3)))
   (1 EXIT ATOM NIL)
   (1 ENTER ATOM ((F 2.3)))
   (1 EXIT ATOM NIL)
   (2 ENTER EQUAL (F F))
      (1 ENTER ATOM (F))
      (1 EXIT ATOM T)
```

```
     (1 ENTER EQL (F F))
     (1 EXIT EQL T)
   (2 EXIT EQUAL T)
   (2 ENTER EQUAL ((2.3) (2.3)))
     (1 ENTER ATOM ((2.3)))
     (1 EXIT ATOM NIL)
     (1 ENTER ATOM ((2.3)))
     (1 EXIT ATOM NIL)
     (3 ENTER EQUAL (2.3 2.3))
        (1 ENTER ATOM (2.3))
        (1 EXIT ATOM T)
        (1 ENTER EQL (2.3 2.3))
        (1 EXIT EQL T)
     (3 EXIT EQUAL T)
     (3 ENTER EQUAL (NIL NIL))
        (1 ENTER ATOM (NIL))
        (1 EXIT ATOM T)
        (1 ENTER EQL (NIL NIL))
        (1 EXIT EQL T)
     (3 EXIT EQUAL T)
    (2 EXIT EQUAL T)
  (1 EXIT EQUAL T) T
```

Notice that EQUAL returns NIL if it recursively has to compare an atom to a cons. Otherwise, it returns T if and only if every call to EQL returns T, and then it returns the "last" T. But our definition for EQL did not include symbol T either. It returns T only when one of ZEROP or EQ returns T.

EXERCISES

E2.7.1 Evaluate the following s-expressions if the result is well defined by Common Lisp.
a. (EQUAL 'A 'A)
b. (EQUAL '(A B) (LIST 'A 'B))
c. (EQUAL 2 3)
d. (EQUAL 2 2)
e. (PROGN (SETQ *LIST* (LIST 'A 'B))
          (SETQ *BIG* (LIST 'C *LIST*))
          (EQUAL *LIST* (CAR (CDR *BIG*))))
f. (EQUAL 2.3 (+ 1.1 1.2))
g. (EQUAL '(A B (C D)) '(A B (C D)))
h. (EQUAL 3 3.0)

2.8 LIST CREATION AND ACCESS FUNCTIONS

We have already seen two functions useful for creating lists: CONS and LIST. A third such function, LIST*, is described below. It is sometimes more convenient than the others.

There are many list-accessing functions provided in Common Lisp that extract an element or some part of a list. Some of the useful ones follow.

- (LIST* ...*list-n*) A call to this function is similar to a call to LIST with all but the last argument, except that the final CDR of the constructed list is the last argument given to LIST*. Thus, for example,

```
eval> (LIST* 'A 'B 'C '(D E))
(A B C D E)

eval> (LIST* 'A 'B 'C)
(A B . C)
```

- (C....R *x*) These functions apply a series of CARs and CDRs to cons cell or NIL. The family of functions CAAR, CADR, and so on, whose names are made up of C followed by two to four letters A or D, followed by an R, are shorthand for writing a series of CARs and CDRs. The expansion rule is that

$$(CrstR\ x)$$

becomes

$$(CrR\ (CsR\ (CtR\ x)))$$

Thus,

```
eval> (CADR '(A (B C D) (E F) G))
(B C D)

eval> (CAADR '(A (B C D) (E F) G))
B

eval> (CADADR '(A (B C D) (E F) G))
C
```

```
eval> (CDADDR '(A (B C D) (E F) G))
(F)
```

Most of these function names have indistinguishable pronounciations. Further-more, any code that uses one of these functions that specifies three or more cons cells accesses is going to be very difficult for others to read. It is usually appropriate to introduce new functions with explanatory names or temporary variables (see chapter 3) to increase the readability of the program.

- (NTH *n list*) This function returns the *n*th element of the list *list*, counting from 0 for the CAR of the list. The function operates identically to taking CDR *n* times followed by CAR. In particular, this means that if *n* is at least the length of the list, NIL is returned. Thus,

```
eval> (NTH 0 '(A B C D E))
A

eval> (NTH 3 '(A B C D E))
D

eval> (NTH 5 '(A B C D E))
NIL
```

- (NTHCDR *n list*) This function applies CDR *n* times to the list and returns the result. Thus,

```
eval> (NTHCDR 0 '(A B C D E))
(A B C D E)

eval> (NTHCDR 2 '(A B C D E))
(C D E)

eval> (NTHCDR 5 '(A B C D E))
NIL
```

Notice in particular that we could therefore define NTH as:

```
(DEFUN NTH (N LIST) (CAR (NTHCDR N LIST)))
```

- (FIRST *list*) An incompatible way of counting elements of a list is assumed by a series of functions: FIRST, SECOND, THIRD, FOURTH, FIFTH, SIXTH, SEVENTH,

EIGHTH, NINTH, and TENTH.[6] These functions pick out the appropriate element of a list by counting the CAR as the first; NTH counts the CAR as the zeroth. If these functions have to CDR off the end of a list to get to where they are going, NIL is returned. Thus,

```
eval> (FIRST '(A B C D E))
A


eval> (THIRD '(A B C D E))
C


eval> (SIXTH '(A B C D E))
NIL
```

- (REST *list*) This function is completely equivalent to (CDR *list*). The name complements the use of FIRST (which is equivalent to CAR). Some programmers prefer to use FIRST and REST when decomposing a list, either recursively or iteratively, because they feel these names are more self-explanatory than the historically inspired terms CAR and CDR.
- (LAST *list*) This function CDRs down the top level of the list and returns the last cons cell in the list. Notice that this is not the same as returning the last element of the list; the last element is the CAR of the LAST of a list. Thus,

```
eval> (LAST '(A B C D E))
(E)


eval> (LAST '((A . B) (C . D) (E . F)))
((E . F))
```

These results are clear if you consider the box notation representation of the lists and recall that LAST returns the last top-level cons cell in a list.

---

[6]If you ever catch yourself using anything more than FOURTH, you are most likely overtaxing your short-term memory of a data pattern you are using. The code that you are writing will be largely undecipherable by mortals. Write a function such as (DEFUN FAVORITE-FOOD (X) (FIFTH X)) whose name accurately describes what the fifth element of the list is supposed to represent.

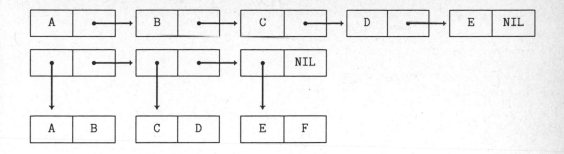

EXERCISES

E2.8.1 Evaluate the following s-expressions:
a. (CADR '(A B C D E))
b. (SECOND '(A B C D E))
c. (NTH 2 '(A B C D E))
d. (CADR (CADR '((A B C) (D E F) (G H I))))
e. (CADADR '((A B C) (D E F) (G H I)))
f. (CDDADR '((A B C) (D E F) (G H I)))
g. (LAST '((A B C) (D E F) (G H I)))
h. (CDR (THIRD '((A B C) (D E F) (G H I))))

E2.8.2 Write two different s-expressions to access symbol C for each of the following lists.
a. (A B C D E)
b. ((A B C) (D E F))
c. ((A B) (C D) (E F))
d. (A (B C D) E F)

2.9 RPLACA **AND** RPLACD: **SURGERY ON CONS CELLS**

The function CONS constructs a cell referring to two objects. Once we have such a cell, we can change its contents with the two predefined functions RPLACA and RPLACD. The first changes the CAR of the cell and the second changes the CDR. Each function takes two arguments: the cons cell to be changed and the replacement value. Both functions return the cons cell as their value. Some examples with the internal representations follow:

```
eval> (SETQ A '(X Y))
(X Y)
```

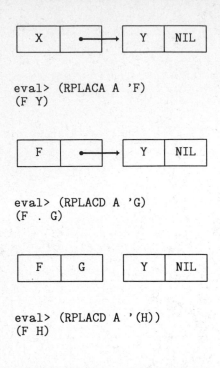

```
eval> (RPLACA A 'F)
(F Y)
```

```
eval> (RPLACD A 'G)
(F . G)
```

```
eval> (RPLACD A '(H))
(F H)
```

Consider again our example of APPEND from the beginning of this chapter:

```
eval> (SETQ X '(R S T))
(R S T)
```

```
eval> (SETQ Y '(U V W))
(U V W)
```

```
eval> (SETQ A (APPEND X Y))
(R S T U V W)
```

```
eval> (SETQ B (APPEND X Y))
(R S T U V W)
```

Recall that A and B actually share structure with Y. Thus, changing the contents of cons cells belonging to Y changes the values of A and B. Thus,

```
eval> (RPLACA Y 'NEW)
(NEW V W)

eval> A
(R S T NEW V W)

eval> B
(R S T NEW V W)

eval> (RPLACD (CDR (CDR (CDR A))) 'END)
(NEW . END)

eval> A
(R S T NEW . END)

eval> B
(R S T NEW . END)

eval> Y
(NEW . END)

eval> (RPLACA A 'START)
(START S T NEW . END)

eval> B
(R S T NEW . END)
```

Notice that the last change to the structure of A did not change the structure of B. That is because the change was to a portion of A that was not shared with B. Prior to that change, however, A and B printed out the same—i.e., they looked equivalent in some manner.

EXERCISES

E2.9.1 Evaluate each of the following s-expressions as though they were typed one after the other to Lisp.

```
(SETQ X '(A B C))
```

```
(SETQ Y (APPEND '(1 2 3) X))
(RPLACA X '4)
Y
(RPLACD X 'NIL)
Y
```

E2.9.2 How would you change C to SEE in each of the following lists?
a. (A B C D E)
b. ((A B C) (D E F))
c. ((A B) (C D) (E F))
d. (A (B C D) E F)

2.10 NCONC **AND** NREVERSE: **DESTRUCTIVE APPENDING AND REVERSING**

Recall what happened when we APPENDed two lists together. When we (APPEND X Y) with X and Y given by

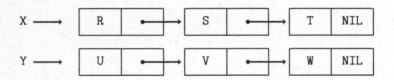

a copy of the list X is made whose third cons cell has a CDR pointing to the beginning of list Y. Now that we know that the contents of a cons cell can be changed, another possibility we could consider is just to change the CDR of the third cons cell of X itself. There is a predefined Lisp function that does just that: NCONC. The following behavior occurs:

```
eval> (SETQ X '(R S T))
(R S T)

eval> (SETQ Y '(U V W))
(U V W)

eval> (SETQ A (NCONC X Y))
(R S T U V W)

eval> X
(R S T U V W)
```

```
eval> (EQ X A)
T
```

We could define NCONC as follows:

```
(DEFUN NCONC (X Y)
     (IF (NULL X)
         Y
         (PROGN (NCONC-AUX X Y)
                X)))
```

```
(DEFUN NCONC-AUX (X Y)
     (IF (NULL (CDR X))
         (RPLACD X Y)
         (NCONC-AUX (CDR X) Y)))
```

Notice that we have to treat the case of an empty first list in a special way. Since there is no cons cell to RPLACD, just the second argument is returned.

In a similar vein, there is a destructive version of REVERSE—namely, NREVERSE.[7] Recall that REVERSE conses up a new top-level list of the old top-level elements. A more efficient way of making a reverse list would be to reuse the cons cells in the following manner:

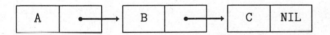

becomes

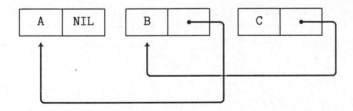

We can define a function with such behavior by:

```
(DEFUN NREVERSE (X)
    (NREVERSE-AUX X 'NIL))

(DEFUN NREVERSE-AUX (REM SOFAR)
    (IF (NULL REM)
        SOFAR
        (NREVERSE-AUX (CDR REM)
                      (PROGN (RPLACD REM SOFAR)
                             REM))))
```

Notice that the recursive call to NREVERSE-AUX relies on the Lisp evaluation procedure evaluating arguments left to right. The old CDR of REM is used as the first argument to NREVERSE-AUX, and once that is evaluated the contents of the CDR of REM are replaced during evaluation of the second argument. In the next chapter we will see a way to make such critical orders of evaluation more explicit in the next chapter using LET and LET*.

An illustration of how the cons cells are recycled by NREVERSE follows:

```
eval> (SETQ L '(A B C))
(A B C)

eval> (NREVERSE L)
(C B A)

eval> L
(A)
```

The original list is destroyed in the process, so NREVERSE should be used only with some prethought.

SUMMARY

Lists can share structure (i.e., they can share cons cells). EQ tests for identity of objects, EQL includes numbers with the same value and type, and EQUAL tests for objects with isomorphic structures.

There are a number of different idioms for using recursion to process a list. One is to CDR down the list and process the body of the desired computation on the way back out of the recursion. Another is to process the body of the computation on the way down, and pass down a partially computed result along with the rest of the list to be processed.

The contents of cons cells can be changed with RPLACA and RPLACD. A large number of list functions that copy list structure in computing their result also have "destructive" versions that change their arguments with these two functions to avoid extra consing. In particular, this chapter introduced functions to append and reverse lists in both nondestructive and destructive versions.

The functions examined in this chapter are shown in Table 2-1.

The special forms examined in this chapter are shown in Table 2-2.

Table 2-1

Function	Args	Description
APPEND	$0 \Rightarrow \infty$	append lists
LOAD	1	load a file
REVERSE	1	reverse top-level list
TYPEP	2	check type of object
SYMBOLP	1	test for a symbol
STRINGP	1	test for a string
-	2	subtract second argument from first
EQ	2	test for same object
EQL	2	test for same object or numbers
EQUAL	2	test for same looking objects
LIST*	$1 \Rightarrow \infty$	make a list with last arg as last CDR
C...R	1	access through cons cells from one to four levels
NTH	2	0-based list element access
NTHCDR	2	0-based list CDR access
FIRST	1	access first list element
SECOND	1	access second list element, etc., through TENTH
REST	1	all but first list element
LAST	1	access last top-level cons
RPLACA	2	replace contents of CAR
RPLACD	2	replace contents of CDR
NCONC	$0 \Rightarrow \infty$	destructively append lists
NREVERSE	1	destructively reverse top-level list

Table 2-2

Special Form	Subforms	Description
DEFVAR	2	declare a global variable and initialize
PROGN	$0 \Rightarrow \infty$	sequentially evaluate subforms
TRACE	$1 \Rightarrow \infty$	trace one or more functions
UNTRACE	$0 \Rightarrow \infty$	untrace some functions

Special form DEFVAR declares a variable to be global and optionally gives it an initial value. A common convention is that all such variables should have names beginning and ending with "*". PROGN provides a mechanism for explicitly sequencing computations.

Special forms TRACE and UNTRACE control the trace facility that lets the programmer watch entry and exit to their functions.

PROBLEMS

P2.1 The Lisp function LENGTH counts the number of elements in the top level of a list. Write a function ALL-LENGTH of one argument that counts the number of atoms that occur in a list at all levels. Thus, the following lists will have the following ALL-LENGTHs.

```
(A B C)                     ==> 3
(A (B C) D (E F))           ==> 6
(((A 1.2) (B (C D) 3.14) (E)))  ==> 7
(NIL NIL (NIL NIL) NIL)     ==> 5
```

P2.2 Write a function ALL-REVERSE of one argument that reverses a list at all levels and thus results in the following transformations:

```
(A B C D)                   ==> (D C B A)
(A (B C) (D E))             ==> ((E D) (C B) A)
((A (B C)) D ((E F G) H))   ==> ((H (G F E)) D ((C B) A))
```

P2.3 Write COUNT-REVERSE-1 and COUNT-REVERSE-2 paralleling the two versions of REVERSE that we studied in section 2.3, using COUNT-APPEND and COUNT-CONS of section 2.4. Write a function COMPARE-REVERSES that takes a list and compares how many more cons cells are used by COUNT-REVERSE-1 than by COUNT-REVERSE-2 to reverse the list. Run COMPARE-REVERSES on a few lists of different lengths. For example,

```
eval> (COMPARE-REVERSES '(A B C))
3

eval> (COMPARE-REVERSES '(A B C D E F))
15
```

You may have to write some auxiliary functions to achieve this. Do not use any global variables other than *COUNT*.

P2.4 Write a function EQUAL-SYMBOLS of two arguments that says any two numbers are equal, a symbol is only equal to itself, and a two list is equal if all their elements are recursively EQUAL-SYMBOLS. Thus, the function has the following results:

```
eval> (EQUAL-SYMBOLS 2.2 3)
T

eval> (EQUAL-SYMBOLS 2.2 'A)
NIL

eval> (EQUAL-SYMBOLS '(B 4 (C D (2.2)) E) '(B 2 (C D (0)) E))
T

eval> (EQUAL-SYMBOLS '(B 4 (C D (2.2)) E) '(B 4 (3 D (2.2)) E))
NIL
```

P2.5 Write a function TYPER that takes a list structure and returns a new one with the same "shape" but with only symbols NUMBER and SYMBOL, corresponding to the type of the original atoms in the list. Thus, for example,

```
eval> (TYPER '(A B 3 D))
(SYMBOL SYMBOL NUMBER SYMBOL)

eval> (TYPER '((A 2.3) (((B C)) 3)))
((SYMBOL NUMBER) (((SYMBOL SYMBOL)) NUMBER))
```

P2.6 Write a destructive version, NTYPER, of TYPER that reuses the cons cells of its argument and thus avoids the necessity of using CONS.

3

CONTROL STRUCTURES

We have seen recursion using recursive function definitions, explicit sequencing using PROGN, and conditional evaluation using IF. Lisp has a much richer set of control primitives, however. Some, such as COND, AND, and OR, are not inherently more powerful than those we have already seen, but they often let us write more understandable code. We can do this by choosing the one that best expresses the structure or "sense" of the desired computation. Other special forms provide new levels of control. For instance, LET and LET* provide a mechanism for introducing new local variables besides those that appear in a functions argument list. In addition, *iteration* is a useful and valid Lisp control structure. Later we will describe the DO special form, which provides a structured approach to iteration. Additionally, DOLIST and DOTIMES provide syntactically simpler specialized versions of DO that cover many of its common uses. These are described in chapter 6. In chapter 12, we will see some other Lisp control structures, maintained in Common Lisp for compatibility with old Lisps, which provide an unstructured approach to iteration.

3.1 SPECIAL FORMS FOR MORE READABLE CODE

Examine again our definition of EQUAL in section 2.7. Notice how the code tends to slide over toward the right of the page with an IF forming the *else* part of each previous IF. There is another special form in Lisp that provides a convenient way to write such strings of *if* tests. Called COND[1] for *conditional*, it takes the form

$$(\text{COND } (test\text{-}1 \; result\text{-}1) \; (test\text{-}2 \; result\text{-}2) \dots).$$

When the Lisp evaluation procedure sees a COND, it evaluates each of the test forms (e.g., *test-1*, *test-2*, etc.) in turn. When one evaluates to non-NIL, the corresponding result form (e.g., *result-1*, *result-2*, etc.) is evaluated and its value is returned as the result of the COND. In such a case, no further test or result forms are evaluated. If all test forms evaluate to NIL, NIL is returned as the result of the COND.[2]

We can rewrite our function as

```
(DEFUN EQUAL (X Y)
```

---

[1] Actually COND historically predates IF in Lisp. Indeed, in some Lisps IF is implemented in terms of COND.

[2] In some Lisps, it is required that at least one of the test forms evaluate to non-NIL; it is illegal to "fall off the end" of a COND.

```
(COND ((ATOM X) (EQL X Y))
      ((ATOM Y) 'NIL)
      ((EQUAL (CAR X) (CAR Y))
       (EQUAL (CDR X) (CDR Y)))
      (T 'NIL)))
```

The final clause (i.e., (T 'NIL)) illustrates a common practice with COND. The test form here is T, which always evaluates to T. Hence, if no other test form has turned up non-NIL, this test form forces its result to be returned. Equally valid clauses with identical behavior could have been

```
('T 'NIL)
(3.14 'NIL)
('(ANY ARBITRARY CONSTANT (FOR INSTANCE THIS LIST)) 'NIL)
```

By convention, the symbol T, is usually used when an "always succeeds" clause is wanted, and this has become an idiom in Lisp programming.[3] Notice that there is no point in writing further clauses after such a "T clause," because they can never be reached.

Notice also that in this particular case we could have left the final clause out and the function would have exactly the same behavior. Putting the clause in makes for a clearer program, stating explicitly what the result will be if none of the other test clauses succeed.

Two other useful special forms are AND and OR. These correspond roughly to logical *and* and *or*. They look like

$$(AND\ form\text{-}1\ form\text{-}2\dots\ form\text{-}n)$$

and

$$(OR\ form\text{-}1\ form\text{-}2\dots\ form\text{-}n)\ .$$

In each case, their argument forms are evaluated left to right until it is first possible to say whether all the forms evaluate to non-NIL (in the case of AND) or whether at least one of the forms evaluates to non-NIL (in the case of OR). Thus, AND evaluates each argument form in turn until one returns NIL—in which case AND returns NIL without evaluating the rest of the forms. If all of the forms return non-NIL, the value of the last is returned. Thus, AND returns "truth" only

---

[3]So much so that it has been transported to various other constructs in some Lisps where there is no such logical explanation of the idiom, and in fact the only justification that can be given is "so that it looks like COND."

if all its arguments return "truth." On the other hand OR returns "truth" if any of its arguments return "truth." It does this by evaluating each argument form in turn until one returns non-NIL, and then it returns the result as the result of the OR. If all argument forms return NIL, the result of the OR is NIL.

We can now rewrite our simple version of EQL in a somewhat clearer way:

```
(DEFUN EQL (A B)
   (OR (EQ A B)
       (AND (OR (AND (TYPEP A 'FIXNUM)
                     (TYPEP B 'FIXNUM))
                (AND (TYPEP A 'SINGLE-FLOAT)
                     (TYPEP B 'SINGLE-FLOAT)))
            (ZEROP (- A B))))))
```

The reorganization of EQL is based on the following observation: If the two arguments are the same object as determined by EQ, they are certainly EQL. If that is not true, the second subform of the OR special form is evaluated. If that is the case, EQL should only return T if the two arguments have the same type and if their difference is zero. The outer AND has two subclauses. The first ensures that the two arguments have the same type, while the second compares them. Here we see the importance of AND giving up evaluating clauses as soon as one of them returns NIL, as the subtraction should not be done unless we are sure that B is a number. This sort of type checking is the most typical use of AND—often more than two clauses are used, however. Within the first clause of the outer AND, there are two possibilities that need to be checked. If either both numbers have type FIXNUM or both have type SINGLE-FLOAT, the comparison in the second subclause should determine the value of the EQL test.

In the foregoing definition of EQL, notice that neither NIL nor T appear explicitly. The former can be returned as the value of a failing AND clause, while the latter can be returned as the result of a call to EQ or ZEROP.

An example of EQUAL using the AND special form where possible follows.

```
(DEFUN EQUAL (X Y)
   (COND ((ATOM X) (EQL X Y))
         ((ATOM Y) 'NIL)
         (T (AND (EQUAL (CAR X) (CAR Y))
                 (EQUAL (CDR X) (CDR Y))))))
```

Here the AND explicitly demonstrates that both the CARs *and* the CDRs must be equal for the two cons cells to be equal. At the same time, the semantics of AND ensure that the CDRs are never needlessly compared if the CARs do not match. Notice also that we have removed the final (T 'NIL) clause in this version of EQUAL without detracting from the understandability of the function definition.

EXERCISES

E3.1.1 For each s-expression, list the predicates that are evaluated in order of evaluation:
a. (AND (NUMBERP 3) (ATOM 'A) (NULL 'T))
b. (AND (NUMBERP 3) (ATOM '(A B)) (NULL 'T))
c. (OR (NUMBERP 3) (ATOM '(A B)) (NULL 'T))
d. (OR (ATOM '(X Y Z)) (NUMBERP 'B) (CONSP 'X))

E3.1.2 Write the following code without using COND:

```
(COND ((EQ DAY 'SATURDAY)
       'FOOTBALL)
      ((EQ DAY 'SUNDAY)
       'DIEM-SUM)
      ((EQ DAY 'WEDNESDAY)
       'LAB)
      (T 'CLASS))
```

3.2 ORGANIZING FOR EFFICIENCY

Look again at the trace of our first definition for EQUAL. Notice in particular how long it took the recursive calls to decide that F is equal to F and NIL is equal to NIL. Also notice that if two EQ lists were given to this EQUAL it would recursively decompose them and compare all of their components. However, any two things that are EQ are certainly EQUAL, since they are the same object.

Thus, it makes sense to first check for EQness of the two arguments to EQUAL because that case is quite common; it is the case of all nonnumeric leafs in comparing any two lists. Since the case of comparing two numbers would still have to be handled by EQL, the test might well be made into an EQL test. Doing this has ramifications for the rest of the function too. In the clause that succeeds when X is an atom, it is no longer necessary to include a test of whether it is EQL to Y. However, it is necessary to check for the atomicity of both X and Y before treating them as cons cells in the last clause of the COND. The result is

```
(DEFUN EQUAL (X Y)
    (COND ((EQL X Y) 'T)
          ((OR (ATOM X)
               (ATOM Y))
           'NIL)
          (T (AND (EQUAL (CAR X) (CAR Y))
                  (EQUAL (CDR X) (CDR Y)))))))
```

Notice that there are exactly the same calls to predefined Lisp functions as before—they simply have been reordered. Notice also that now there is an explicit T in the function definition.

3.3 LET **AND** LET*: **BINDING LOCAL VARIABLES**

So far, whenever we have computed a value we have handed it directly to a function needing it. Sometimes we may need to hand a computed value to two or more different places, or we may need to save a result while we do some order-critical computations (where side effects are involved). We saw an example of the latter in our definition of NREVERSE and NREVERSE-AUX—we were saved there by making use of the left to right evaluation of arguments by the Lisp evaluation procedure.

The special form LET provides a way of introducing temporary variables into a function. Temporary variables can save the result of a computation. The general form is

```
(LET ((var-1  value-1)
      (var-2  value-2)
           .

           .

           .
      (var-n  value-n))
  body)
```

Here *var-1*, *var-2*, ... *var-n* are symbols (LET does not evaluate them) that will be used as names of introduced variables. They can be referred to by any code that appears in the *body* form. When the LET is entered, each of the s-expressions *value-1*, *value-2*, ... *value-n* is evaluated in turn. When they are all done, the new variables are given their values. Thus, *value-3*, say, cannot legitimately refer to *var-1*.

Suppose we represent points in the plane as a list of two numbers, the first being the point's *x* coordinate and the second its *y* coordinate. Then we could compute the distance between two points with

```
(DEFUN DISTANCE (P1 P2)
    (LET ((XDIFF (- (CAR P1) (CAR P2)))
          (YDIFF (- (CAR (CDR P1)) (CAR (CDR P2)))))
        (SQRT (+ (* XDIFF XDIFF) (* YDIFF YDIFF)))))
```

(Notice that SQRT is a function of one numeric argument that computes its square root.) Without the benefit of temporary variables, we either would have had to extract the *x* and *y* components from each point list twice and computed their difference twice, or we would have had to define a function SQARE to compute the square of the difference. LET is more appropriate when we won't be using the auxilary function anywhere else.

With LET, we can now redefine NREVERSE in a clearer manner as

```
(DEFUN NREVERSE (X)
    (NREVERSE-AUX X 'NIL))


(DEFUN NREVERSE-AUX (REM SOFAR)
    (IF (NULL REM)
        SOFAR
        (LET ((NEWREM (CDR REM)))
            (PROGN (RPLACD REM SOFAR)
                   (NREVERSE-AUX NEWREM REM)))))
```

The essential sequential ordering of the computations is now quite explicit.

Now consider a third example. Suppose that we have a list of names of people that could be surnames or first-name/surname pairs, so that it might look as follows:

```
((BILL BROWN) EINSTEIN NEWTON (ADA LOVELACE)
 (JAN BROWN) BULLWINKLE)
```

Suppose further that we want to pass each name to a function PROCESS-NAME that takes two arguments—a surname and a first name—but the latter can be NIL. Then we could write something similar to

```
(DEFUN PROCESS-NAME (SURNAME FIRSTNAME)
  ...)

(DEFUN PROCESS-LIST-OF-NAMES (LIST)
  (IF (NULL LIST)
      'T
      (LET ((NAME (CAR LIST)))
           (LET ((NAME (IF (ATOM NAME)
                           NAME
                           (CAR (CDR NAME))))
                 (FNAME (IF (ATOM NAME)
                            'NIL
                            (CAR NAME))))
```

```
(PROGN (PROCESS-NAME NAME FNAME)
       (DO-SOMETHING-ELSE NAME FNAME)
       (PROCESS-LIST-OF-NAMES (CDR LIST)))))))
```

to feed PROCESS-NAME. Notice that there are two variables called NAME in this example, one in each LET. This is poor practice because it makes the program harder to read and debug, but we will use this example to illustrate a point. The value for FNAME is computed after the value for the inner NAME has been computed, but references to the variable NAME within FNAME's value are to the first, or outer, variable NAME. This is because the new variable NAME is not available until all of the values of all of the variables in the inner LET have been computed.

A variation on LET is LET*. It sequentially binds each new variable as its value is computed, and so later values can use variables introduced by the current LET*. Thus, for example, the following two functions are equivalent, but the latter suffers less from "right-crawl."

```
(DEFUN PAINT-COST (COLOR)
   (LET ((PAIR (ASSOC COLOR
                   '((BLUE . 8.00)
                     (RED . 5.50)
                     (CHARTREUSE . 13.25)))))
        (LET ((PRICE (IF (NULL PAIR)
                         *DEFAULT-PAINT-PRICE*
                         (CDR PAIR))))
             (+ PRICE
                (* *TAX-RATE* PRICE)))))


(DEFUN PAINT-COST (COLOR)
   (LET* ((PAIR (ASSOC COLOR
                   '((BLUE . 8.00)
                     (RED . 5.50)
                     (CHARTREUSE . 13.25))))
          (PRICE (IF (NULL PAIR)
                     *DEFAULT-PAINT-PRICE*
                     (CDR PAIR))))
         (+ PRICE
            (* *TAX-RATE* PRICE))))
```

Notice how the convention of starting and ending global variables with an "*" makes this function much easier to understand; there is no need to search for a variable binding for such variables.

EXERCISES

E3.3.1 What do each of these evaluate to?
```
a.  (LET ((A 3))
        (CONS A
              (LET ((A 4))
                  A)))
b.  (LET ((A 3))
        (LET ((A 4)
              (B A))
          (CONS A B)))
c.  (LET ((A 3))
        (LET* ((A 4)
               (B A))
           (CONS A B)))
```

3.4 DEFUN, COND **AND** LET **HAVE IMPLICIT** PROGNS

In chapter 2, we saw the special form PROGN, which looked like:

$$(PROGN\ form\text{-}1\ form\text{-}2\ldots form\text{-}n)$$

It evaluates each of its argument forms in turn and returns the value of the last as the value of the PROGN. This special form is only useful if at least all but the last arguments have side effects. It provides a method for sequencing forms with side effects.

A number of Lisp constructs save the user from having to type an explicit PROGN by allowing sequences of forms in their bodies; this is known as "having an *implicit* PROGN." In particular, the bodies of DEFUN and LET are implicit PROGNs—they each can be a series of statements that are evaluated in order with the result of the last being returned as the result of the enclosing form. Thus, the following three functions have equivalent behavior (although the third is a somewhat strange way to go about it):

```
(DEFVAR *COUNT* 0)

(DEFUN COUNT-CONS-1 (X Y)
    (PROGN (SETQ *COUNT* (+ 1 *COUNT*))
           (CONS X Y)))
```

```
(DEFUN COUNT-CONS-2 (X Y)
    (SETQ *COUNT* (+ 1 *COUNT*))
    (CONS X Y))


(DEFUN COUNT-CONS-3 (X Y)
    (LET ((CONS-CELL (CONS 'NIL 'NIL)))
        (RPLACA CONS-CELL X)
        (RPLACD CONS-CELL Y)
        (SETQ *COUNT* (+ 1 *COUNT*))
        CONS-CELL))
```

The special form COND is also more general than previously indicated. Each of its clauses may contain an implicit PROGN. Thus, the general form looks like

```
(COND (test-1 form-1-a form-1-b ...result-1)
      (test-2 form-2-a form-2-b ...result-2)
      ...)
```

If a test form evaluates to non-NIL, each of the following forms is evaluated and the result of the last is returned as the result of the COND.

3.5 COMMENTING CODE

Comments can make programs understandable. They can describe the expected class of inputs to a function and the resulting outputs. They can explain how clever algorithms really do produce the claimed result. They can describe the assumptions about, and effects on, global data structures that the function alters.

Comments can be easily interspersed with Lisp code. Whenever Lisp sees a semicolon, it ignores it and everything else until the next new line. The following conventions are adhered to by many Lisp programmers and are used throughout this book. In addition, many automated programming aids (such as editors) understand about these conventions and make some inferences from them in choosing the best way to display a program on a screen or in a listing. There are other sets of conventions used by various groups of programmers—it is important to use a consistent set of conventions within a project.

Our conventions are as follows:

1. Any s-expression that is top level within a file is preceded and followed by a blank line.

2. If a comment is outside the scope of a function three semicolons are used, flush against the left margin.

3. If a comment is within a function but on a line of its own, two successive semicolons are used, and they are indented to the same place a piece of Lisp code would logically appear.

4. When a comment is placed on a line that also contains Lisp code, at least one space is left after the Lisp code, a single semicolon is used, and the comment follows. Often editors will ensure that all such comments have their semicolons line up on a particular column on the page. Another possibility is to use a tab because these are ignored by Lisp.

5. A much more optional convention is that Lisp code be typed in uppercase lettering[4] and that comments appear in lowercase lettering with the usual capitalization for punctation.[5]

Here is a function from section 3.2 with comments written according to these conventions:

```
;;; Given a paint color compute the selling price of a
;;; standard can of paint, including the tax.


(DEFUN PAINT-COST (COLOR)
  ;; a few colors have special prices
  (LET* ((PAIR (ASSOC
                COLOR
                '((BLUE . 8.00)
                  (RED . 5.50)
                  (CHARTREUSE . 13.25)))) ;at this price!!
         (PRICE (IF (NULL PAIR)
                    ;; this should be SETQed before use
                    *DEFAULT-PAINT-PRICE*
                    (CDR PAIR)))) ;get the price from the cons
    (+ PRICE
       ;; tax rate is a fraction of 1.00
       (* *TAX-RATE* PRICE))))
```

---

[4] This does not work in Franz Lisp, which is case-sensitive; so while `CAR` is undefined, `car` works as expected.

[5] The ZWEI editor for Lisp machines has an `ELECTRIC-SHIFT-LOCK` mode that detects whether you are typing Lisp code or comments and automatically sets the case of type-in to follow this convention. It is even smart enough to handle strings correctly within Lisp code.

3.6 DO: **A SPECIAL FORM FOR ITERATION**

We have seen many examples of functions that can be defined recursively. Often, however, the structure of a computation has a much more natural expression as an iterative procedure. The primitive for iteration within Common Lisp is DO.[6] The key property of DO is that it involves multiple iteration variables that are all stepped according to their own stepping rules in parallel. It takes the general form

```
(DO ((var-1  init-1  stepper-1)
     (var-2  init-2  stepper-2)
     .

     .

     .

     (var-n  init-n  stepper-n))
    (end-test
     end-form-1
     .

     .

     .

     end-form-k
     return-value)
   body-1
   body-2
   .

   .

   .

   body-m)
```

It looks something like a LET with a set of variables—and values to which they get bound—all in parallel. In fact, the operation up through the binding of each *var-i* to the value of each *init-i* is identical to that of LET. Then the *end-test* is evaluated. If it returns non-NIL, each of the optional *end-form-j*'s are evaluated and their values discarded. Finally, the *return-value* is evaluated and its value is returned as the value of the DO. Thus, there is a COND-clause like structure following the variable bindings. If the *end-test* returns NIL, the DO continues. Each of its *body-l* expressions is evaluated in turn. If any expression of the form

---

[6]DO was inherited from Maclisp and all Maclisp descendants have left it intact. Thus, the Common Lisp definition is quite commonly accepted, which is quite surprising for the complexity of its description; usually such large organisms mutate quickly.

(RETURN *value*) is evaluated, the DO is exited and *value* is returned as its value. If not, the iteration is complete. The next iteration starts by evaluating each of the *stepper* forms in terms of the current bindings of the DO variables, and once they are all done the variables are all bound to the new values in parallel. Now the iteration continues as before by evaluating the end test and then the body.

    As an example, let's redefine iteratively a Lisp function that we have studied recursively.

```
(DEFUN LENGTH (X)
     (DO ((LST X (CDR LST))
          (COUNT 0 (+ 1 COUNT)))
         ((NULL LST)
          COUNT)))
```

There is a no body of the DO in this particular example—it is optional.

    Two variables are introduced by the DO: LST and COUNT. They get bound to the argument list and 0, respectively, and they are each stepped in parallel. At each iteration, LST is stepped another CDR down the list, while COUNT is increased by one. When the end of the argument list is reached, the DO is exited with the current value of COUNT. Thus, the following behavior happens internally:

```
eval> (LENGTH '(A B))

      LST = (A B)
      COUNT = 0
      (NULL LST) = (NULL '(A B)) = NIL

      LST = (CDR LST) = (B)
      COUNT = (+ 1 COUNT) = 1
      (NULL LST) = (NULL '(B) = NIL

      LST = (CDR LST) = NIL
      COUNT = (+ 1 COUNT) = 2
      (NULL LST) = (NULL 'NIL) = T

  2
```

    Notice that the end test is performed *after* the variables have received their new bindings.

    Now compare an iterative formulation of the function REVERSE with our previous recursive formulation.

```
;;; iterative formulation

(DEFUN I-REVERSE (LST)
    (DO ((REM LST (CDR REM))
         (SOFAR 'NIL (CONS (CAR REM) SOFAR)))
        ((NULL REM)
         SOFAR)))


;;; recursive formulation


(DEFUN R-REVERSE (LST)
    (R-REVERSE-AUX LST 'NIL))

(DEFUN R-REVERSE-AUX (REM SOFAR)
    (IF (NULL REM)
        SOFAR
        (R-REVERSE-AUX (CDR REM) (CONS (CAR REM) SOFAR))))
```

The variables REM and SOFAR play identical roles in the two versions. The function R-REVERSE does the same as the initial forms in the DO of I-REVERSE. The recursive calls to R-REVERSE are equivalent to supplying the stepping values in the DO.[7]

The next example shows a DO-loop whose controlling variable is an integer. The variable I is stepped from N down to 1, and the iteration stops as soon as it stepped past there to 0.

```
eval> (DEFUN MAKE-ASCENDING-LIST (N)
          (DO ((I N (- I 1))
               (LST '()
                    (CONS I LST)))
              ((ZEROP I)
               LST)))
MAKE-ASCENDING-LIST
```

---

[7] In fact, a good Lisp compiler should compile almost the same code for the recursive **R-REVERSE-AUX** and the new iterative **I-REVERSE**. Using a technique called *tail recursion* analysis, the compiler should recognize that **R-REVERSE-AUX** is a recursive implementation of an inherently iterative process. Even a good Lisp compiler will not recognize the iterativeness of our previous recursive definition of **LENGTH**. The foregoing iterative definition (of **LENGTH**) does, however, suggest another recursive implementation of **LENGTH** using an auxiliary function in the spirit of **REVERSE-AUX**. Can you see it?

```
eval> (MAKE-ASCENDING-LIST 4)
(1 2 3 4)
```

So far, all the examples have essentially used one variable as a driver for the iteration, stopping on some condition met by the single variable. That is by no means always the case, as the following example shows. In this case, the DO has a body. (Notice that a DO body makes sense only if it has side effects or uses RETURN.)

```
(DEFUN GET-LONGEST (LIST1 LIST2)
    (DO ((REM1 LIST1 (CDR REM1))
         (REM2 LIST2 (CDR REM2)))
        (NIL)
      (COND ((NULL REM1) (RETURN LIST2))
            ((NULL REM2) (RETURN LIST1)))))
```

In GET-LONGEST, the end test of the DO is NIL, so it can only be exited by a RETURN from the body. Care must be taken in using NIL as an end test to ensure that there is a guaranteed way that the DO will eventually be exited from its body. Notice that an end test is required, even if it is NIL.

A common habit of many DO users is to use stepping variable names that are already the names of variables containing a value to be iterated upon. Thus, they would write our iterative REVERSE as

```
(DEFUN REVERSE (LST)
    (DO ((LST LST (CDR LST))
         (NEW 'NIL (CONS (CAR LST) NEW)))
        ((NULL LST)
         NEW)))
```

The stepping variable LST is a new variable introduced by the DO. It is initialized to the value of the outer LST; the one used as a function argument. All variable references in initialization forms are to variables introduced outside the scope of the DO. Many other programmers (including the author) do not like this particular style of variable naming. They find it confusing to have two variables with the same name, especially since they do start out referring to the same thing but then quickly diverge.

It is permissible to leave out a stepper form for any variable. In that case, the variable is initialized but its value is not changed at the time all other variables are stepped. Stylistically, it might be clearer to delete such variables from the DO and have them initialized in a LET wrapped around it.

EXERCISES

E3.6.1 Evaluate each of the following s-expressions:
```
a. (LET ((COUNT 0)) ;gets SETQed below
        (DO ((LST '(A B C D E) (CDR LST)))
            ((NULL LST)
             COUNT)
            (SETQ COUNT (+ 1 COUNT))))
b. (LET ((COUNT 0)) ;gets SETQed below
        (DO ((I 3 (+ 1 I)))
            ((EQL I 9)
             COUNT)
            (SETQ COUNT (+ 1 COUNT))))
c. (DO ((LST1 '(A B C D E) (CDR LST1))
        (LST2 '(E D C B A) (CDR LST2))
        (COUNT 0 (+ 1 COUNT)))
       ((EQ (CAR LST1) (CAR LST2))
        COUNT))
```

E3.6.2 What does this function do?

```
(DEFUN ANON (LIST)
    (DO ((LST (CDR LIST) (CDR LST))
         (HEAD (CAR LIST) (CAR LST))
         (LASTHEAD LIST HEAD))
        ((NULL LST)
         'NIL)
        (IF (EQ HEAD LASTHEAD)
            (RETURN LST))))
```

SUMMARY

The special forms examined in this chapter are shown in Table 3-1.

Special form COND provides a more general test and branch control structure than does IF. Forms AND and OR evaluate just enough of their argument subforms to determine whether the combination is logically true under conjunction or disjunction. They sometimes make the intent of conditional evaluations more clear.

The special forms LET and LET* are used to introduce new variables and to give them initial values. The first binds all of its variables in parallel, while the second does them sequentially. The special form DO also introduces variables and gives them initial values in parallel. Then it iteratively evaluates body statements and gives all the variables new values, again in parallel. End tests

Table 3-1

Special Form	Subforms	Description
COND	$1 \Rightarrow \infty$	conditionally evaluate expressions
AND	$0 \Rightarrow \infty$	conditionally evaluate logical conjunction
OR	$0 \Rightarrow \infty$	conditionally evaluate logical disjunction
LET	$2 \Rightarrow \infty$	parallel binding of variables
LET*	$2 \Rightarrow \infty$	sequential binding of variables
DO	$2 \Rightarrow \infty$	iteration primitive

and explicit returns can terminate the iteration. For all three special forms, the introduced variables remain "in force" only within, or during, the evaluation of the special form. The variables disappear on exit, and, furthermore, are not accessible from functions called within the form. The *scope* of the introduced variable is the special form.

When a variable is referenced in a Lisp function, the Lisp system must determine its value. It looks outwards through s-expressions of increasing scope, that contain the variable reference. The first such s-expression that is a special form binding a variable of the desired name determines the variable that is being referenced. The initialization forms for variables in LET, LET*, and DO, while structurally within the scope of their special forms, are treated as lying lexically outside the forms. The only other variable introducing form we have seen is function definition; the argument list lists arguments whose scope is the whole function. The foregoing class of variables are referred to as *lexical* or *local* variables. If no variable is found within the scope of the function to match a variable reference, the reference is assumed to be to a global variable. All global variables are accessible to all functions, except where their name has been shadowed by a newly introduced lexical variable.

PROBLEMS

P3.1 Rewrite function EQUAL-SYMBOLS from problem 2.4 using some of the special forms introduced in this chapter.

P3.2 Some Lisps provide TCONC structures, which make it easy to add elements to the end of a list. A TCONC is the cons of a list and its last cons cell. This cons cell is then modified as elements are added to the end of the underlying list and removed from the front—thus TCONCs provide a first-in first-out structure. Write the following functions:

- (MAKE-TCONC) Makes a fresh and empty TCONC; that is, (NIL).
- (TCONC *tconc element*) Adds an element to an existing TCONC.
- (LCONC *tconc list*) Adds a list of elements to an existing TCONC.
- (REMOVE-HEAD *tconc*) Removes the first element from a TCONC and returns it.

All but the last of these functions should return the TCONC itself. The most difficult part about writing these functions is dealing with the cases of emptiness—in
particular, a null list to be LCONCed, an empty TCONC in any of the last three
cases, or a TCONC with only one element in the last case. For example,

```
eval> (SETQ TC (MAKE-TCONC))
(NIL)

eval> (TCONC TC 'A)
((A) A)

eval> (REMOVE-HEAD TC)
A

eval> TC
(NIL)

eval> (TCONC TC 'B)
((B) B)

eval> (TCONC TC 'C)
((B C) C)

eval> (LCONC TC 'NIL)
((B C) C)

eval> (LCONC TC '(D E F))
((B C D E F) F)

eval> (REMOVE-HEAD TC)
B

eval> TC
((C D E F) F)
```

P3.3 Why are TCONCs more efficient than ordinary lists for these operations?

P3.4 Define an iterative function RANGE that takes a list of numbers (at least
one long) and returns a list of length 2 of the smallest and largest numbers.
Recall predicates < and > from section 1.9. Function RANGE should have the
following behavior:

```
eval> (RANGE '(0 7 8 2 3 -1))
(-1 8)
```

```
eval> (RANGE '(7 6 5 4 3))
(3 7)
```

Be sure that your solution only iterates down the list once.

P3.5 Write another function, VALID-RANGE, that returns the same result as RANGE if all elements of the argument list are numbers, but that returns the atom INVALID if the list contains a nonnumber.

P3.6 Write a function that finds the maximum number that occurs at any depth in a list. For example,

```
eval> (MAX-NO '((A 3) (B (C 4.5)) 3.2))
4.5
```

P3.7 The sequence of numbers 0, 1, 1, 2, 3, 5, 8, 13 ... are known as the Fibonacci numbers, where the fourth Fibonacci number is 5 and the fifth is 8, and so on. Each Fibonacci number is the sum of the previous two. If we let $F(n)$ represent the nth Fibonacci number, $F(0) = 0$, $F(1) = 1$, and $F(n) = F(n-1) + F(n-2)$. Write a recursive definition RECF to compute Fibonacci numbers. Then write an iterative version. Compare your recursive and iterative implementations by trying them for $n = 16, 17, 18$, or so. What's the difference and why?

4

MORE
LIST
OPERATIONS

We have seen that Lisp programs are represented as lists. Lists also are the primary data structures of Lisp. There are three very common ways in which they are used. They are used as record structures, as sets, and as associative stores.

When used as record structures, the programmer uses a particular pattern for many list instances. For example, the `CAR` might be a person's name represented as a list of two symbols, the `CADR` might be the person's age as a number, or the `CADDR` might be the person's occupation. Thus, the lists

```
((MARY SMITH) 33 LAWYER)
((JOE BROWN) 27 DENTIST)
((BOB BLACK) 45 TEACHER)
```

might each represent a person and be processed uniformly by some set of functions. The list component accessing and modifying functions of chapter 2 provided a powerful set of tools for using lists in this way.

In this chapter, we look in more detail at the other two common uses of lists: sets and associations.

4.1 LISTS AS SETS

A list that has no repeats among its top-level elements can be viewed as a representation of a set of its top-level elements. There are a number of predefined Lisp functions that are motivated by such a view of lists. The most important and useful is `MEMBER`, a predicate that tests for membership of a set represented as a list. Other useful, but less indispensable functions are ones to compute unions and intersections of sets represented in this manner.

The Lisp function `MEMBER` is a predicate of two arguments that tests whether its first argument, or *key*, is a top-level member of the second argument, which is a list. It returns `NIL` (i.e., "false") if the key is not a list member and non-`NIL` (i.e., "truth") if it is. By default, the function `MEMBER` compares each element of the list with the key using `EQL`. We will see how to change the default (to `EQUAL` or `EQ` for instance) in chapter 12.

Function `MEMBER` is an example of a predicate that returns more information than simply `T` in the case of success or truth. It returns the remainder of the list from the point at which the key occurs. Thus,

```
eval> (MEMBER 'X '(A B C D))
NIL

eval> (MEMBER 'C '(A B C D))
(C D)
```

```
eval> (MEMBER '(A FLAT) '((C SHARP) D (F SHARP) (A FLAT) G B))
NIL

eval> (SETQ *TUNE* '((C SHARP) D (F SHARP) (A FLAT) G B))
((C SHARP) D (F SHARP) (A FLAT) G B))

eval> (MEMBER (FOURTH *TUNE*) *TUNE*)
((A FLAT) G B)
```

The function MEMBER could be defined recursively as:

```
(DEFUN MEMBER (ELEMENT LIST)
    (COND ((NULL LIST)
            'NIL)
          ((EQL ELEMENT (CAR LIST))
           LIST)
          (T (MEMBER ELEMENT (CDR LIST)))))
```

The function MEMBER can be implemented iteratively as a DO with a body. When the searched-for item is found, the remainder of the searched list is returned. If the item is not found, NIL is finally returned.

```
(DEFUN MEMBER (ITEM LST)
    (DO ((ELEMENTS LST (CDR ELEMENTS)))
        ((NULL ELEMENTS)
         'NIL)
       (IF (EQL ITEM (CAR ELEMENTS))
           (RETURN ELEMENTS))))
```

The following functions are sometimes useful for manipulating sets represented as lists of elements. Each has two variants: nondestructive and destructive.

- (UNION *list1 list2*) This function returns a new list containing all elements that appear in the top level of either of the two argument lists. There is neither a guaranteed order for the resulting list, nor determinate behavior if either of the original lists contains duplicated elements. Elements are compared using EQL.

- (NUNION *list1 list2*) This function is the same as UNION, but it may destroy the argument lists.

- (INTERSECTION *list1 list2*) This function returns a new list containing all elements that appear in the top level of both of the two argument lists. There is neither a guaranteed order for the resulting list, nor determinate behavior if either of the original lists contains duplicated elements. Elements are compared using EQL.

- (NINTERSECTION *list1 list2*) This function is the same as INTERSECTION, but it may destroy the argument lists.

Some examples of these functions are

```
eval> (UNION '(A B C) '(D B E))
(E D A B C)

eval> (INTERSECTION '(A B C) '(D B E))
(B)
```

EXERCISES

E4.1.1 Evaluate the following s-expressions:
a. (MEMBER 'C '(A B C D E))
b. (MEMBER 'C '(A B D E))
c. (MEMBER 3 '(6 5 4 3 2 1))
d. (MEMBER '(C D) '((A B) (C D) (E F)))

4.2 LISTS AS DATABASES

In addition to straightforward sets, lists also provide convenient representations for *associations* of keys and values.

 The function ASSOC uses a *key* argument to search for an *associated* value in an *association list*. An association list has the form

$$((key\text{-}1 . value\text{-}1)\ (key\text{-}2 . value\text{-}2) \ldots (key\text{-}n . value\text{-}n))$$

Thus, it is a list of cons cells, the CAR of each of which is a key, and the CDR is the associated value. ASSOC searches the list linearly until either it drops off the end and returns NIL or it finds a key that is EQL[1] to the desired key, in which case it returns the cons cell containing the key. Thus,

---

[1] Again we will see how to change this default comparison function in chapter **7**.

```
eval> (ASSOC 3 '((1 PARTRIDGE)
                  (2 TURTLE DOVES)
                  (3 FRENCH HENS)
                  (4 TURTLE DOVES)
                  (5 GOLD RINGS)))
(3 FRENCH HENS)

eval> (SETQ *LANGUAGES* '((APL . WEIRD)
                          (FORTRAN . BORING)
                          (LISP . WONDERFUL)
                          (BASIC . TOTALLY-BOGUS))))
((APL . WEIRD) (FORTRAN . BORING) (LISP . WONDERFUL)
 (BASIC . TOTALLY-BOGUS))

eval> (ASSOC 'LISP *LANGAUAGES*)
(LISP . WONDERFUL)

eval> (CDR (ASSOC 'LISP *LANGUAGES*))
WONDERFUL

eval> (CDR (ASSOC 'COBOL *LANGUAGES*))
NIL

eval> (RPLACD (ASSOC 'FORTRAN *LANGAUAGES*) 'USEFUL)
(FORTRAN . USEFUL)

eval> (CDR (ASSOC 'FORTRAN *LANGUAGES*))
USEFUL
```

The foregoing examples illustrate two common usage patterns of ASSOC.

First, since ASSOC returns NIL when an entry matching the key is not found and CDR of NIL is NIL, it is often the case that instead of checking whether an entry was found, the CDR of the result is simply used. As long as NIL is not a valid value to be associated with a key, a result of NIL indicates failure to find a matching entry.

Second, a value associated with a key can be changed by altering the CDR of a cons cell returned by ASSOC—this is one reason ASSOC returns the complete cons cell rather than just its CDR.

The function ASSOC could have been defined as

```
(DEFUN ASSOC (KEY ASSOCIATION-LIST)
    (COND ((NULL ASSOCIATION-LIST)
             'NIL)
```

```
                ((EQL KEY (CAR (CAR ASSOCIATION-LIST)))
                 (CAR ASSOCIATION-LIST))
                (T (ASSOC KEY (CDR ASSOCIATION-LIST)))))
```

Another example of using ASSOC is

```
eval> (SETQ *ADJECTIVE-OPPOSITES*
              '((BIG . LITTLE)
                (LITTLE . BIG)
                (GOOD . BAD)
                (BAD . GOOD)
                (HOT . COOL)
                (COOL . HOT)))
((BIG . LITTLE) (LITTLE . BIG)
 (GOOD . BAD) (BAD . GOOD)
 (HOT . COOL) (COOL . HOT))

eval> (SETQ *NOUN-OPPOSITES*
              '((BROTHER . SISTER)
                (SISTER . BROTHER)
                (DOG . CAT)
                (CAT . DOG)
                (APPLE . ORANGE)
                (ORANGE . APPLE)))
((BROTHER . SISTER) (SISTER . BROTHER)
 (DOG . CAT) (CAT . DOG)
 (APPLE . ORANGE) (ORANGE . APPLE))

eval> (DEFUN FLIP (PHRASE)
          (LIST (CDR (ASSOC (CAR PHRASE)
                            *ADJECTIVE-OPPOSITES*))
                (CDR (ASSOC (CAR (CDR PHRASE))
                            *NOUN-OPPOSITES*))))
FLIP

eval> (FLIP '(BIG SISTER))
(LITTLE BROTHER)

eval> (FLIP '(BAD APPLE))
(GOOD ORANGE)

eval> (FLIP '(HOT DOG))
(COOL CAT)
```

Another predefined Common Lisp function provides an interesting example of how DO can be used. The function PAIRLIS takes a list of keys and values and puts association pairs at the head of an association list *alist*. In the following Common Lisp definition, the DO steps three variables simultaneously, two of which can be viewed as drivers for the iteration since they are both used to construct a value for the third.

```
(DEFUN PAIRLIS (KEYS VALUES ALIST)
    (DO ((REMKEYS KEYS (CDR REMKEYS))
         (REMVALS VALUES (CDR REMVALUES))
         (NEWALIST ALIST
                    (CONS (CONS (CAR REMKEYS)
                                (CAR REMVALS))
                          NEWALIST)))
        ((NULL REMKEYS)
         NEWALIST)))
```

Consider the following example:

```
eval> (PAIRLIS '(FRED SUE JIM)
               '(24 32 25)
               '((JOE . 18) (DAVID . 22) (JOHN . 21)))
((FRED . 24) (SUE . 32)
             (JIM . 25) (JOE . 18)
             (DAVID . 22) (JOHN . 21))
```

A more complete implementation of PAIRLIS would cause an error in the body of the DO if REMVALS were ever empty, or in the end forms if REMVALS were not empty, thus checking that the same number of keys and values were passed to the function.

EXERCISES

E4.2.1 Evaluate the following s-expressions:
a. (ASSOC 'SQUARE '((TRIANGLE . 3)
                    (SQUARE . 4)
                    (HEXAGON . 6)))
b. (ASSOC 'PENTAGON '((TRIANGLE . 3)
                      (SQUARE . 4)
                      (HEXAGON . 6)))

E4.2.2 Choose a better name for the following function:

```
(DEFVAR *BROTHERS*
        '((FRED JOE JIM)
          (SUE DAVID JOHN)
          (JOE FRED JIM)
          (JOHN DAVID)
          (JIM JOE FRED)
          (DAVID JOHN)))

(DEFUN F (X Y)
    (MEMBER X (CDR (ASSOC Y *BROTHERS*))))
```

4.3 LIST COPYING FUNCTIONS

To round out the set of Lisp functions that deal with lists, we examine some that copy lists. There are variations on how deeply they go in a list to copy it, and there are versions that also do substitutions while copying.

■ (COPY-LIST *list*) This function is equivalent to (APPEND *list* NIL). It copies the cons cells in the top level of the list and returns that copy. Thus,

```
eval> (SETQ X '(A (B C D) (E F) G))
(A (B C D) (E F) G)

eval> (SETQ Y (COPY-LIST X))
(A (B C D) (E F) G)

eval> (EQ X Y)
NIL

eval> (EQ (CADR X) (CADR Y))
T

eval> (EQ (CDADR X) (CDADR Y))
T
```

■ (COPY-ALIST *list*) This function is intended for copying association lists, although it is applicable to any list. It walks down the top level of a list, copying the cons cells and checking each CAR. If one is a cons cell, that too is copied. Thus, COPY-ALIST copies all the structure of an association list without looking into the structure of either the keys or the values.

```
eval> (SETQ X '(A (B C D) (E F) G))
(A (B C D) (E F) G)

eval> (SETQ Y (COPY-ALIST X))
(A (B C D) (E F) G)

eval> (EQ X Y)
NIL

eval> (EQ (CADR X) (CADR Y))
NIL

eval> (EQ (CDADR X) (CDADR Y))
T
```

■ (COPY-TREE *object*) This function takes any Lisp object. If it is not a cons cell, it returns it; otherwise, it makes a new cons cell whose CAR and CDR are the result of COPY-TREE of the CAR and CDR of the original. Thus, COPY-TREE walks down a tree structure (made from cons cells), copying all the nonleaf nodes. For example,

```
eval> (SETQ X '(A (B C D) (E F) G))
(A (B C D) (E F) G)

eval> (SETQ Y (COPY-TREE X))
(A (B C D) (E F) G)

eval> (EQ X Y)
NIL

eval> (EQ (CADR X) (CADR Y))
NIL

eval> (EQ (CDADR X) (CDADR Y))
NIL
```

The definition of COPY-TREE is simple:

```
(DEFUN COPY-TREE (OBJECT)
    (IF (CONSP OBJECT)
        (CONS (COPY-TREE (CAR OBJECT))
```

```
                    (COPY-TREE (CDR OBJECT)))
            OBJECT))
```

The following functions perform susbstitutions in a tree. That is, they map over all cons cells in a list, down to all depths, making substitutions of new elements for old. There are two variations: one that substitutes for just one element and another that substitutes for all keys of an association list. There is a second dimension of variation: destructive and nondestructive versions.

■ (SUBST *new old tree*) This function makes a copy of *tree* and replaces all pointers EQL to *old* with a pointer to *new*. List structure may be shared between the original tree and the new, but the original is not changed in any way.

```
eval> (SUBST 'BROOKS 'SUCKER
            '((DEAR MR/MS SUCKER)
              (YOU MAY ALREADY HAVE WON ONE MILLION DOLLARS)
              (YES YOU MR/MS SUCKER COULD ALREADY BE RICH!)))
((DEAR MR/MS BROOKS)
 (YOU MAY ALREADY HAVE WON ONE MILLION DOLLARS)
 (YES YOU MR/MS BROOKS COULD ALREADY BE RICH!))
```

A Lisp definition for SUBST is

```
(DEFUN SUBST (NEW OLD TREE)
   (COND ((EQL OLD TREE)
          NEW)
         ((ATOM TREE)
          TREE)
         (T (LET ((NEWCAR (SUBST NEW OLD (CAR TREE)))
                  (NEWCDR (SUBST NEW OLD (CDR TREE))))
              (IF (AND (EQL NEWCAR
                            (CAR TREE))
                       (EQL NEWCDR
                            (CDR TREE)))
                  TREE
                  (CONS NEWCAR NEWCDR))))))
```

Notice how consing is avoided by only doing it when either the CAR or the CDR of a particular cons cell was changed by the recursive application of SUBST. This makes the result share unchanged portions of the original tree that is being substituted into. EQL is used as the comparison of the old and new CARs (and CDRs) rather than EQ because there is no guarantee that an unchanged

number—2 for instance—will occupy the same storage when returned from
the recursive call. This version of SUBST consumes the minimum number of
cons cells possible without altering the original tree structure. A less sparing
SUBST could have been defined as:

```
(DEFUN SUBST (NEW OLD TREE)
    (COND ((EQL OLD TREE)
           NEW)
          ((ATOM TREE)
           TREE)
          (T (CONS (SUBST NEW OLD (CAR TREE))
                   (SUBST NEW OLD (CDR TREE)))))))
```

but this will copy the list structure even when there are no changes to be
made.

- (NSUBST *new old tree*) This function is a destructive version of SUBST. It
  changes the contents of cons cells in the tree argument rather than copying.

- (SUBLIS *alist tree*) This function is similar to SUBST except that there are
  many old/new pairs that can be substituted. They are the key/value pairs of
  an association list *alist*. The function ASSOC is used to search the association
  list for possible substitutions. Like SUBST, this function does not affect its tree
  argument, *tree*, and may copy only the minimum amount necessary, sharing
  structure with the original.
  A definition for SUBLIS could be

```
(DEFUN SUBLIS (ALIST TREE)
    (LET ((NEWPAIR (ASSOC TREE ALIST)))
        (COND ((NOT (NULL NEWPAIR))
               (CDR NEWPAIR))
              ((ATOM TREE)
               TREE)
              (T (LET ((NEWCAR (SUBLIS ALIST (CAR TREE)))
                       (NEWCDR (SUBLIS ALIST (CDR TREE))))
                   (IF (AND (EQL NEWCAR
                                 (CAR TREE))
                            (EQL NEWCDR
                                 (CDR TREE)))
                       TREE
                       (CONS NEWCAR NEWCDR)))))))
```

- (NSUBLIS *alist tree*) Again, this is a destructive version of a nondestructive
  function.

SUMMARY

Lists can be used to represent sets, and as associative databases.
    The functions described in this chapter are shown in Table 4-1.

Table 4-1

Function	Args	Description
MEMBER	2	test for top-level list membership
UNION	2	form union of sets represented as lists
NUNION	2	destructively form union
INTERSECTION	2	form intersection
NINTERSECTION	2	destructively form intersection
ASSOC	2	associatively retrieve on key
PAIRLIS	3	augment an association list
COPY-LIST	1	copy top level of a list
COPY-ALIST	1	copy an association list
COPY-TREE	1	copy a list to all levels
SUBST	3	substitute single change throughout a list
NSUBST	3	destructive version
SUBLIS	2	substitute associated pairs throughout
NSUBLIS	2	destructive version

The MEMBER function tests for set membership and returns the rest of a list
starting with the desired element. The ASSOC function returns a cons cell that
includes both the searched-for key and its associated value. This is so that the
case of a null value can be distinguished from not finding an association at all
and so that the database can be updated with RPLACD on the returned cons cell.

PROBLEMS

P4.1   Write a function MY-COPY-ALIST that behaves in the same way as COPY-
ALIST.

P4.2   Write a function that inverts an association list. It should act something
like:

```
eval> (INVERT-ALIST '((MARY . LAWYER)
                      (JOHN . DOCTOR)
                      (SUE . DOCTOR)
                      (FRED . DENTIST)
                      (JANE . DOCTOR)
                      (BILL . LAWYER)))
((DENTIST FRED)
 (DOCTOR JANE SUE JOHN)
 (LAWYER BILL MARY))
```

The particular order of the professions and of the people within them are unimportant. Do not use any global variables.

P4.3 This problem involves constructing a system that encodes parent-child relationships and that can then answer questions about other relationships and deduce the sex of some of the people involved.   Write functions that add pairs of the form *(child . parent)* to one of the two association lists *MOTHERS* and *FATHERS*. The functions should be IS-FATHER-OF, IS-MOTHER-OF, and IS-PARENT-OF. They all take two arguments: a parent and a child. They should all return T on success and NIL on failure. Note that IS-PARENT-OF should only work if the sex of the parent is known. People whose sex is known should appear in the *FEMALES* list or the *MALES* list—for efficiency, ensure that they appear only once. Write query functions SEX-OF? and GRANDMOTHERS-OF?. The following is an example of how they should work:

```
eval> (IS-FATHER-OF 'BILL 'MARY)
T

eval> (IS-MOTHER-OF 'JANE 'MARY)
T

eval> (IS-MOTHER-OF 'MARY 'JILL)
T

eval> (GRANDMOTHERS-OF? 'JILL)
(JANE)

eval> (SEX-OF? 'JILL)
UNKNOWN

eval> (SEX-OF? 'MARY)
FEMALE

eval> (IS-MOTHER-OF 'SALLY 'LELAND)
T

eval> (IS-FATHER-OF 'LELAND 'JILL)
T
```

```
eval> (GRANDMOTHERS-OF? 'JILL)
(JANE SALLY)
```

To save the recomputation of "grandmothers" every time that they are requested, add an association list *GRANDMOTHERS* keyed on grandchildren. Under what condition should an entry be added to this list?

5

PROGRAMMING STYLE

There are many styles of programming in Lisp. Some individuals develop habits of style and idiom and their own favorite constructs, which combine to give their own unique style. On the other hand, just from looking at their code one can often guess the book from which a Lisp user learned to program.

The examples given throughout this book are written in a certain style, with the intent that it should meet three goals—that programs written in this style should be

- Understandable.
- Debuggable.
- Maintainable.

What do these terms mean?

Understandable
It should be clear to someone who knows Lisp what a Lisp program is doing locally. The intent of every s-expression and its effects should be clearly understandable. While this goal is desirable on aesthetic grounds, it also has practical implications. As the user is writing a program, they will want to check pieces already written to determine what arguments to pass, or what values to receive, and they will need to understand the precise computations and restrictions assumed by the existing parts of the program. Even though it is their own code they are looking at, the more understandable it is to an outsider, the easier it will be for programmers to understand their own code. In addition, understandability is a necessary prerequisite for attainment of the next two goals.

Debuggable
Much to the surprise of the builders of the first digital computers, programs written for them usually did not work. The human programmers produced programs with errors or *bugs*. After a few iterations of "fixing" the programs, they usually did work. We still don't know how to write programs that are correct the first time. Thus, every program will have to be *debugged*. If this fact is appreciated at the time the program is first written, it may be possible to structure the program so that the task will be considerably eased. In addition, many of the techniques we will discuss for writing understandable programs will help to produce programs with fewer bugs.

Maintainable
Apart from homework exercises, programs are rarely written, used once, and then forgotten. Often, a program will be used by many other people, and as they discover bugs or suggest changes or extensions, the original program will

have to be modified or *maintained*. Usually people other than the original programmer will have to change the code. It is desirable that it be easy for them. Clearly, understandability and debuggability contribute significantly to the ease of maintainability. There are a few additional techniques that can help too.

Notice that even if the original programmer is the only user of a piece of Lisp code, and hence the only maintainer, it is still important to keep the goal of maintainability in mind at the time of writing the program. The reasons are at least twofold. First, after a month it is easy to forget some of the details of a program, and after a year, the original writer has almost no advantage over a newcomer. After six years, the program is unrecognizable as being the programmer's own creation. Second, the program might be successful beyond the programmer's wildest dreams, and it will be distributed far and wide, and others will have to maintain it.

Given these definitions, it is clear that these three goals are laudable for programming in any language. Lisp does not hold a monopoly on their desirability. On the other hand, due partly to the nontyping of Lisp variables, it is often easier in Lisp to write programs that do not meet these goals.

A fourth goal is that the program should be *transportable*. That is, the program sources should be able to be taken to a machine with a different architecture or operating system and perform unchanged on it. We will not pursue this goal explicitly in this book as that is precisely the goal of Common Lisp, and it is supposed to all happen anyway, "behind our backs."

We will continue to discuss our three main goals throughout the rest of the book, but we already know enough Lisp to give some serious consideration to these issues in writing code now.

5.1 UNDERSTANDABILITY

The writing of understandable programs is based on the *principle of local transparency*. This means that it is desirable that any piece of code can be explained by examining only a small window around it. Thus, every piece of Lisp code should be locally transparent in the sense that someone reading the code (call them the *reader*) can peer through that small window and get a local understanding of how the program works. Some of the implications of this principle are listed and explained below. Keep it in mind yourself, though, in writing every piece of code.

- Choose variable names that are descriptive of their value. Lisp allows hyphens to be included, so two or three word names for variables are quite acceptable— for instance, HIGHEST-SCORE, CURRENT-SENTENCE, VERB or BEST-GUESS. Such naming conventions satisfy the principle of local transparency because looking at just the context of the variable name suffices to tell a reader what it is for— there is no need to try to find what it is bound for this level of understanding.

- Choose descriptive function names. The name should give some indication of the purpose of, and value returned from, the function.
- Avoid shadowing an existing variable name with a variable of the same name. If the reader sees a variable reference and scans back up the function they might miss the innermost introduction of a variable instance with that name but find an earlier one and mistake the instance to which the reference is made.
- Always use names for global variables that begin and end with "*". This clearly sets them off distinctly from lexical variables, and the reader does not need to go searching for a binding for the variable within the function. This is a clear invocation of the principle of local transparency.
- Use global variables only as pointers to a global database and try to avoid passing around values between functions by way of global variables. When the latter practice is violated it makes it extremely difficult to follow what is going on between two functions. One cannot look locally at a function and determine how it is operating, because it relies on side effects of another function, that is lexically separate. This violates the principle of local transparency.
- Avoid using SETQ wherever possible. When SETQ is used, it is no longer possible simply to find where the variable was introduced in order to understand what its value will be. Instead, one must understand the whole control structure and examine all the SETQs of the variable in order to guess at where its actual value will come from.
- If a variable is SETQed, make a comment to that effect where it is first introduced. Thus, when the reader sees a reference to a variable and scans back up the function to find where it was introduced, they will know immediately that the value bound there may not be the one the variable has at the point of interest and more thorough analysis will be necessary. Thus, when the principle of local transparency is violated, inspection based on its assumption will discover the violation.
- Use functions that express the meaning rather than ones that happen to have the right value. This means that one should use (or write) a predicate when using a function in a conditional. For example, use (HAS-BROTHER-P PERSON) rather than (BROTHER-OF PERSON). One also should use NOT when testing for logical falseness, and NULL when testing for the empty list. This makes clear whether a quantity is the result of a test or the end of a walk down a list. To test that a list is non-empty, one should write (IF (NOT (NULL X)) ...) rather than (IF X ...) because this too makes the intent clearer.[1]
- Use LET rather than LET* whenever possible. This makes it clear when the values that variables are getting bound to are independent rather than used sequentially by later variables values.
- Remove unstepped variables from a DO and put them in a surrounding LET.

---

[1] A good Lisp compiler should compile the two forms identically.

This is to avoid confusion from failing to check that a stepper form is present for every variable.

■ When using AND or OR, do not rely on fortuitous results of functions to let the evaluation of the terms of the logical operator continue past it. An example of this bad practice would be including a clause that is a side-effecting function, taking an argument that must be a number and that returns T. The NUMBERP ensures that X is a number as required by each of the next two clauses. Notice also that the third clause always returns non-NIL so the logical property of AND is not used after the first clause.

```
(AND (NUMBERP X)
     (ALWAYS-RETURNS-T X)
     (+ 1 X))
```

Without the fortuitous name chosen for the function in the second clause, it would be impossible to figure out what was intended here without looking at the source of that function. A better way to write the foregoing would be

```
(COND ((NUMBERP X)
       (ALWAYS-RETURNS-T X)
       (+ 1 X))
      (T NIL))
```

5.2 DEBUGGABILITY

The following two techniques can help debugging and can make bugs show up earlier and in places closer to their true source. We will introduce more techniques later in the book.

■ Make functions into reasonably small chunks so that each one can be tested on hand-generated data before being integrated into the complete system.

■ Check for impossible cases in a COND. Even when you *know* that only three cases can happen,—for example, variable X has as its value one of the symbols TOP, BOTTOM, or MIDDLE—don't simply test for the first two and get the third case on a catch-all COND statement. Thus, instead of writing

```
(COND ((EQ X 'TOP) (TOP-FUNCTION Y))
      ((EQ X 'BOTTOM) (BOTTOM-FUNCTION Y))
      (T (MIDDLE-FUNCTION Y)))
```

it is better to write

```
(COND ((EQ X 'TOP) (TOP-FUNCTION Y))
      ((EQ X 'BOTTOM) (BOTTOM-FUNCTION Y))
      ((EQ X 'MIDDLE) (MIDDLE-FUNCTION Y))
      (T <signal-an-error>))
```

We will see in the next chapter how to signal an error. Meanwhile, we see that in testing the second piece of code we will find if we are passing X an illegal value. In the first case, we might discover it in MIDDLE-FUNCTION, or it might happen that our piece of code gets exited and we never know that there was a bug, but instead we will simply get the wrong program result eventually.

5.3 MAINTAINABILITY

So far, we have not studied or written any large sets of Lisp programs, so some of the issues in maintainability will seem rather abstract.

- Try to keep some sort of ordering convention for arguments to functions. For example, if there are a few functions that all take one particular argument, WORLD-MODEL say, along with others, different for each function, you could always have WORLD-MODEL as the first argument. Suppose further that many of these functions take two arguments—OBJECT and MOTION—to describe an action to be carried out in the modelled world. Perhaps these arguments could always be the second and third arguments to those functions. This makes it easier for a maintainer to add in new code, as the argument orders will tend to follow an easily remembered pattern, rather than every function being a special case.

- Make explicit in comments any hidden assumptions about the behavior of functions, both at the point where it is assumed, and at the point where it is guaranteed. For example, one function, ALL-NOUNS say, might return a list of nouns used in a story. Another function, KEYWORD-COMPARE say, which wants to compare this list to some other for intersections, might assume that both lists are always sorted alphabetically, resulting in a straightforward linear comparison algorithm. This fact should be commented in KEYWORD-COMPARE, where it calls ALL-NOUNS, and in ALL-NOUNS, where the alphabetic sort is done. Thus, the maintainer will realize the connection and not make ALL-NOUNS "more efficient" by removing the sort, nor will he or she be puzzled about how the intersection algorithm can possibly work in KEYWORD-COMPARE.

    All the points of style in the previous sections can be internalized reasonably quickly when writing large volumes of code and soon become second nature.

5.4 EXAMPLE OF A STYLISH REALISTIC FUNCTION

Suppose we are writing a program to do symbolic algebra. For instance, we might be writing a system that can differentiate and integrate expressions such as $x^3 \cos x$. An important piece of such a program will be an algebraic simplifier, something that can take an expression like $(2x + 4) + (3x - 7)$ and return an expression $5x - 3$. For now, we will consider a simpler problem: simplifying expressions involving "+", numbers, and variables. We will represent expressions using standard Lisp prefix notation. Thus, we would like to write a function that can do things like

```
eval> (SIMPLIFY-PLUS '(+ 2 3))
5

eval> (SIMPLIFY-PLUS '(+ X (+ Y -2 Z) 2))
(+ Z Y X)

eval> (SIMPLIFY-PLUS '(+ 3 X -3))
X

eval> (SIMPLIFY-PLUS '(+ 5 -5))
0
```

How can we write this? First, we notice that we need to collect up all the numeric terms and actually add them together. Let's ignore the collapsing of imbedded +-terms for the moment. This certainly has an iterative flavor—we need to look at each element of the list (after the +) and accumulate it into a running total. If we were only going to collect the numeric terms, we could write

```
(DEFUN SIMPLIFY-PLUS (EXP)
    (DO ((ARGLIST (CDR EXP) (CDR ARGLIST))
         (CONSTANT 0
                   (IF (NUMBERP (CAR ARGLIST))
                       (+ CONSTANT (CAR ARGLIST))
                       CONSTANT)))
        ((NULL ARGLIST)
         CONSTANT)))
```

The variable name `CONSTANT` was chosen because it accumulates all the numeric, or constant, parts of the expression. Notice that `ARGLIST` is initialized to the `CDR` of the expression to be simplified in order to skip over the +. Then the list is stepped down using `CDR`, and at each iteration we examine the `CAR` of the remaining arguments. If it is a number, it is added to CONSTANT and the result becomes the new value of CONSTANT, otherwise the old value of CONSTANT remains. The stepping rule for CONSTANT employs a common idiom for selectively skipping elements of a list in some sort of accumulation process. CONSTANT has its old value passed to it unless the current CAR of ARGLIST is a number.

With this definition, our examples become:

```
eval> (SIMPLIFY-PLUS '(+ 2 3))
5

eval> (SIMPLIFY-PLUS '(+ X (+ Y -2 Z) 2))
2

eval> (SIMPLIFY-PLUS '(+ 3 X -3))
0

eval> (SIMPLIFY-PLUS '(+ 5 -5))
0
```

We got two of them correct!

Of course, we have to do something with the nonnumeric terms in the sum. We should make a list of them, and then symbolically add them to the numeric portion. This suggests the following:

```
(DEFUN SIMPLIFY-PLUS (EXP)
    (DO ((ARGLIST (CDR EXP) (CDR ARGLIST))
        (CONSTANT 0
                (IF (NUMBERP (CAR ARGLIST))
                    (+ CONSTANT (CAR ARGLIST))
                    CONSTANT))
        (OTHERS '()
                (IF (NUMBERP (CAR ARGLIST))
                    OTHERS
                    (CONS (CAR ARGLIST) OTHERS))))
        ((NULL ARGLIST)
        (LIST* '+ CONSTANT OTHERS))))
```

Again we used the idiom of conditionally stepping a variable with itself to skip over items in a list. The items skipped for OTHERS exactly complement those taken for CONSTANT. In the case of a nonnumber, the term is consed onto the front of the list OTHERS. Our examples now work like this

```
eval> (SIMPLIFY-PLUS '(+ 2 3))
(+ 5)


eval> (SIMPLIFY-PLUS '(+ X (+ Y -2 Z) 2))
(+ 2 (+ Y -2 Z) X)


eval> (SIMPLIFY-PLUS '(+ 3 X -3))
(+ 0 X)


eval> (SIMPLIFY-PLUS '(+ 5 -5))
(+ 0)
```

This time we got none of them correct! We need to be more careful with how we put together the CONSTANT and the OTHERS with the +-sign at the end. If there are no OTHERS, we can just return the numeric result. If the numeric result is zero, we can leave it out. If there is only one term in OTHERS and zero constant, we can just return the single term. Otherwise, we should put together a +, a number, and then the OTHERS terms. Our function now becomes:

```
(DEFUN SIMPLIFY-PLUS (EXP)
    (DO ((ARGLIST (CDR EXP) (CDR ARGLIST))
         (CONSTANT 0
                   (IF (NUMBERP (CAR ARGLIST))
                       (+ CONSTANT (CAR ARGLIST))
                       CONSTANT))
         (OTHERS 'NIL
                 (IF (NUMBERP (CAR ARGLIST))
                     OTHERS
                     (CONS (CAR ARGLIST) OTHERS))))
        ((NULL ARGLIST)
         (COND ((NULL OTHERS)
                CONSTANT)
               ((ZEROP CONSTANT)
                (IF (NULL (CDR OTHERS))
                    (CAR OTHERS)
                    (CONS '+ OTHERS)))
               (T (LIST* '+ CONSTANT OTHERS))))))
```

It's getting bigger! Notice that we have no particular reason to have the numeric constant at the front of our result other than the ease of consing it onto the front of the list of OTHERS. With the foregoing definition, our examples become

```
eval> (SIMPLIFY-PLUS '(+ 2 3))
5

eval> (SIMPLIFY-PLUS '(+ X (+ Y -2 Z) 2))
(+ 2 (+ Y -2 Z) X)

eval> (SIMPLIFY-PLUS '(+ 3 X -3))
X

eval> (SIMPLIFY-PLUS '(+ 5 -5))
0
```

Now we are back up to 3 out of 4 correct answers!

Notice that the NUMBERP test is duplicated in two stepping rules, taking the same argument in each. Fortunately, NUMBERP is a simple computation, but if it were complex the overhead of doing it twice might lead to a very inefficient program (in the limit, twice as slow as it need be). In such a case, we might want to have only one of CONSTANT and OTHERS be an iterated variable and use a SETQ to update the other. This would lead to the code:

```
(DEFUN SIMPLIFY-PLUS (EXP)
    (LET ((CONSTANT 0))
        (DO ((ARGLIST (CDR EXP) (CDR ARGLIST))
             (OTHERS 'NIL
                     (COND ((NUMBERP (CAR ARGLIST))
                            (SETQ CONSTANT
                                  (+ CONSTANT (CAR ARGLIST)))
                            OTHERS)
                           (T (CONS (CAR ARGLIST) OTHERS)))))
            ((NULL ARGLIST)
             (COND ((NULL OTHERS)
                    CONSTANT)
                   ((ZEROP CONSTANT)
                    (IF (NULL (CDR OTHERS))
                        (CAR OTHERS)
                        (CONS '+ OTHERS)))
                   (T (LIST* '+ CONSTANT OTHERS)))))))
```

This is more efficient, but now it is difficult to see at a glance where CONSTANT gets updated because it happens in the stepping rule for variable OTHERS. Perhaps it's time to move down the updating of both CONSTANT and OTHERS into the body of the DO. This gives the following code:

```
(DEFUN SIMPLIFY-PLUS (EXP)
    (LET ((CONSTANT 0)     ; SETQed in the DO body
          (OTHERS 'NIL))   ; SETQed in the DO body
        (DO ((ARGLIST (CDR EXP) (CDR ARGLIST)))
            ((NULL ARGLIST)
             (COND ((NULL OTHERS)
                    CONSTANT)
                   ((ZEROP CONSTANT)
                    (IF (NULL (CDR OTHERS))
                        (CAR OTHERS)
                        (CONS '+ OTHERS)))
                   (T (LIST* '+ CONSTANT OTHERS))))
          (IF (NUMBERP (CAR ARGLIST))
              (SETQ CONSTANT
                    (+ CONSTANT (CAR ARGLIST)))
              (SETQ OTHERS (CONS (CAR ARGLIST) OTHERS))))))
```

Now we have two SETQs, which is bad from the point of view of transparency of where the values for the variables came from, but this is prefereable to having a strange SETQ in another variable's DO stepping rule in one case or duplicating an expensive function call in the other case (although NUMBERP is not expensive, we have been acting as though it was to illustrate the point).

Getting back to progress on the original problem, we still have to take into account the nested +-terms. We could check for that explicitly and splice its arguments into the list of arguments with which we are dealing already. It will be somewhat tricky to keep the iteration going, and what if the nested + has a nested +? Since the data structure is recursively defined, perhaps we should use a recursive simplification function. If we notice a +-term as the CAR of ARGLIST, we can recursively call SIMPLIFY-PLUS on it. That will guarantee that the result is either

1. A constant

2. A single variable

3. A +-expression with no constant term, but some number of other terms, none of which is a number

4. A +-expression with a constant term first, and some other terms following it, none of which is a number.

Wherever we make the recursive call, we may get both a number that needs to be accumulated into CONSTANT and more terms that need to be merged into OTHERS. This suggests that the idea of moving down the stepping of both CONSTANT and OTHERS to the body of the DO was the right idea. Otherwise, we would be cross SETQing the two of them in their stepping rules within the DO.

When we put this all together, we get the following function:

```
;;; The final version of the +-expression simplifier.
;;; There are four possibilities for the value of SIMPARG:
;;; 1. a numeric constant.
;;; 2. a single variable.
;;; 3. a "+" expression with no numeric terms.
;;; 4. a "+" expression with a numeric term first.


(DEFUN SIMPLIFY-PLUS (EXP)
  (LET ((CONSTANT 0)      ; SETQed in the DO body
        (OTHERS 'NIL))    ; SETQed in the DO body
      (DO ((ARGLIST (CDR EXP) (CDR ARGLIST)))
          ((NULL ARGLIST)
           (COND ((NULL OTHERS)
                    CONSTANT)
                 ((ZEROP CONSTANT)
                  (IF (NULL (CDR OTHERS))
                      (CAR OTHERS)
                      (CONS '+ OTHERS)))
                 (T (LIST* '+ CONSTANT OTHERS))))

        ;; body of the DO
        (LET* ((ARG (CAR ARGLIST))
               (SIMPARG (IF (AND (CONSP ARG)
                                 (EQ '+ (CAR ARG)))
                            (SIMPLIFY-PLUS ARG)
                            ARG)))
          (COND ((NUMBERP SIMPARG) ;case 1 above
                 (SETQ CONSTANT
                       (+ CONSTANT SIMPARG)))
                ((AND (CONSP SIMPARG)
                      (EQ '+ (CAR SIMPARG)))
                 (LET ((FST (CADR SIMPARG)))
                   (COND
                     ((NUMBERP FST) ;case 4
                      (SETQ CONSTANT
                            (+ CONSTANT FST))
                      (SETQ OTHERS
                            (APPEND (CDDR SIMPARG)
                                    OTHERS)))
                     (T (SETQ OTHERS ;case 3
                              (APPEND (CDR SIMPARG)
                                      OTHERS))))))
                ;; case 2
                (T (SETQ OTHERS
                         (CONS SIMPARG OTHERS)))))))))
```

Notice that in the body of the DO we introduce a new variable ARG, which is bound to the current term to be processed purely so that we can refer to it many times by name rather than as (CAR ARGLIST). We then make sure we have a simplified term, SIMPARG. If ARG is not another +-expression, it becomes the value of SIMPARG directly. Otherwise, it is first simplified by a recursive call to SIMPLIFY-PLUS. No matter where SIMPARG got its value from, it still must fall into one of the four categories previously mentioned. The remaining code tests which one it is and updates the variables CONSTANT and OTHERS appropriately. Variable FST is potentially a number in the case that SIMPARG is another +-expression. Notice that now we are making use of the earlier fortuitous ordering of the terms within a +-expression; namely, that any constant term, if it exists, will be first.

Notice further that by testing explicitly for the existence of a "+" at the head of any subexpression we let pass any composite terms that are not additions (e.g., (* X Y)) without accidentally accumulating its terms into the sum.

SUMMARY

Programs should be written with the goals of understandability, debuggability, and maintainability in mind. In particular, the principle of local transparency says that any small piece of a program should be understandable by itself. The application of this principle leads to a large number of coding conventions that aid in the achievement of all three goals.

PROBLEMS

P5.1 Write a function SIMPLIFY that simplifies both + expressions and * expressions. The bulk of the work should be done by the same code for each, although it may be in the form of auxilary functions rather than in SIMPLIFY itself. Your program also should simplify exponential expressions of the form:

$$(POWER \; arg \; exponent)$$

by simplifying each of *arg* and *exponent* and collapsing the result in the case of an exponent equal to zero or one.

Examine the following examples:

```
eval> (SIMPLIFY '(+ (* X 0) (* 1 Y)))
Y

eval> (SIMPLIFY '(+ (* 5 (POWER X (+ 5 -1))) 1)
                  (* 4 (POWER Y (+ 4 -1)) 0) 0))
```

```
(* 5 (POWER X 4))

eval> (SIMPLIFY '(* 1 (POWER X (+ 1 -1))))
1
```

Run it on some more examples to demonstrate its correctness.

P5.2 Write a symbolic differentiator that differentiates an expression with respect to a given variable. It should know how to differentiate sums, products, and exponentials—you can assume that exponents are independent of the variable with respect to which they are being differentiated. Some examples are

```
eval> (DERIV '(* X Y) 'X)
(+ (* X 0) (* 1 Y))

eval> (DERIV '(+ (POWER Y 4) (POWER X 5)) 'X)
(+ (* 5 (POWER X (+ 5 -1)) 1) (* 4 (POWER Y (+ 4 -1)) 0) 0))
```

Your DERIV function might not come out with exactly these expressions, but it should get algebraically equivalent expressions.

P5.3 Attach your simplifier to your differentiator so that you get results such as:

```
eval> (DIFF '(* X Y) 'X)
Y

eval> (DIFF '(+ (POWER Y 4) (POWER X 5) 3) 'X)
(* 5 (POWER X 4))
```

Try your function DIFF on a few examples. What are the major shortcomings of your simplifier?

P5.4 The next few problems ask you to write an English language front end for problem P4.3 of chapter 4. It should be able to handle a dialog of the complexity of this one:[2]

```
eval> (HEAR '(FRED IS JOE'S FATHER))
T

eval> (HEAR '(SUE IS THE MOTHER OF JOE))
T
```

---

[2]The first input sentence will be read as (FRED IS JOE (QUOTE S) FATHER). Thus, we sneak in possessive apostrophes through the Lisp shorthand for quoting expressions.

```
eval> (HEAR '(WHO IS JOE'S MOTHER))
SUE

eval> (HEAR '(LILY IS THE MOTHER OF JOE'S FATHER))
T

eval> (HEAR '(WHO IS FRED'S MOTHER))
LILY

eval> (HEAR '(GRACE IS JOE'S MOTHER'S MOTHER))
SEMANTICALLY-CONFUSED

eval> (HEAR '(GRACE IS THE MOTHER OF JOE'S MOTHER))
T

eval> (HEAR '(WHO ARE JOE'S GRANDMOTHERS))
(GRACE LILY)

eval> (HEAR '(WHAT IS LILY'S SEX))
FEMALE

eval> (HEAR '(WHAT IS JOE'S SEX))
UNKNOWN

eval> (HEAR '(JOE'S FATHER IS THE FATHER OF JUDY))
T

eval> (HEAR '(WHO IS JUDY'S FATHER))
FRED

eval> (HEAR '(WHO IS JOE'S FATHER))
FRED

eval> (HEAR '(WHO IS FEMALE))
(GRACE LILY SUE)

eval> (HEAR '(WHAT'S UP))
UNPARSABLE

eval> (HEAR '(WHO IS JOE'S UNCLE))
UNABLE-TO-ANSWER

eval> (HEAR '(WHO IS JOE'S FATHER FRED))
UNPARSABLE
```

The key to solving this problem is recognizing that the domain of discourse is quite limited so that the level of understanding of the input sentences can be quite shallow. For instance, whether a noun or verb is singular or plural can be ignored. In fact, since IS and ARE are the only two verbs that will ever be seen, there need be no concept of verb meaning.

There are two major functions to write: PARSE and PROCESS. The latter is the subject of the next problem.

Function PARSE takes a list of symbols and returns NIL or a data structure representing the sentence for a syntactically correct English sentence.

The function PARSE should try calling functions PARSE-QUERY and PARSE-ASSERTION on the input (if the first succeeds, there is no need to call the second). They will in turn call other functions on parts of the input, such as PARSE-VERB, PARSE-NOUN, PARSE-NOUN-PHRASE, and so on. It will make things easier if each of these parse functions returns NIL if it can't find what was wanted at the head of the input, and a cons cell if it can. The CAR of the cons cell should contain a description of what was found and the CDR should contain what remains of the input. For instance,

```
eval> (PARSE-ASSERTION '(WHO IS JOE'S FATHER))
NIL

eval> (PARSE-QUERY '(WHO IS JOE'S FATHER))
((QUERY (NOUN-PHRASE (NOUN FATHER) (NAME JOE))))

eval> (PARSE '(WHO IS JOE'S FATHER))
(QUERY (NOUN-PHRASE (NOUN FATHER) (NAME JOE)))

eval> (PARSE-NOUN-PHRASE '(JOE'S FATHER IS THE FATHER OF JUDY))
((NOUN-PHRASE (NOUN FATHER) (NAME JOE)) IS THE FATHER OF JUDY)

eval> (PARSE-NOUN-PHRASE '(FRED IS JUDY'S FATHER))
((NAME FRED) IS JUDY (QUOTE S) FATHER)        ; !!note the hack!!

eval> (PARSE-ASSERTION '(FRED IS JUDY'S FATHER))
((ASSERTION (NAME FRED)
            (NOUN-PHRASE (NOUN FATHER) (NAME JUDY))))
```

Notice how a very limited type of NOUN-PHRASE is used; it is merely a possessive form.

The following tables might help. You will not need (nor should you use) any other global variables (apart from those in problem P4.3). You can assume that any word whose type is not specified, is a proper name.

```
(DEFVAR *WORDS*
        '((FATHER . NOUN)
          (MOTHER . NOUN)
          (SEX . NOUN)
          (MALE . NOUN)
          (FEMALE . NOUN)
          (GRANDMOTHER . NOUN)
          (IS . VERB)
```

```
            (ARE . VERB)
            (THE . ARTICLE)
            (A . ARTICLE)
            (OF . PREPOSITION)
            (WHO . Q-WORD)
            (WHAT . Q-WORD)))

(DEFVAR *PLURALS*
        '((FATHERS . FATHER)
          (MOTHERS . MOTHER)
          (GRANDMOTHERS . GRANDMOTHER)
          (MALES . MALE)
          (FEMALES . FEMALE)))
```

P5.5 Now write the function PROCESS that takes the structure produced by the previous problem, divines the semantic meaning of the original sentence, and calls the appropriate database functions, such as IS-FATHER-OF, GRANDMOTHERS-OF?, and so on. Queries should be easy to handle. But notice that there were some complex assertions in the examples given. For example,

a. (SUE IS THE MOTHER OF JOE))
b. (LILY IS THE MOTHER OF JOE'S FATHER))
c. (JOE'S FATHER IS THE FATHER OF JUDY))
d. (THE MOTHER OF JOE IS SUE))

Notice that in cases a, b, and d a person is explicitly named on one side of the IS. In these cases, whether the subject or predicate of IS was formerly unknown is clear. In cases a and d the assertion becomes a call to a single database update function (i.e., IS-MOTHER-OF). In case b, however, it is necessary to do a database query, and then use that for an argument to the update. Essentially, the translation of sentence b is:[3]

(IS-MOTHER-OF 'LILY (FATHER-OF? 'JOE))

Sentence c is more ambigous. Since IS is symmetric and no explicit name appears on either side for the person being discussed, it is necessary to try to find out if either of the two descriptions (JOE'S FATHER and THE FATHER OF JUDY) resolves to a name when the database is queried, and if so, use that name to update the database entry for the other description.

---

[3]Notice that you should not actually produce the s-expression and then evaluate it—the two calls to database routines should be with variable arguments.

You might find it useful to define a function `FIND-RELATIVE` that takes two arguments, a relationship and a person, and does the appropriate data-base look up. For example,

```
(FIND-RELATIVE 'FATHER 'JOE) ==> (FATHER-OF? 'JOE)
```

P5.6   Write the function `HEAR`.

6

INPUT
AND
OUTPUT

So far, we have only seen output from Lisp as a result of evaluating expressions. No matter how much computation has gone on, just a single s-expression has been printed at the end. The one exception to this observation is TRACE, which prints out status reports during evaluation of s-expressions. In this chapter, we will see how to print arbitrary things, either to the terminal or to a file, *during* evaluation of Lisp expressions.

Similarly, the only input we have provided to Lisp is a single s-expression typed to be evaluated immediately, or a file of s-expressions (using LOAD) to be treated as a series of single inputs. In this chapter, we will see more general methods of input, which will enable us to write interactive programs.

Both input and output have much broader capabilities in Common Lisp than will be presented here, but they are not necessary except for very specialized input/output requirements.

6.1 FORMAT: **AN INTRODUCTION**

We will start by looking at FORMAT, which is the most useful, but not simplest, way of making pretty output. The general form of the function FORMAT is

$$(\text{FORMAT } stream\ control\text{-}string\ arg\text{-}1 \ldots arg\text{-}n)$$

Function FORMAT usually returns NIL as its result, but it might send output to the terminal or a file before returning.

The argument *stream* specifies where the output should be printed. If it is the symbol T, output is printed on the user's terminal. Later we will see how to direct output to a file.

The argument *control-string* is a string to be printed with some embedded escape sequences to splice in the printing of the remaining arguments to FORMAT. A string is a Common Lisp data type that was briefly encountered in chapter 1. Examples of strings are "abcdef", "DEFUN", "123", and "% @+~". Notice that strings are typed in by encasing them in double quotes. A string is an atom, but it is not a symbol or a number. It is another sort of atom—namely, a string. Like numbers, NIL, and T, strings evaluate to themselves, so there is no need to quote them.

Here are some examples of FORMAT with output directed to the terminal, and no arguments following the control string.

```
eval> (FORMAT T "Here are some characters to print.")
Here are some characters to print.
NIL
```

```
eval> (FORMAT 'T '"We used quotes this time.")
We used quotes this time.
NIL
```

Each character in the control string is printed and then `FORMAT` exits with result
`NIL`—that is what is printed on the line following the printed control string. The
behavior of `FORMAT` changes when the escape character "~", *tilde*, appears in the
control string. In that case, one or more characters are read following the tilde
and treated as a *control directive* telling `FORMAT` to do something besides copy
characters from the control string to the output. The most important control
directives are "%" and "S". The first directs that a new line should be started
in the output, while the second says to take the next unused argument following
the control string and print it immediately, using the same print rules that Lisp
uses to print the result of evaluating an s-expression typed to the `eval>` prompt.
For example:

```
eval> (FORMAT T "Start a new line after this.~%It worked!")
Start a new line after this.
It worked!
NIL

eval> (SETQ X '(A B C))
(A B C)

eval> (FORMAT T "~%The list ~S has length ~S.~%" X (LENGTH X))

The list (A B C) has length 3.

NIL

eval> (FORMAT T
             "A string prints like this: ~S and ~~ like that!"
             "string")
A string prints like this: "string" and ~ like that!
NIL
```

Notice that a string printed with a ~S directive has double quotes printed
around it. A third directive was used in the previous example: ~~ is the way to
print a single tilde on the output device.

EXERCISES

E6.1.1 Write a format statement that prints output such as

```
Length: 22.7
Width:  13.3
Height: 1.0
```

given three variables—L, W, and H—containing the three quantities.

E6.1.2 What will the output string look like for each of these expressions?
a. (FORMAT T "The word is ~S." "bazola")
b. (FORMAT T "The symbol is '~S'." 'BAZOLA)
c. (FORMAT T "Using ~~S makes a string print like: ~S." "this")
d. (FORMAT T "Using ~~~S will be different." 'A)

6.2 OPENING AND CLOSING A FILE

The first argument to FORMAT can specify any output stream. An *output stream* is a place at which characters can be output one after the other. The terminal (specified by T) is an output stream. Files also can become output streams. A file for output can be created and opened using the OPEN function. Its form is

```
(OPEN file-name :DIRECTION :OUTPUT)
```

The *file name* is evaluated and should be a string specifying a file. The details of how a file name string corresponds to files manipulated by the operating system will vary across Common Lisp implementations.

The second and third arguments are *keywords*. We will see them in more detail in chapter 7. For now, it suffices to know that they are symbols that evaluate to themselves and that we will always use precisely these two keywords in opening a file for output.

The result of OPEN is an output stream that can be passed to FORMAT as its first argument. All output from FORMAT is then directed to that file. The file is closed by calling the function CLOSE on the output stream. Consider the following:

```
eval> (DEFUN DUMP-OUTPUT (FILE OUTPUT)
          (LET ((STREAM (OPEN FILE :DIRECTION :OUTPUT)))
```

```
                    (FORMAT STREAM
                            "Here's today's output: % % S %"
                            OUTPUT)
                    (CLOSE STREAM)))
    DUMP-OUTPUT

    eval> (DUMP-OUTPUT "foo.bar" '(A LIST OF STUFF))
    T
```

This will write a file named "`foo.bar`" on your directory. Its contents will be

```
Here's today's output:

(A LIST OF STUFF)
```

6.3 THE STANDARD PRINT FUNCTIONS

The standard printing functions, from which FORMAT can be built, are PRIN1, PRINC, and PRINT.[1] They each take one or two arguments. The first argument is the object to be printed, and the second is an optional stream specification. In a normal Lisp environment, when the second argument is not supplied it is treated as though it were T, specifying the terminal. There are ways to change this default via global variables, but we will not look into that.

Each of these functions prints a representation of the object on the output stream. PRIN1 and PRINC have slightly different rules about how they print objects. PRIN1 prints objects so that they can be read back into Lisp as objects EQUAL to those printed. PRINC "prettifies" objects a little. The only difference we will notice is that strings printed by PRIN1 have double quotes around them, while PRINC removes the quotes. Function PRINT starts a new line on the specified output stream and then passes its argument to PRIN1.

A fourth printing function is TERPRI. It takes zero or one argument, and in the latter case the argument specifies an output stream. The same rule for defaulting that argument is followed as above. Function TERPRI starts a new line on the specified output stream. Thus, PRINT could almost be defined as

---

[1] In fact, usually all of these functions are built on top of a function **WRITE-CHAR**, which writes single characters to an output stream.

```
eval> (DEFUN PRINT (OBJECT STREAM)
         (TERPRI STREAM)
         (PRIN1 OBJECT STREAM))
```

Some examples of these functions in action are

```
eval> (PROGN (PRINT 'FOO)
             (PRINC " is a generic symbol!")
             (TERPRI)
             'FOO)
FOO is a generic symbol!

FOO

eval> (PROGN (PRINT 'FOO)
             (PRINT " is a generic symbol!")
             'FOO)
FOO
" is a generic symbol!"
FOO

eval> (PROGN (PRINC "The prompt ")
             (PRIN1 "eval> ")
             (PRINC "is printed using PRINC")
             '!)
The prompt "eval> " is printed using PRINC
!
```

The printing characteristics of the three printing functions can be controlled by three global parameters: *PRINT-BASE*, *PRINT-LEVEL*, and *PRINT-LENGTH*. The effect of each of these parameters is

- *PRINT-BASE* Determines the number base used to output integers.
- *PRINT-LEVEL* If this is NIL, deep lists get printed normally. If it is a positive number, after depth *PRINT-LEVEL* a list is printed as #.
- *PRINT-LENGTH* If this is NIL, long lists get printed normally. If it is a positive number, after length *PRINT-LENGTH* three dots are printed instead of the remaining elements.

Since Lisp uses these functions to print the results of its interactions with the user, we can experiment with the use of the parameters by seeing what is printed in response to an expression to be evaluated! Here are some examples:[2]

```
eval> (SETQ *PRINT-BASE* 8)
10                              ;printed in base 8!

eval> (+ 6 6)
14

eval> 65
101

eval> (SETQ *PRINT-LEVEL* 2)
2

eval> (SETQ *PRINT-LENGTH* 3)
3

eval> '(A B C D E)
(A B C ...)

eval> '((B B) ((C C) B (C C)) ((C C)))
((B B) (# B #) (#))

eval> '(A (B C (D E) F) (G H I J) K L)
(A (B C # ...) (G H I ...) ...)
```

Consider how we might write a printing function with such characteristics. We will assume that we can use PRINC to print atoms, but let's try to write our own print function, which can have its printing level and printing length controlled. Printing a list naturally decomposes into two control ideas. The first is that the elements of the list should be printed one after the other, or iteratively, preceded and followed by a left and right parenthesis, respectively. The second is that elements of the list should be printed by a recursive call to the print function itself. The first control aspect suggests iterating over the elements of the list until the maximum print length is reached. The second suggests that the recursive call should include information on how deep the nesting of lists found is so far, so that the function will know when the maximum print level is reached. Combining these ideas suggests the following definition:

---

[2]Notice that *PRINT-BASE* always prints as 10 regardless of the base!

```
;;; Both LEVEL and LENGTH can be NIL or numbers.  The
;;; recursive calls decrease numeric LEVELs whereas
;;; they pass on a constant LENGTH.  Variable LEVEL can
;;; be interepreted as how many more levels of the list
;;; should be printed before '#' is substituted.  NIL
;;; means infinity.  Print length control is by
;;; iteration, counting down from the value of LENGTH
;;; until zero is reached, when '...'  is substituted.
;;; Again NIL means infinity, and counting down from -1
;;; guarantees that zero will not be reached.


(DEFUN OUR-PRINC (OBJECT LEVEL LENGTH)
    (COND ((AND (CONSP OBJECT)
                (NUMBERP LEVEL)
                (< LEVEL 1))
           (PRINC "#"))
          ((CONSP OBJECT)
           (LET ((LOWERLEVEL (IF (NUMBERP LEVEL)
                                 (- LEVEL 1)
                                 LEVEL)))
                (PRINC "(")
                (OUR-PRINC (CAR OBJECT) ; first element
                           LOWERLEVEL
                           LENGTH)
                (DO ((REM (CDR OBJECT) (CDR REM))
                     (LEN (IF (NUMBERP LENGTH)
                              (- LENGTH 1)
                              -1)
                          (- LEN 1)))
                    ((NULL REM))
                  ;; iteration body
                  ;; LEN is max number of elements still
                  ;; to be printed. Negative LEN means
                  ;; infinity.
                  (COND ((ZEROP LEN)
                         (PRINC " ...")
                         (RETURN 'NIL))  ; exit DO
                        ((NOT (CONSP REM)) ; dotted list
                         (PRINC " . ")
                         (OUR-PRINC REM
                                    LOWERLEVEL
                                    LENGTH)
                         (RETURN 'NIL))  ; exit DO
                        (T (PRINC " ")
```

```
                    (OUR-PRINC (CAR REM)
                               LOWERLEVEL
                               LENGTH))))
              (PRINC ")" STREAM)))
         (T (PRINC OBJECT)))
       ;; always return the argument as the result
       OBJECT)
```

EXERCISES

E6.3.1 With *PRINT-BASE*, *PRINT-LEVEL*, and *PRINT-LENGTH* having values 7, 3, and 4, respectively, what will the values of the following s-expressions
be printed as?
a. (+ 5 5)
b. (LIST (* 5 5) '((B C (D E) E F) A) 'G 'H 'I 'J)
c. '((A B C D E) (F G H I J) (K L M N) (O P Q R S) (T U V))
d. '(((A B) (C (D E)) (F (G H) I)) J K)

E6.3.2 What will be printed by each of these print statements, given that
PRINT-LEVEL and *PRINT-LENGTH* are both NIL?
a. (PRIN1 '"Hi there!")
b. (PRINC '"Hi there!")
c. (PRINC 'HELLO)
d. (PRINC "HELLO")
e. (PRIN1 '(THIS IS A "string"))
f. (PRINC '(THIS IS A "string"))

6.4 MORE FORMAT

Consider again the ~S directive for FORMAT. It simply asks that the next unused
argument following the control string be printed using PRIN1. Another directive,
~A, asks that the argument be printed with PRINC—this is useful for suppressing
double quotes around strings. For instance,

```
eval> (FORMAT T
              "~%Intro Lisp was a ~A course!"
              (IF (EQ GRADE 'A)
                  "good"
                  "bad"))
Intro Lisp was a good course!
NIL
```

Another useful FORMAT directive is ~nT. This directive is little different in that it takes a numeric argument, n, after the tilde and before T. FORMAT spaces out to column n with white space, unless it has already been reached, in which case it inserts a single blank. For instance,

```
eval> (DEFUN PRINT-PEOPLE (PEOPLE-ALIST)
          (FORMAT T "~%Person~10TLocation")
          (DO ((ENTRIES PEOPLE-ALIST (CDR ENTRIES)))
              ((NULL ENTRIES)
               (FORMAT T "~%"))
            (FORMAT T
                    "~%~S~10T~S"
                    (CAAR ENTRIES)
                    (CDAR ENTRIES))))
PRINT-PEOPLE

eval> (PRINT-PEOPLE '((FRED . CHICAGO)
                      (ANNE . SEATTLE)
                      (JIM . NEWARK)
                      (BARTHOLOMEW . KANSAS-CITY)
                      (JOCELYN . ATLANTA)))
Person      Location
FRED        CHICAGO
ANNE        SEATTLE
JIM         NEWARK
BARTHOLOMEW KANSAS-CITY
JOCELYN     ATLANTA


NIL
```

In summary, the directives for FORMAT that we will use are

- ~% Start a new line.
- ~S Print an argument using PRIN1.
- ~A Print an argument using PRINC.
- ~~ Print a tilde.
- ~nT Space out to column n unless already past there, in which case skip a single space.

There is much more to the full Common Lisp FORMAT. The control string can contain instructions of bewildering complexity. The function FORMAT is described in the Common Lisp manual in 23 pages of dense prose. If you read it and survive, you will know that you can type

```
eval> (FORMAT T
               "~%{~{~#[ ~;~A~:;~A, ~]~}} i.e. ~R variable~:P."
               '(X Y Z)
               3)
{X, Y, Z} i.e. three variables.
NIL
```

You probably will be content with learning much less about `FORMAT`.

EXERCISES

E6.4.1 Write two format statments, one to produce a header and one that can be repeatedly called with new values for L, W, and H so that the following style output will appear:

```
Length  Width   Height
------  -----   ------
 22.7   13.3     1.0
 27.6    3.5     1.25
```

E6.4.2 Write a format statement that substitutes a person's name into the sentence "Dear x, You may already be a winner!". The person's surname is in the variable `NAME` and their sex, either M or F, in the variable `SEX`.

6.5 SIGNALLING ERRORS

The user can signal an error in Common Lisp with the `ERROR` function. It causes a break in the processing that is not recoverable in the sense that the user must abandon the current computation and return to a top-level "eval>" prompt. However, before doing so it is usually possible to obtain some debugging information.

 The form of a call to `ERROR` is

$$\text{(ERROR } \textit{control-string arg-1} \ldots \textit{arg-n)}$$

It simply hands the control-string and subsequent arguments to FORMAT, with the output stream specified to be the terminal, and then breaks processing, irrecoverably. The form of that break will differ between Common Lisp implementations. Usually it leaves the user typing at some type of debugger, but the meaning and form of commands expected and accepted by debuggers can differ.

A typical use of ERROR would be

```
(DEFUN OUR-REVERSE (LST)
    (DO ((REM LST (CDR REM))
         (SOFAR 'NIL
                (CONS (CAR REM) SOFAR)))
        ((NULL REM)
         SOFAR)
        ;; body of the DO
        (IF (ATOM REM)
            (ERROR "Reverse of illformed list: ~S"
                   LST))))
```

Notice that this definition catches all errors that can cause REVERSE to fail. Thus,

```
eval> (OUR-REVERSE '(A B C))
(C B A)


eval> (OUR-REVERSE 'A)

>>ERROR: Reverse of illformed list: A
>> quit


eval> (OUR-REVERSE '(A B . C)

>>ERROR: Reverse of illformed list: (A B . C)
>>
```

It is good practice to check explicitly for error conditions and to call ERROR with an explanatory message. In this way, many of your bugs will advertise themselves before they can hide in later parts of your program. In particular, as discussed in chapter 5, it is excellent practice to catch "impossible" cases explicitly at the end of a COND expression and to signal an error. Such cases will never occur once the program is debugged fully, but the error messages will serve you well during that process.

The ERROR function is also useful in debugged applications programs to catch errors caused by incorrect input to the application. In principle, a robust error-checking program could detect errors and query the user rather than trap out to a Lisp level error. On the other hand, the former technique is often simpler, especially in an applications program intended for expert users only.

6.6 READ: **AN INPUT FUNCTION**

The primitive function for reading s-expressions in Lisp is READ. It reads characters from an input stream until a valid s-expression is completed. It returns an atom or a list. It treats parentheses and "white space" characters (i.e., space, tab, carriage return, line feed, form feed, and vertical tab) as delimiters. A call to it takes the form

(READ *stream eof-errorp eof-value*)

All three arguments are optional, but of course if the second is supplied, so must be the first, and so on. The meanings of the arguments are:

- *stream* must be an input stream. As is the case for output streams, the symbol T means the terminal. Input streams also can be created by applying the OPEN function to a file name. Thus,

(OPEN *filename* :DIRECTION :INPUT)

returns an input stream (it can be closed later with CLOSE) from which READ will read s-expressions. The *stream* argument defaults to T if it is not supplied. The remaining two arguments only make sense in the case of input files as the stream. The function READ gobbles characters from the input stream. They are never seen twice; thus, if READ is called twice on the same stream, the second call will only see characters following those read by the first.

- *eof-errorp* is a flag. If non-NIL, it says that an error should be signalled if READ comes to the end of the file while trying to read a valid s-expression. If the file contains only the characters "FOO", READ will successfully read the s-expression, which is the symbol FOO the first time it was called, even though that means reading right up to the end of the file (and it must actually peek ahead and see the end of the file to delimit FOO). The second time READ is called it will signal an error. If READ were reading a list and had yet to read the closing parenthesis when it reached the end of file, an error would be signalled if the *eof-errorp* flag were non-NIL. If *eof-errorp* is not supplied, it defaults to T. This does not affect READ when the input stream is the terminal because there is no end of file possible.

- *eof-value* is a value that is not examined by READ, but which, if *eof-errorp* is NIL, is handed back as the result of READ when the end of a file is reached during a call to READ. Thus, if there is an unknown number of expressions to be read from a file, READ should be repeatedly called with *eof-errorp* set to NIL, but with some unique value, that cannot possibly be found in the file, supplied for eof-value. The result of READ can be compared to this unique value and the user program thus will be able to detect when the file end is reached without generating an error. The problem of finding a unique value to pass as `eof-value`, something that cannot possibly be read from the file, is simple. The stream object itself is an internal data structure that cannot be printed or read as a text object. Thus, supplying that and testing EQness with the result of READ suffices.

We can now write our own version of LOAD (we first saw LOAD in chapter 2):

```
(DEFUN LOAD (FILENAME)
    (LET ((STREAM (OPEN FILENAME :DIRECTION :INPUT)))
        (DO ((FORM NIL (READ STREAM NIL STREAM)))
            ((EQ FORM STREAM)
             (CLOSE STREAM))
            ;; body of the DO
            (EVAL FORM))))
```

Suppose that we wanted to load a file of s-expressions and also see the result of each one (this is sometimes useful in a file of definitions, as each function name is returned by DEFUN and so is printed out—an error that chokes the READer in mid-file can be better located with this feedback). In some Lisps, such a function is called DSKIN. Notice that we explicitly give the PRINT function a stream argument of T, forcing the output on the terminal.

```
(DEFUN DSKIN (FILENAME)
    (LET ((STREAM (OPEN FILENAME :DIRECTION :INPUT)))
        (DO ((FORM NIL (READ STREAM NIL STREAM)))
            ((EQ FORM STREAM)
             (CLOSE STREAM))
            ;; body of the DO
            (PRINT (EVAL FORM)
                   'T))))
```

Now suppose we have data sets that always consisted of exactly 187 numbers, and we want to sum them, but at the same time we want to ensure that we have precisely 187 numbers and signal an error if we don't. Then we could write a function such as

```
(DEFUN SUM-DATA-SET (FILENAME)
    (LET ((STREAM (OPEN FILENAME :DIRECTION :INPUT)))
        (DO ((SUM 0.0
                  (+ (READ STREAM 'T) SUM))
             (I 187 (- I 1)))
```

```
((ZEROP I)
 (IF (NOT (EQ STREAM (READ STREAM NIL STREAM)))
     (ERROR "Extra data in file: ~S" FILENAME)
     (CLOSE STREAM))
SUM)))))
```

Notice how we use two different techniques to detect too few and too many values in the file.

There is a global variable, *READ-BASE*, that controls the base in which READ reads in numbers. Note that if a number is followed by a decimal point, but no further digits, it is taken as a base 10 integer regardless of the value of *READ-BASE*. If there are digits following the decimal point, the number is assumed to be a floating point number.

Consider the following examples:

```
eval> (SETQ *PRINT-BASE* 10.)
10

eval> (SETQ *READ-BASE* 8.)
8

eval> (LIST 77 77. 1000 1000.01)
(63 77 512 1000.01)
```

In the list of numbers read, the first and third were read in base 8 as integers, because they were simply strings of digits with no decimal points. The second number was read as a base 10 integer because it included a decimal point but no following digits. The last number was read as a base 10 floating point number because it included both a decimal point and digits following it.

Notice that there is no explicit relationship between *PRINT-BASE* and *READ-BASE*.

SUMMARY

The most general output function is FORMAT, but it can be understood in terms of simpler functions PRIN1, PRINC, and PRINT. The standard input function is READ. Both input and output functions use streams, abstract sources, or sinks of characters. Streams can be created from disk files using the function OPEN. They can be released using the function CLOSE.

The functions introduced in this chapter are shown in Table 6-1.

Table 6-1

Function	Args	Description
FORMAT	$2 \Rightarrow \infty$	print formatted output
OPEN	3	open a file
CLOSE	1	close a file
PRIN1	$1 \Rightarrow 2$	print an s-expression
PRINC	$1 \Rightarrow 2$	print more prettily
PRINT	$1 \Rightarrow 2$	print on a new line
TERPRI	$0 \Rightarrow 1$	start a new line
READ	$0 \Rightarrow 3$	read an item from a stream

The printers and readers can be controlled with the global variables which are shown in Table 6-2.

Table 6-2

Variable	Description
PRINT-BASE	number base for output
PRINT-LEVEL	maximum printing depth
PRINT-LENGTH	maximum printing length
READ-BASE	number base for output

PROBLEMS

P6.1 Sometimes it can be useful to be able to look ahead in an input stream and to see what was coming without actually taking it out of the stream. Write three functions:

(MAKE-BUFFER *stream*)

(PEEK-NEXT *buffer*)

(GET-NEXT *buffer*)

The first function takes an open input stream and returns some list structure that we will call a *buffer*. You will have to decide what should be in the list.

Function GET-NEXT returns the next thing to be read from the stream, which was used to make its buffer argument. Repeatedly calling GET-NEXT on a file reads s-expressions one at a time. When the end of a file is reached, the stream itself should be returned. Thus, GET-NEXT acts just like READ (with appropriate end of file arguments). The function PEEK-NEXT, however, always returns what would next be returned by GET-NEXT were it to be called—for example,suppose a file contains symbols A, B, and C. Then, after MAKE-BUFFER is called, the following should happen:

```
eval> (PEEK-NEXT BUFFER)
A

eval> (GET-NEXT BUFFER)
A

eval> (PEEK-NEXT BUFFER)
B

eval> (PEEK-NEXT BUFFER)
B

eval> (GET-NEXT BUFFER)
B

eval> (PEEK-NEXT BUFFER)
C
```

P6.2   Rewrite function SIMPLIFY from problem P5.1 to include error handling.

P6.3   Process the grading file for an introductory Lisp course. It consists of records of student's names and the scores they received for homework assignments and for the final exam. There are 7 homework assignments, each worth 10 points, and a final exam, worth 30. Not everyone does every homework assignment. Those scores are missing. If the final exam was turned in, it is the last score for a person. The grading file might look like

```
ANNE 10 10 9 10 8 7 8 27
BILL 5 4 3 2 1
COLIN 7 6 78  6 9 8 22
DIANNA 7 7  7 7 8 8 24
EUSTACIA 5 7 5 8 4 9 6 28
FRED 8 7 4 6 8 9 10 23
```

Write a program to read such a grade file and to print out a total score for each student, as shown in the following example:

```
Student    Score
-------    -----
ANNE        89
BILL        15
COLIN       xx
DIANNA      68
EUSTACIA    72
FRED        75
```

Make sure that your program checks for valid scores. In the case of COLIN, two scores were accidentally elided. The program caught the error and signalled the problem in the table. Your program can signal an error and give up in cases that are more confused than this (e.g., a list in the file).

Your program should use no globals and should be able to handle arbitrarily many students in the class. In particular, when the data for ANNE is printed out, not much past BILL should have been read of the input file.

P6.4   Write a pair of functions START-DRIBBLE and END-DRIBBLE that switch on and off, respectively, a record of all input and output being sent to an output file. The function START-DRIBBLE should take a file name as an argument, and the function END-DRIBBLE need take no arguments. (Hint: You actually won't need to write the END-DRIBBLE function. Instead, simply detecting the call to END-DRIBBLE is enough.) So that a user knows the conversation is being recorded, you should use a prompt different from "eval". Thus, for instance, after a dialogue such as

```
eval> (START-DRIBBLE "foo.baz")

dribbler> (LIST 'A 'B 'C)
(A B C)

dribbler> (+ 3 4)
7

dribbler> (END-DRIBBLE)
T

eval>
```

the file "foo.baz" should contain the following:[3]

---

[3]Note that this record is not exactly what was typed, because the quotes have been expanded. Making an exact copy can be done within Common Lisp but is not necessary for this assignment.

```
dribbler> (LIST (QUOTE A) (QUOTE B) (QUOTE C))
(A B C)

dribbler> (+ 3 4)
7

dribbler> (END-DRIBBLE)
```

7

FUNCTIONS

We have seen that functions, cons cells, and atoms are the fundamental concepts of Lisp. In this chapter, we turn our attention to functions. First, we examine some more general ways to pass arguments to them, and then see how they can be used successfully as data objects.

7.1 OPTIONAL ARGUMENTS

We have seen many Lisp functions that take optional arguments and have defaults (e.g., READ) and other functions that take arbitrarily many arguments (e.g., LIST). So far, we have not been able to define such functions ourselves. The special form DEFUN allows more general argument list specifications to allow such argument specifications.

Optional arguments are specified with an argument list that looks like:

$$(rarg\text{-}1 \ldots rarg\text{-}n \ \text{\&OPTIONAL} \ oarg\text{-}1 \ldots oarg\text{-}m)$$

Here, each *rarg-i* is a required argument and each *oarg-j* is an optional argument. As usual, required arguments are specified by symbols. The symbol &OPTIONAL is not treated as an argument name. It is an *argument list keyword* and is a syntactic device. Optional arguments may be specified by symbols alone or by lists of a symbol and a default value expression. Thus, an optional argument specification can look like

$$optional\text{-}arg$$

or like

$$(optional\text{-}arg \ default\text{-}value)$$

The former case is treated as though it were

$$(optional\text{-}arg \ \text{'NIL})$$

When a function with optional arguments is entered, each of the supplied arguments is matched up, left to right, with the required arguments of the function, and if any are left over they are matched with the optional arguments. If there are insufficient arguments supplied for an optional argument to be given a value, its *default-value* expression is evaluated in an environment where all arguments to the left of it have been evaluated and bound, and the default argument is bound to the result.

Consider the following example:

```
eval> (DEFUN FUZZY-EQUAL-P (X Y &OPTIONAL (FUZZ 0.001))
          (< (ABS (- X Y)) FUZZ))
FUZZY-EQUAL-P

eval> (FUZZY-EQUAL-P 0.1513 0.1517)
T

eval> (FUZZY-EQUAL-P 0.1513 0.1517 0.0001)
NIL

eval> (FUZZY-EQUAL-P 0.151 0.153)
NIL
```

(Notice that the function **ABS** returns the absolute value of its single argument.)
In the following example, one of the default arguments depends on some of
the required parameters when no value for it is supplied:

```
(DEFUN CLASS-STATS (CLASSNAME PASSED FAILED
                    &OPTIONAL (TOTAL (+ PASSED FAILED))
                              (STREAM 'T))
   (FORMAT STREAM
           "~%~S~10T~S~20T~S~30T~A"
           CLASSNAME
           PASSED
           FAILED
           (LET ((INCOMPLETES (- TOTAL
                                 (+ PASSED FAILED))))
                (IF (ZEROP INCOMPLETES)
                    " "
                    INCOMPLETES))))

(DEFUN PRINT-HEADER (&OPTIONAL (STREAM T))
   (FORMAT STREAM
           "~%Class~10TPassed~20TFailed~30TIncomplete"))
```

With the following sequence of calls,

```
(PRINT-HEADER)
(CLASS-STATS 'CS-102 62 1)
(CLASS-STATS 'CS-227C 3 5 65)
```

the output, on the terminal, would be

```
Class     Passed    Failed    Incomplete
CS-102    62        1
CS-227C   3         5         57
```

Notice that READ might have been defined starting with

```
(DEFUN READ (&OPTIONAL (STREAM T)
                       (EOF-ERRORP 'T)
                       (EOF-VALUE STREAM))
  ...)
```

EXERCISES

E7.1.1 What would the first line of a Lisp definition for PRINT look like?

E7.1.2 Given a function definition that starts out like:

```
(DEFUN TESTFUN (A B &OPTIONAL
                C (D (CONS A B)) (E (APPEND C D)) F)
  ...)
```

what would the values of A, B, C, D, E, and F be on entry to the function with the following call?

```
(TESTFUN 'FRED '(IS WELL) '(SUE KNOWS) '(EVERYTHING))
```

7.2 ARBITRARILY MANY ARGUMENTS

Arbitrarily many arguments can be specified as legal to a function by using the argument list keyword **&REST** as the second to last item in the argument list, and following it with a single argument name. The form of an argument list with a *rest* argument is

$$(rarg\text{-}1 \ldots rarg\text{-}n \text{ \&REST } restarg)$$

When such a function is called, all the supplied arguments are matched left to right with the required arguments *rarg-i*'s. If any remain, a list is made of them and the *restarg* is bound to that list. Thus,

```
(DEFUN MAKE-EXPRESSION (OPERAND &REST ARGUMENTS)
    (COND ((OR (EQ OPERAND '+)
               (EQ OPERAND '*))
           (CONS OPERAND ARGUMENTS))
          ((OR (EQ OPERAND 'COS)
               (EQ OPERAND 'SIN))
           (IF (OR (NULL ARGUMENTS)
                   (NOT (NULL (CDR ARGUMENTS))))
               (ERROR "Incorrect number of trig args: ~S"
                      ARGUMENTS)
               (CONS OPERAND ARGUMENTS)))
          (T (ERROR "Unknown operand: ~S" OPERAND)))))
```

would provide a robust way of making algebraic expressions, doing error checking not possible if we had simply used the LIST function.

```
eval> (MAKE-EXPRESSION '+ 3 'X 'Y)
(+ 3 X Y)


eval> (MAKE-EXPRESSION 'COS 'THETA)
(COS THETA)
```

The definition of the function LIST, in its entirety, could be

```
(DEFUN LIST (&REST X) X)        ; !!!
```

The definition of FORMAT could start out as

```
(DEFUN FORMAT (STREAM CONTROL &REST PARAMETERS) ...)
```

A function can have both optional arguments and a rest argument. The argument list must specify the required arguments, the optional arguments, and finally the rest argument. When the function is called, the supplied arguments are matched first, left to right, with those supplied. If any remain, they are bound to the optional arguments. If all the optional arguments are provided for, any remaining arguments are turned into a list for the rest argument, which otherwise is bound to NIL.

EXERCISES

E7.2.1 What would the first line of a Lisp definition for ERROR look like?

E7.2.2 Given a function definition that starts out with

```
(DEFUN NEWTEST (A B &REST C)
  ...)
```

what would the values of A, B, and C be for each of the following calls?
a. (NEWTEST 'A 'B 'C)
b. (NEWTEST 1 2)
c. (NEWTEST '(A B) '(C D) '(E F) '(G H))
d. (NEWTEST '(A B) '(C D) '(E F) '(G H) '(I J))

7.3 KEYWORD ARGUMENTS

We saw the function OPEN in section 6.2. It took a file name as its first argument and then two more arguments that we referred to as keywords. Recall that a typical call to it looked like

```
(OPEN "foo.lisp" :DIRECTION :INPUT)
```

The function OPEN is one of hundreds of Common Lisp functions that take *keyword arguments*. Many of the functions that we have already seen optionally take keyword arguments, in addition to their required arguments. For instance,

```
(LOAD "foo.lisp" :PRINT 'T)
```

says to load a file called "foo.lisp" and print the value of each expression within the file as it is loaded (recall that LOAD usually is mute).

Keywords provide a mechanism for supplying a large number of arguments to a function without having to remember the order in which the arguments should be supplied. This is especially useful when in the average case only a small fraction of the total number of possible arguments are actually supplied.

Keywords are all symbols whose values are themselves, and they are printed with a colon preceding them. Thus, :PRINT, :DIRECTION, :INPUT, and :OUTPUT are all keywords. These are not the same as "argument list keywords" such as &OPTIONAL and &REST. The latter have undefined values and are not "keywords" that appear in a call to a function.

Keywords in a call to a function follow the required arguments of the function. They are evaluated as ordinary arguments, since in the calling form the function call is treated as a standard function call. The result should be a list of alternating keywords and values. For instance, in the previous example the second argument :PRINT evaluates to the keyword :PRINT and the third argument evaluates to T. Thus, it would be equally valid to have typed

```
(LOAD "foo.lsp" (CADR '(:DIRECTION :PRINT :INPUT)) 'T)
```

in the above example. It is the *values* that must be keywords, not the form of the argument in the calling form. The value following each keyword can in general be anything. It often referred to as the *value of the keyword argument*. Thus, T is the value of the :PRINT keyword argument. In the first example of this section, the value of the :DIRECTION keyword argument was itself another keyword—namely, :INPUT.

A user-defined function can take keyword arguments, either by using a rest argument and parsing the list of arguments itself or by explicitly asking for keywords using the argument list keyword[1] &KEY[2]. We will not go into such esoterica in this book—you can find all the details in the Common Lisp manual if you are so inclined.

7.4 FUNCALL: PASSING A FUNCTION AS AN ARGUMENT

Almost any part of Lisp can be treated as data. It is possible to pass functions around as values and apply them to arbitrary sets of arguments.

Suppose we wanted to be able to call a different function depending on the value of an expression. For instance, recalling our parent-child relationship examples from the problems in chapter 5, we might want a general FIND-RELATIVE function that would dispatch on the type of relative desired to the appropriate function to find people with that relationship in the database. (If you have done the problems in chapter 5, you will know how useful this is.) For instance, we might write the function as:

---

[1] Isn't this keyword word ambiguous and something of a key word itself in understanding all this?

[2] Just in case you thought you understood all of this, be aware that some 51 Common Lisp functions, including MEMBER and ASSOC, take a :KEY keyword argument, which is unrelated to the argument list keyword &KEY, except that the latter is used in the definitions of those functions in order to define the :KEY keyword argument!

```
(DEFUN FIND-RELATIVE (RELATION PERSON)
    (COND ((EQ RELATION 'FATHER)
           (FATHER-OF? PERSON))
          ((EQ RELATION 'MOTHER)
           (MOTHER-OF? PERSON))
          ((EQ RELATION 'GRANDMOTHER)
           (GRANDMOTHERS-OF? PERSON))
          (T (ERROR "Unknown family relationship ~S"
                    RELATION))))
```

Now suppose we write a new function to find grandfathers. We would have to go back to our FIND-RELATIVE and change its definition. It would be nicer if we could somehow simply associate the symbol GRANDFATHER with the function GRANDFATHERS-OF? in a table somewhere.[3] For instance, we might keep the following correspondence between relationship names and function names:

```
(SETQ *RELATIONSHIP-FUNCTIONS*
    '((FATHER . FATHER-OF?)
      (MOTHER . MOTHER-OF?)
      (GRANDMOTHER . GRANDMOTHERS-OF?)))
```

We need only two Lisp primitives to do what we want: (1) we need to be able to get hold of the function associated with a symbol, and (2) we need to be able to call that function once we have it. There are two functions that do just these things.

$$(\text{SYMBOL-FUNCTION } symbol)$$

returns the *functional object* associated with the symbol given it as an argument. We call the associated functional object the *functional value* of a symbol. We can ignore what a functional object looks like, because the function FUNCALL enables us to call it with any set of arguments we wish. It takes the form

$$(\text{FUNCALL } functional\text{-}object\ arg\text{-}1\ \ldots\ arg\text{-}n)$$

---

[3]This would even open up the possibility of being able to *tell* our natural language interface how to find a person's grandfathers—it becomes fairly easy to be able to interpret and act on a sentence such as (USE GRANDFATHERS-OF? TO COMPUTE GRANDFATHER).

and calls the functional object with the arguments it received. Thus, the first two of the following forms are equivalent, and in fact the third is also.

```
(MEMBER 'A X)
```

```
(FUNCALL (SYMBOL-FUNCTION 'MEMBER) 'A X)
```

```
(FUNCALL #'MEMBER 'A X)
```

The third of these forms requires a little more explanation. As 'S is read as (QUOTE S), so #'S is read as (FUNCTION S). FUNCTION is a special form, which for the case of a symbol as its argument is equivalent to (SYMBOL-FUNCTION 'S). Later in this chapter we will see what happens for nonsymbol "arguments."

Now we are equipped to write a better version of FIND-RELATIVE:

```
(DEFUN FIND-RELATIVE (RELATION PERSON)
     (LET ((FUN-NAME (CDR (ASSOC RELATION
                               *RELATIONSHIP-FUNCTIONS*))))
         (IF (NULL FUN-NAME)
             (ERROR "Unknown family relationship ~S"
                 RELATION)
             (FUNCALL (SYMBOL-FUNCTION FUN-NAME) PERSON))))
```

Notice that no function called FUN-NAME is being used here. Rather the *value* of the variable FUN-NAME is a symbol whose functional value is being applied to an argument.

The function FIND-RELATIVE can remain unchanged and we can simply add new entries to the *RELATIONSHIP-FUNCTIONS* association list to add new relation-to-procedure mappings.

EXERCISES

E7.4.1 Evaluate the following s-expressions:
a. (FUNCALL #'LIST 'A 'B 'C 'D)
b. (FUNCALL #'MEMBER 'C '(A B C D))
c. (FUNCALL #'LIST* '(A B) '(C D) '(E F) '(G H))
d. (FUNCALL (SYMBOL-VALUE 'CONS) 'A 'B)

7.5 APPLY: **FOR LISTS OF ARGUMENTS**

We can use FUNCALL only when we know in advance precisely how many arguments are to be supplied. Sometimes we may have a variable number of arguments, and they may be in a list. The function APPLY applies a function object to an aribtrary number of values, which may be listed as follows:

$$\text{(APPLY }fun\text{-}obj\ arg\text{-}1\ \ldots\ arg\text{-}n\ arg\text{-}more)$$

The functional object *fun-obj* has its argument list matched to each of *arg-1* through *arg-n*, and then the final argument to APPLY is a list of the remaining available arguments.[4] Some typical uses of APPLY are

```
eval> (APPLY #'+ '(1 2 3 4 5 6))
21

eval> (APPLY #'* 2 3 '(4 5 6))
720
```

Notice that our general definition of APPLY is equivalent to

$$\text{(APPLY }fun\text{-}obj\ (\text{LIST* }arg\text{-}1\ \ldots\ arg\text{-}n\ arg\text{-}more))$$

A second typical use of APPLY is to pass down an undetermined number of arguments from one function to another. We saw the function ERROR, for instance, taking a control string and an arbitrary number of arguments that would together be fed to the function FORMAT. Here is a more explicit example of that technique. Suppose we have a large program with modules, and we would occasionally like to send the user a message (on the terminal, regardless of output files) and indicate which module sent the message. We could write the following general-purpose message routine:

```
(DEFUN USER-MESSAGE (SUBSYSTEM CONTROL &REST ARGS)
```

---

[4]In some Lisps—for example, Maclisp and Franz Lisp—APPLY is allowed only two arguments; all the arguments for the function to be applied to must be supplied as a single list.

```
(FORMAT T "~%Message from module: ~S~%" SUBSYTEM)
(APPLY <#'FORMAT
        'T
        CONTROL
        ARGS))
```

A typical call would be

```
(USER-MESSAGE 'PATH-PLANNER
              "Was blocked at exit ~S by obstacle ~S."
              EXIT-TRY
              OBSTACLE)
```

with the resultant sort of message appearing on the user's screen:

```
Message from module: PATH-PLANNER
Was blocked at exit LEFT-DOOR by obstacle TIGER.
```

Finally, notice that with APPLY we could write FUNCALL as

```
(DEFUN FUNCALL (FUNC &REST ARGS)
       (APPLY FUNC ARGS))
```

but this would be rather inefficient as the consing necessary to turn the rest argument ARGS into a list would be largely wasted. The real FUNCALL manages to avoid actually doing it. The moral is that sometimes FUNCALL is the right function to use, and sometimes APPLY is the right function.

EXERCISES

E7.5.1 Evaluate the following s-expressions:
a. (APPLY #'LIST 'A 'B 'C '(D E))
b. (APPLY #'MEMBER '(C (A B C D)))
c. (APPLY #'LIST* '(A (B)) '(C (D)) '(E (F)) '(G (H)))
d. (APPLY (SYMBOL-VALUE 'CONS) '(A B))

7.6 THE VALUE AND FUNCTIONAL VALUE OF A SYMBOL

We have seen previously that all symbols can have a global value and a function associated with them. There are a number of functions for accessing these values:

- (BOUNDP *symbol*) This function returns NIL if the symbol has never been given a value in the global environment; otherwise it returns T.
- (SYMBOL-VALUE *symbol*) In the case that the symbol is bound in the global environment (as can be checked with BOUNDP), this returns the value of the symbol. Otherwise, it causes an error.
- (FBOUNDP *symbol*) This function returns NIL if the symbol does not have a functional definition of some sort; otherwise, it returns non-NIL. Special forms, macros (which we will see in chapter 9), and ordinary functions are all FBOUNDP.
- (SYMBOL-FUNCTION *symbol*) As we saw above, this retrieves the functional definition of a symbol.
- (FUNCTIONP *object*) This is a predicate to test whether the object is a true functional object (rather than, say, the functional value of a special form or a macro) and returns non-NIL only in that case. Such a functional object is something that it makes sense to pass to FUNCALL or APPLY along with its arguments.

All of FUNCALL, APPLY, BOUNDP, and so on, will be very useful tools for writing interpreters for other languages within Lisp. For now, however, we will write an interpreter for Lisp itself!

Early in the book, we saw the function EVAL, which is precisely the function the Lisp system uses to evaluate expressions. We now have enough tools to write our own simple version of EVAL.

Let's call our version of the evaluator, or interpreter, OUR-EVAL. If given a list as an expression, it should try to apply the function named by the CAR of that list to the evaluations of all the rest of the elements of the list. First, of course, it should check that the symbol in the CAR is a defined function. This ignores the case of special forms. For now, let's check only for the QUOTE special form.

When given an atom, there are two possibilities: either the atom is a symbol in which case its value should be returned, or it is a self-evaluating atom (e.g., a number or a string), so the atom itself can be returned.

Given these considerations, OUR-EVAL can be defined as

```
(DEFUN OUR-EVAL (EXPRESSION)
  (COND ((CONSP EXPRESSION)
         (LET ((FUN-NAME (CAR EXPRESSION))
               (ARGLIST (CDR EXPRESSION)))
```

```
            ;; handle the special form QUOTE
            (COND ((EQ FUN-NAME 'QUOTE)
                   (CAR ARGLIST))
                  ((AND (SYMBOLP FUN-NAME)
                        (FBOUNDP FUN-NAME)
                        (FUNCTIONP (SYMBOL-FUNCTION
                                       FUN-NAME)))
                   ;; if its a good function then
                   ;; apply it to its evaluated arguments
                   (APPLY (SYMBOL-FUNCTION FUN-NAME)
                          (DO ((ARGS ARGLIST (CDR ARGS))
                               (EVARGS
                                ()
                                (CONS (OUR-EVAL (CAR ARGS))
                                      EVARGS)))
                              ((NULL ARGS)
                               (NREVERSE EVARGS)))))
                  (T (ERROR "Unknown function: ~S"
                            FUN-NAME)))))
    ;; a smbol has a value
    ((SYMBOLP EXPRESSION)
     (IF (BOUNDP EXPRESSION)
         (SYMBOL-VALUE EXPRESSION)
         (ERROR "Unbound variable: ~S"
                EXPRESSION)))
    ;; all other atoms evaluate to themselves
    (T EXPRESSION)))
```

EXERCISES

E7.6.1 Evaluate the following s-expressions:
a. (BOUNDP '*PRINT-LENGTH*)
b. (BOUDNP '*A-NEW-SYMBOL*)
c. (FBOUNDP 'SETQ)
d. (FUNCTIONP '(SYMBOL-FUNCTION SETQ))
e. (FBOUNDP 'LENGTH)
f. (FUNCTIONP '(SYMBOL-FUNCTION LENGTH))
g. (FBOUNDP 'FUNCTION)
h. (FUNCTIONP '(SYMBOL-FUNCTION FUNCTION))
i. (FBOUNDP 'A-REALLY-FUNNY-SYMBOL-HO-HO-HO)

E7.6.2 List the calls to OUR-EVAL with the argument with which it will be supplied in evaluating the following s-expressions:

a. (OUR-EVAL '(+ 1 2 3))
b. (OUR-EVAL '(LIST (CONS 'A 'B) 'C (CAR '(D E F)))))
c. (OUR-EVAL '(CONS (+ 2 3) (OUR-EVAL '(QUOTE (4 U)))))

7.7 LAMBDA

The basis for Lisp was the lambda calculus—a formalism for functions. Internally, Lisp functions are represented[5] as lists in the form of LAMBDA expressions. A LAMBDA expression has the following form:

$$(\text{LAMBDA } arglist \ body)$$

A LAMBDA expression is somewhat like DEFUN except that it makes an unnamed function[6]—note that it is the expression itself which is the function and that LAMBDA itself is neither a special form nor a function. Such functions can be handed to APPLY and FUNCALL, just as functions defined by DEFUN can be. For example,

```
eval> (FUNCALL
        '(LAMBDA (N) (+ 1 N))
        3)
4
```

Although simply quoting the list works fine in interpreted Lisp, we will see later that it is preferable to indicate to the compiler[7] that we are passing more than just a list to FUNCALL. The special form FUNCTION does this and we recall the shorthand for typing it—that is, #'.

```
eval> (APPLY
        #'(LAMBDA (A B C) (* A (+ B C)))
        '(4 3 5))
32
```

---

[5] Except that compiled functions are represented as machine code procedures—we will see more of this later.

[6] Which is exactly the opposite way to which Lisp was originally developed. DEFUN was built on top of LAMBDA.

[7] We have not yet talked about compilation, but we will in chapter 8.

It is good to get into the habit of using #' now.

Various Lisps have various rules about what variables may be referred to in the body of a LAMBDA expression. The rules usually depend on whether the code is to be compiled or interpreted (Common Lisp rules make no such distinction), and where the function is to be passed (either down to another function, or up as a result, or part of a result, from the current function). We will stick with some simple rules that are slightly more restrictive than Common Lisp allows—you won't need more except for very advanced programs.

A variable within a LAMBDA that is embedded within a DEFUN can be any variable that might legitimately be referred to at that location within the enclosing function, to a variable in the LAMBDA's own arguments, or to a variable introduced by a special form within the LAMBDA. We will only consider cases in which the result of FUNCTION with a LAMBDA expression as a subform is passed to other functions called within the enclosing DEFUN. We will not consider cases in which it is passed back as the result of the outer function. Notice that when a LAMBDA function is passed down to another function and then invoked with APPLY there, it may be referring to variables not within the function from which it is being called, but rather to variables in the function in which it was created.

The major utility we will have for functional LAMBDA expressions is to pass easy to define functions to the mapping functions of Lisp.

EXERCISES

E7.7.1 Evaluate the following s-expressions:
```
a. (APPLY #'(LAMBDA (X Y) (CONS X (CONS X Y)))
          '(DO-BE DO))
b. (APPLY #'(LAMBDA (X Y) (CONS X (CONS X Y)))
          'DO-BE
          '(DO))
c. (APPLY #'(LAMBDA (X Y) (CONS X (CONS X Y)))
          'DO-BE
          '((DO)))
d. (FUNCALL #'(LAMBDA (A B) (SQRT (+ (* A A) (* B B))))
            (- 4 1)
            (- 3 7))
e. (FUNCALL #'(LAMBDA (A &REST B) (MEMBER A B))
            'X
            'U
            'V
            'W
            'X
            'Y)
```

7.8 MAPPING FUNCTIONS

We have seen how to iterate with the DO special form. There is an older form of iteration in Lisp—*mapping*. Under mapping, a function is successively applied to elements of one or more lists.[8] The most common form is MAPCAR. It takes the form

(MAPCAR *function arglist-1 ... arglist-n*)

The function "*function*" must take n arguments. First, it is applied to the CARs of each *arglist-i*. Then it is applied to the CADRs, and so on, until the end of the shortest list is reached. The results of each application of the function are collected into a list that is returned as the value of the MAPCAR. Some examples are

```
eval> (MAPCAR #'NUMBERP
              '(A 3 B 2 4 C 7))
(NIL T NIL T T NIL T)

eval> (MAPCAR #'(LAMBDA (N) (+ 1 N))
              '(5 3 6 7 2))
(6 4 7 8 3)

eval> (MAPCAR #'(LAMBDA (KEY VALUE) (CONS KEY VALUE))
              '(MIAMI DENVER OAKLAND LOS-ANGELES)
              '(DOLPHINS BRONCOS RAIDERS RAMS))
((MIAMI . DOLPHINS) (DENVER . BRONCOS) (OAKLAND . RAIDERS)
 (LOS-ANGELES . RAMS))
```

In the first of these examples, a predefined predicate NUMBERP was applied to elements of a list, and the results accumulated. The second example was a LAMBDA expression, again applied to a single list of values. The first two examples both used functions of a single variable. The third example used a function of two variables, and so it is mapped over two lists. First, it is handed the CARs of the two lists, then the CADRs of the two, and so on. This example constructs an association list.

There are five variations on MAPCAR. The six functions form three logical pairs. The three sets of functions have different ways of producing their results from mapping their functional argument over their list arguments. Within each

---

[8]It is very easy to write very inefficient iteration constructs using mapping functions. They are included here only for the sake of completeness. It is extremely rare that it makes sense to use anything other than MAPCAR or MAPCAN. Modern Lisp compilers tend to rewrite the mapping constructs as DOs before they compile them anyway!

pair, there are two ways the arguments are derived from the argument lists for the mapped function.

The function that pairs with MAPCAR is MAPLIST. Instead of being given CARs of the argument list, the mapped function is successively given the lists, then their CDRs, and so on. As an example,

```
eval> (MAPLIST #'(LAMBDA (LIST)
                    (APPLY #'+ LIST))
            '(5 3 6 7 2))
(23 18 15 9 2)
```

Notice that there were 10 additions done to compute the result, whereas a more direct DO, or recursive, implementation could have done it in 4.

The next pair of functions is MAPC and MAPL. They behave the same as MAPCAR and MAPLIST, respectively, but instead of collecting the results of each function application into a list, they simply return their second argument, which is the first list of arguments that are supplied to the mapped function. Thus, MAPC and MAPL are to be used primarily for side effect. For example, we can redo our table printing function from chapter 6:

```
(DEFUN PRINT-PEOPLE (PEOPLE-ALIST)
    (FORMAT T "~%~%Person~10TLocation")
    (MAPC #'(LAMBDA (ENTRY)
                (FORMAT T "~%~S~10T~S" (CAR ENTRY) (CDR ENTRY)))
          PEOPLE-ALIST)
    NIL)
```

with result

```
eval> (PRINT-PEOPLE '((FRED . CHICAGO)
                      (ANNE . SEATTLE)
                      (JIM . NEWARK)
                      (JOCELYN . ATLANTA)))

Person    Location
FRED      CHICAGO
ANNE      SEATTLE
JIM       NEWARK
JOCELYN   ATLANTA
NIL
```

The final pair of functions is MAPCAN and MAPCON. They apply the mapping function to arguments in the same way as do MAPCAR and MAPLIST. Instead of

CONSing the results together, however, they NCONC them together. The most common use for these two functions is to filter one or more lists, picking out only entries that satisfy some test. Two examples are

```
eval> (MAPCAN #'(LAMBDA (ELEMENT)
                  (IF (NUMBERP ELEMENT)
                      (LIST ELEMENT)
                      NIL))
              '(A 3 B 2 4 C 7))
(3 2 4 7)

eval> (MAPCAN #'(LAMBDA (EVENT A-TIME B-TIME)
                  (IF (< A-TIME B-TIME)
                      (LIST EVENT)
                      NIL))
              '(1500M 800M 400M 200M)
              '(225 116 56 27)
              '(231 117 54 26))
(1500M 800M)
```

In the first case, when a nonnumber was encountered then NIL was returned, which gets absorbed by the NCONCing of the results and disappears. If a number is encountered that is made into a list of one element that is then returned, the NCONCer splices that into the result list. The second example picks out elements from one list that depend on the relative properties of entries appearing at the same distance along two other lists.

The following is an example of MAPCON. Recall that MAPCON is handed the remainders of the argument lists at each step. The function SETIFY, defined below, takes a list of symbols and removes all duplicates. Thus, it turns a "bag" into a "set." Again, we use the idiom of filtering out elements of a list.[9]

```
eval> (DEFUN SETIFY (BAG)
        (MAPCON #'(LAMBDA (MOREBAG)
                    (IF (MEMBER (CAR MOREBAG) (CDR MOREBAG))
                        NIL
                        (LIST (CAR MOREBAG))))
                BAG))
SETIFY
```

---

[9]Again, this is not a very efficient method of carrying out this operation. The number of EQL comparisons made by calls to MEMBER is roughly $n^2/2$ (where n is the number of list elements), whereas sorting the list (say, on lexigraphic order of the symbols) would take $n \log n$ comparisons and then only n EQL tests to check for collisions.

```
eval> (SETIFY '(A B A C B D A D))
(C B A D)
```

EXERCISES

E7.8.1   Evaluate the following s-expressions:
a. (MAPCAR #'LIST '(A B C D) '(W X Y Z))
b. (MAPLIST #'LIST '(A B C D) '(W X Y Z))
c. (MAPC #'LIST '(A B C D) '(W X Y Z))
d. (MAPL #'LIST '(A B C D) '(W X Y Z))
e. (MAPCAN #'LIST '(A B C D) '(W X Y Z))
f. (MAPCON #'LIST '(A B C D) '(W X Y Z))

E7.8.2   Choose the correct mapping function in each of the following cases:
```
a. (DEFUN GRANDCHILREN-OF (PERSON)
        (<mapper> #'CHILDREN-OF (CHILDREN-OF PERSON)))
b. (DEFUN PRINT-LIST (LIST)
        (<mapper> #'PRINT LIST)
        (LENGTH LIST))
c. (DEFUN NORM (VECTOR)
        (SQRT (APPLY #'+
                     (<mapper> #'(LAMBDA (X) (* X X))
                               VECTOR))))
d. (DEFUN WINNERS (LIST)
        (LENGTH (<mapper> #'(LAMBDA (ITEM)
                              (IF (WINNERP ITEM)
                                  (LIST 'T)
                                  'NIL))
                          LIST)))
```

7.9 LAMBDA IS TRANSPARENT

Functions defined as LAMBDA expressions were able to take the place of named functions when handed to APPLY or FUNCALL. For example,

```
eval> (DEFUN PLUS-ONE (N) (+ 1 N))
PLUS-ONE

eval> (FUNCALL #'PLUS-ONE 4)
5

eval> (FUNCALL #'(LAMBDA (N) (+ 1 N)) 4)
5
```

Likewise, LAMBDA expressions can take the place of symbols naming functions in s-expressions. For example,

```
eval> (PLUS-ONE 5)
6

eval> ((LAMBDA (N) (+ 1 N)) 5)
6
```

Thus, a function can be defined and applied in a single step. Note that the LAMBDA expression is used exactly as a function name would be. It is the CAR of the list and the remaining elements are the argument forms that will be evaluated and provide bindings for the variables of the LAMBDA list.

```
eval> ((LAMBDA (XDIFF YDIFF)
               (SQRT (+ (* XDIFF XDIFF)
                        (* YDIFF YDIFF))))
       (- 7 4)
       (- 5 1))
5
```

Before LET was invented, LAMBDA was a standard way of introducing new variables within Lisp functions. The rules for what variables can be referred to within a LAMBDA used as a local function are exactly the same as those for when a LAMBDA is passed as an argument to FUNCALL or MAPCAR.

Consider the following example:

```
(DEFUN ADD-ASSOC-ENTRY (KEY NEWVALUE ALIST)
    ((LAMBDA (ENTRY)
             (COND ((NULL ENTRY)
                    (CONS (LIST KEY NEWVALUE)
                          ALIST))
                   (T (RPLACD ENTRY
                              (CONS NEWVALUE (CDR ENTRY)))
                      ALIST)))
     (ASSOC KEY ALIST)))
```

Such code is a little hard to read because the new variables occur at the beginning of the LAMBDA, but the values to which they get bound do not appear until the end. For this reason, LET, which bundles these two up together at the start of the form, was invented. It is usually implemented in terms of LAMBDA—we will see how to do that when we study macros in chapter 9.

SUMMARY

User-defined functions can have optional arguments, and orthogonally, an unlimited number of arguments. Argument list keywords &OPTIONAL and &REST are placed in the argument list in the function definition to achieve this.

Many Common Lisp functions use alternating keywords, such as :PRINT and :DIRECTION, to receive a large number of options. These keywords evaluate to themselves.

There was one special form covered in this chapter. FUNCTION turns its subform into a functional object. A symbol has its functional value extracted from it. A list that is headed by the distinguished symbol LAMBDA is also turned into a function. LAMBDA is the primitive for defining functions in Lisp.

As ' is shorthand for QUOTE, so is #' shorthand for FUNCTION.

The functions introduced in this chapter are shown in Table 7-1. The list includes a number of functions to test for the existence of symbol values and functional values and their values. Functions FUNCALL and APPLY provide mechanisms for calling functions where the identity of the function is determined at runtime. There are six mapping functions that provide a means for iterating over a list of arguments and various ways of collecting the results.

Table 7-1

Function	Args	Description
ABS	1	absolute value of a number
SYMBOL-FUNCTION	1	functional value of a symbol
FUNCALL	$1 \Rightarrow \infty$	call a function with arguments
APPLY	$2 \Rightarrow \infty$	apply a function to argument list
BOUNDP	1	predicate for boundness of symbol
SYMBOL-VALUE	1	retrieve symbol value
FBOUNDP	1	predicate for functional boundness
FUNCTIONP	1	see whether a real function
MAPCAR	$2 \Rightarrow \infty$	map function over list items
MAPLIST	$2 \Rightarrow \infty$	map over sublists
MAPC	$2 \Rightarrow \infty$	over items but ignore results
MAPL	$2 \Rightarrow \infty$	over sublists but ignore results
MAPCAN	$2 \Rightarrow \infty$	over items and nconc results
MAPCON	$2 \Rightarrow \infty$	over sublists and nconc results

PROBLEMS

P7.1   Write a function that evaluates expressions written in infix notation, containing only Lisp functions that can take two arguments. Example expressions and the values they should yield are

```
(3 + 4)                        ==> 7
(3 * 4)                        ==> 12
(3 - 2)                        ==> 1
(3 + (4 * 5))                  ==> 23
((4 * 5) - (3 + (2 * 4)))      ==> 9
```

Assume that the expressions contain only numbers and defined Common Lisp functions. In this version, dispense with error checking completely.

P7.2   Write another version of the evaluator that produces the same result for correct input expressions, but one that checks for every conceivable error in the input and signals them with diagnostic messages.

P7.3   Suppose PRIMITIVE-ERROR is the function that ERROR uses to force a break in processing after it has called FORMAT. Write a function MY-ERROR that behaves just like ERROR.

P7.4   Write an interpreter for a strongly typed algorithmic language without user procedure calls (unless you are ambitious). A typical program would be

```
INTEGER I %
LIST L %
BEGIN
    PRINT ("List? ") %
    L := READ () %
    I := 0 %
    WHILE <> (L NIL) DO
                    BEGIN
                        I := + (I 1) %
                        L := CDR (L) %
                    END %
    PRINT ("Length is: " I) %
END
```

Write a function RUN so that if the foregoing program was contained in the file "prog.inp" the following would happen:

```
eval> (RUN "prog.inp")

List? (A B C)
```

```
Length is: 3
DONE!
```

The BNF for the language follows. You should write a parser that reads the file and accepts this language, turning the input program into some internal form. Variables only can be referenced in the body of the program if they have been declared.

```
<program> ==> <declaration> <program>
<program> ==> <block>
<declaration> ==> <type> <var> %
<block> ==> begin <statement>* end
<statement> ==> <block> %
<statement> ==> <var> := <expression> %
<statement> ==> <expression> %
<statement> ==> WHILE <expression> DO <block> %
<expression> ==> <term>
<expression> ==> <function> ( <expression>* )
<term> ==> <var>
<term> ==> <number>
<term> ==> <string>
<term> --> NIL
```

The legal types and functions are defined by the following associations, which also provide interpretations for them. The types specify a predicate that must be true of any value assigned to the variable during execution of the program. The functions specify a Lisp function (predefined or user defined) that is to be used as the interpretation of the algorithmic reference. Feel free to add more types and functions and to define their interpretations.

```
(SETQ *TYPES*
    '((LIST . LISTP)
      (INTEGER . FIXNUMP)))    ;this one needs definition!
(SETQ *FUNCS*
    '((READ . READ)
      (+ . +)
      (<> . NEQL)              ;and this one,
      (CDR . CDR)
      (PRINT . PRINT-LIST)))   ;and this one too.
```

The parsed input must now be interpreted. Ensure that no variable is ever given a value that doesn't satisfy its type predicate. No global variables other than *TYPES* and *FUNCS* should be necessary.

8

HOW
LISP
WORKS

This chapter is not essential to the rest of the book. It is intended to give an idea of what happens inside the machine when Lisp runs on it. This gives some basis for making efficiency trade-offs in writing large programs, and also motivates, to some extent, the use of macros described in chapter 9.

We have referred a number of times to the *interpreter* and the *compiler*. What is the difference between interpretation and compilation of Lisp programs?

When a Lisp program is interpreted, the lists that represent the functions are examined by APPLY and EVAL, which cooperate to walk recursively down the list structure. They must associate symbols and values to handle argument lists when functions are entered and to handle LAMBDA argument lists in internal LAMBDA applications. (All other variable introduction mechansisms—for example, LET and DO—are usually implemented in terms of LAMBDA.)

When a Lisp program is compiled, an assembly language program is produced that has an effect identical to that which would be achieved by interpreting the functions that are compiled. The resulting program can be much more efficient because it is a program for a particular set of functions rather than a general-purpose interpreter. Speedups on the order of a factor of 20 are routinely achieved by compiling Lisp programs.

We will examine in more detail an interpreter and a compiler to get a better feel for the efficiency issues. We will consider only a reduced version of Lisp; the primitives CAR, CDR, CONS, EQ, +, and ZEROP, the special forms QUOTE and IF, user-defined functions, and internal LAMBDA expressions.

8.1 THE INTERPRETER

A Lisp interpreter (the function EVAL) is a computer program, and as such it must be written in some language. In the past, the usual practice was to write it in assembly language or some algorithmic language such as C. It cannot be written in the interpretive Lisp itself; who would interpret the interpreter? Today, an interpreter is usually written in Lisp itself and is compiled by a compiler running in an *existing* Lisp, but the compiler produces machine code for the new target machine. The compiled code then can run on the new machine as a Lisp interpreter.[1]

We will write our own interpreter for our Lisp subset in Common Lisp. We will use an existing Common Lisp to interpret it interpreting our Lisp subset.[2] We will use the built-in Common Lisp functions to do the actual computations of the program, and we will rely completely on Common Lisp DEFUN to provide a function definition mechanism.

---

[1] And one of its first tasks usually is to interpret the compiler compiling itself! This process is called *bootstrapping*.

[2] We also can use Common Lisp to interpret the same things itself to compare results!

First, consider the problem of writing APPLY. We will write a version called OUR-APPLY. We will restrict it to two arguments—a function and a list of arguments for that function. The function always will be in the form of a LAMBDA list, because that is what DEFUN puts in a symbol's functional value slot. Recall that a LAMBDA looks like:

$$(\text{LAMBDA } var\text{-}list\ body)$$

The function OUR-APPLY must associate the argument variables in the LAMBDA with the values in the argument list and then evaluate the body of the LAMBDA in the context of those associations. This means that our evaluation function, call it OUR-EVAL, must take a second argument describing a variable binding environment. This is an extra layer of complexity over our OUR-EVAL of chapter 7, which could only handle global variables. OUR-APPLY looks like

```
(DEFUN OUR-APPLY (FUNC ARGLIST)
     (LET ((LAMBDA-ARGS (CADR FUNC))
           (LAMBDA-BODY (CADDR FUNC)))
       (IF (NOT (EQL (LENGTH LAMBDA-ARGS)
                     (LENGTH ARGLIST)))
           (ERROR "Wrong no args~%Function: ~S~%Args: ~S"
                  FUNC
                  ARGLIST)
           (OUR-EVAL LAMBDA-BODY
                     (MAPCAR #'(LAMBDA (VAR VAL)
                                 (CONS VAR VAL))
                             LAMBDA-ARGS
                             ARGLIST)))))
```

An error check makes sure the number of supplied arguments matches the number expected. OUR-EVAL is handed an association list of symbols and values that represents the bindings implied by invoking the function on its arguments.[3] To see what gets handed to OUR-EVAL, consider the following:

```
eval> (DEFUN XCONS (X Y) (CONS Y X))
XCONS

eval> (TRACE OUR-EVAL)
(OUR-EVAL)
```

---

[3]In fact, this is how it was done in early Lisps.

```
eval> (OUR-APPLY (SYMBOL-FUNCTION 'XCONS) '(A B))

(1 ENTER OUR-EVAL ((CONS Y X) ((X . A) (Y . B))))
...
```

The main part of our Lisp interpreter will be OUR-EVAL—it will use OUR-APPLY to handle any user-defined functions. We first need a few auxiliary functions. The first is useful in recursively evaluating the arguments to a user-defined function or an embedded LAMBDA expression. It is defined as

```
(DEFUN OUR-EVAL-ARGLIST (ARGLIST ENV)
    (MAPCAR #'(LAMBDA (ARG) (OUR-EVAL ARG ENV))
          ARGLIST))
```

It takes a list of arguments and a binding environment (an association list of variables and values) and returns a list of arguments evaluated in that environment.

The next function is the part of the interpreter that must call on Common Lisp to do all the primitive operations of our Lisp subset. If we were writing a real interpreter in assembler, we would need to have assembly code for each of the primitives. This function merely dispatches on function name to the appropriate built-in Common Lisp function. We assume here that the arguments have been evaluated already and that ARGLIST is a list of the results.

```
(DEFUN OUR-EVAL-PRIMOP (FUN-NAME ARGLIST)
    (COND ((EQ FUN-NAME 'CAR)
           (CAR (CAR ARGLIST)))
          ((EQ FUN-NAME 'CDR)
           (CDR (CAR ARGLIST)))
          ((EQ FUN-NAME 'CONS)
           (CONS (CAR ARGLIST) (CADR ARGLIST)))
          ((EQ FUN-NAME 'EQ)
           (EQ (CAR ARGLIST) (CADR ARGLIST)))
          ((EQ FUN-NAME '+)
           (+ (CAR ARGLIST) (CADR ARGLIST)))
          ((EQ FUN-NAME 'ZEROP)
           (ZEROP (CAR ARGLIST)))
          (T (ERROR "Unknown primop: ~S"
                    FUN-NAME))))
```

The last few auxiliary functions are predicates that help us dispatch inside OUR-EVAL.

```
(DEFUN PRIMOP-P (FUN-NAME)
    (MEMBER FUN-NAME '(CAR CDR CONS EQ + ZEROP)))


(DEFUN APPLYABLE-P (FUN-NAME)
    (AND (SYMBOLP FUN-NAME)
         (FBOUNDP FUN-NAME)
         (FUNCTIONP (SYMBOL-FUNCTION FUN-NAME))))


(DEFUN LAMBDA-P (FUN-NAME)
    (AND (LISTP FUN-NAME)
         (EQ (CAR FUN-NAME) 'LAMBDA)))
```

Now we are in a position to define OUR-EVAL. It is a modification of the version that we constructed in Chapter 7. It takes an expression to be evaluated and an optional environment. The environment is an association list of symbols and values representing bindings of local variables.

```
(DEFUN OUR-EVAL (EXPRESSION &OPTIONAL (ENV 'NIL))
   (COND
     ((CONSP EXPRESSION)
      (LET ((FUN-NAME (CAR EXPRESSION))
            (ARGLIST (CDR EXPRESSION)))
         (COND ((EQ FUN-NAME 'QUOTE)
                (CAR ARGLIST))
               ;; special form IF
               ((EQ FUN-NAME 'IF)
                (IF (OUR-EVAL (CAR ARGLIST) ENV)
                    (OUR-EVAL (CADR ARGLIST) ENV)
                    (OUR-EVAL (CADDR ARGLIST) ENV)))
               ;; handle primitives
               ((PRIMOP-P FUN-NAME)
                (OUR-EVAL-PRIMOP FUN-NAME
                          (OUR-EVAL-ARGLIST ARGLIST
                                            ENV)))
               ;; handle user defined functions
               ((APPLYABLE-P FUN-NAME)
                (OUR-APPLY (SYMBOL-FUNCTION FUN-NAME)
                          (OUR-EVAL-ARGLIST ARGLIST
                                            ENV)))
               ;; handle embedded LAMBDAs
               ((LAMBDA-P FUN-NAME)
                ;; need to augment the existing environment
                ;; with the new LAMBDA variables
```

```
                          (OUR-EVAL
                            (CADDR FUN-NAME)
                            (PAIRLIS (CADR FUN-NAME)
                                      (OUR-EVAL-ARGLIST ARGLIST ENV)
                                      ENV)))
                       (T (ERROR "Unknown function: ~S"
                                  FUN-NAME)))))
        ((SYMBOLP EXPRESSION)
         (LET ((LEXENTRY (ASSOC EXPRESSION ENV)))
              (COND ((NOT (NULL LEXENTRY))
                     (CDR LEXENTRY))
                    ((BOUNDP EXPRESSION)
                     (SYMBOL-VALUE EXPRESSION))
                    (T (ERROR "Unbound variable: ~S"
                               EXPRESSION)))))
        (T EXPRESSION)))
```

There are four aspects of this extension of OUR-EVAL that need explaining.

The special form IF is essentially reduced to the Common Lisp special form IF. Note that we did not use OUR-EVAL-ARGLIST to evaluate the three arguments to IF because IF only evaluates one of its second and third arguments.

If the expression is a call to one of our primitive operations, the arguments are evaluated and the results are passed to the function OUR-EVAL-PRIMOP.

If an embedded LAMBDA expression is detected, its arguments are evaluated and its variables are bound to those values by augmenting the environment as the variable NEWENV. The body of the LAMBDA is then passed to a recursive call to OUR-EVAL with the new environment. Notice that all variables in the original environment still appear in the association list for the new.

Finally, the handling of symbols has been extended. If they appear in the environment association list, the value associated there with a symbol is used as its value. Otherwise, its global value is used if there is one or an error is signalled. Notice that if a LAMBDA expression has introduced a new variable with the same name as the old, the old will be shadowed in the association list by the new.

Given the two definitions

```
(DEFUN P1 (X) (+ 1 X))

(DEFUN TF (X)
    ((LAMBDA (Y)
       (IF (ZEROP Y)
           X
           (P1 Y)))
     (+ X -5)))
```

we see a trace of our evaluator:

```
eval> (OUR-EVAL '(TF 7))

(1 ENTER OUR-EVAL ((TF 7)))
  (1 ENTER OUR-EVAL-ARGLIST ((7) NIL))
    (2 ENTER OUR-EVAL (7 NIL))
    (2 EXIT OUR-EVAL 7)
  (1 EXIT OUR-EVAL-ARGLIST (7))
  (1 ENTER OUR-APPLY ((LAMBDA (X)
                        ((LAMBDA (Y)
                            (IF (ZEROP Y) X (P1 Y)))
                         (+ X -5))))
                      (7)))
    (2 ENTER OUR-EVAL (((LAMBDA (Y)
                           (IF (ZEROP Y) X (P1 Y)))
                        (+ X -5))
                       ((X . 7)))))
      (1 ENTER OUR-EVAL-ARGLIST (((+ X -5)) ((X . 7))))
        (3 ENTER OUR-EVAL ((+ X 5) ((X . 7))))
          (2 ENTER OUR-EVAL-ARGLIST ((X -5) ((X . 7))))
            (4 ENTER OUR-EVAL (X ((X . 7))))
            (4 EXIT OUR-EVAL 7)
            (4 ENTER OUR-EVAL (-5 ((X . 7))))
            (4 EXIT OUR-EVAL -5)
          (2 EXIT OUR-EVAL-ARGLIST (7 -5))
          (1 ENTER OUR-EVAL-PRIMOP (+ (7 -5)))
          (1 EXIT OUR-EVAL-PRIMOP 2)
        (3 EXIT OUR-EVAL 2)
      (1 EXIT OUR-EVAL-ARGLIST (2))
      (3 ENTER OUR-EVAL ((IF (ZEROP Y) X (P1 Y))
                         ((Y . 2) (X . 7))))
        (4 ENTER OUR-EVAL ((ZEROP Y)
                            ((Y . 2) (X . 7))))
          (1 ENTER OUR-EVAL-ARGLIST ((Y)
                                      ((Y . 2) (X . 7))))
            (5 ENTER OUR-EVAL (Y ((Y . 2) (X . 7))))
            (5 EXIT OUR-EVAL 2)
          (1 EXIT OUR-EVAL-ARGLIST (2))
          (1 ENTER OUR-EVAL-PRIMOP (ZEROP (2)))
          (1 EXIT OUR-EVAL-PRIMOP NIL)
        (4 EXIT OUR-EVAL NIL)
        (4 ENTER OUR-EVAL ((P1 Y) ((Y . 2) (X . 7))))
          (1 ENTER OUR-EVAL-ARGLIST ((Y)
                                      ((Y . 2) (X . 7))))
```

```
            (5 ENTER OUR-EVAL (Y ((Y . 2) (X . 7))))
            (5 EXIT OUR-EVAL 2)
          (1 EXIT OUR-EVAL-ARGLIST (2))
          (2 ENTER OUR-APPLY ((LAMBDA (X) (+ 1 X)) (2)))
            (5 ENTER OUR-EVAL ((+ 1 X) ((X . 2))))
              (1 ENTER OUR-EVAL-ARGLIST ((1 X) ((X . 2))))
                (6 ENTER OUR-EVAL (1 ((X . 2))))
                (6 EXIT OUR-EVAL 1)
                (6 ENTER OUR-EVAL (X ((X . 2))))
                (6 EXIT OUR-EVAL 2)
              (1 EXIT OUR-EVAL-ARGLIST (1 2))
              (1 ENTER OUR-EVAL-PRIMOP (+ (1 2)))
              (1 EXIT OUR-EVAL-PRIMOP 3)
            (5 EXIT OUR-EVAL 3)
          (2 EXIT OUR-APPLY 3)
        (4 EXIT OUR-EVAL 3)
      (3 EXIT OUR-EVAL 3)
    (2 EXIT OUR-EVAL 3)
  (1 EXIT OUR-APPLY 3)
(1 EXIT OUR-EVAL 3)
3
```

A natural question upon examining the code for OUR-EVAL is: Why was an embedded LAMBDA expression treated as a function and passed to OUR-APPLY along with its arguments? An embedded LAMBDA expression is a function, but it is defined lexically within the function that calls it and therefore must have access to the variables within the calling functions. Therefore, if we had passed it to OUR-APPLY, the latter would have had to take an extra argument, the binding environment. We would then have trouble extending OUR-APPLY to the general argument structure (i.e., lexical scoping) used by Common Lisp. Perhaps we could store the environment in a global variable. But then we would have trouble resetting it to NIL when OUR-EVAL calls OUR-APPLY on a normal function and getting back the original environment on return. The solution presented here is perhaps cleaner.

Notice that if the call to OUR-APPLY for a normal function in OUR-EVAL did not effectively reset the environment to NIL, the scoping rules for variable reference would be vastly different. Any variable that was currently active in any function could be referenced (unless shadowed by a variable of the same name). As it happens, that is the rule used by most older Lisp interpreters. It is called *dynamic scoping* of variables. It is very inefficient to write a compiler that produces code that uses dynamic scoping, so most Lisp compilers follow the *lexical scoping* rules that we have previously defined. Common Lisp interpreters follow the same rules, as does the interpreter we defined above. (For example, notice how Y disappears from the environment as soon as function P1 is entered. Y would remain in a dynamically scoped Lisp.)

8.2 THE COMPILER

Now we will look at what a typical compiler might do with functions TF and P1 and see what must happen for the expression (TF 7) to be evaluated under these conditions.

We will use a simple machine model: a two-address machine, with registers and a stack. We will assume that compiled Lisp functions are passed with their arguments in register a1, a2, and so on, and return their results in register r. The stack will be used to hold variables created by embedded LAMBDA expressions, and for return addresses. We will use (sp)0 to refer to the top of the stack, (sp)-1 to refer to the next to top element, and so on. A not very smart Lisp compiler might compile our two functions in the following way (instructions have a source on the left and destination on the right):

```
(DEFUN P1 (X) (+ 1 X))

P1:        move    a1,r
           add     #1,r  % add 1 to arg1 and leave as result
           return


(DEFUN TF (X) ((LAMBDA (Y) (IF (ZEROP Y) X (P1 Y))) (+ X -5)))

TF:        move    a1,tmp
           add     #-5,tmp      % add -5 to arg1
           push    tmp,sp       % create new variable (i.e. Y)
           tst     (sp)0        % compare it to zero
           jmp.ne  else         % branch if non-zero
           move    a1,r         % arg1 is the result
           jmp     exitlam      % go exit from the lambda
else:      push    a1,sp        % save arg1 of this function
           move    (sp)-1,a1    % pass Y to the called function
           call    P1           % call it
           pop     sp,a1        % restore arg1
           move    r,r          % pick up result from P1
exitlam:   pop     sp,tmp       % throw away lambda variable
           return
```

Notice that a smarter compiler could have figured out that saving the argument to TF was not necessary because it was unused after return from function P1. Also, since the result of P1 became the result of TF, there was no need to generate the useless move r,r. Thus, three instructions could be saved easily.

To evaluate (TF 7), the argument only needs to be put into register a1 and the foregoing code needs to be called. Sixteen machine instructions later, the result will be in register r.

Compare this to all the work that needs to be done under an interpretive scheme. More than 16 CDR's are needed to be done just to walk over the list structures! Furthermore, in the foregoing interpreter, at least 9 cons cells are generated and then are discarded to handle passing of arguments and to maintain the lexical environment. Thus, compiled code is much more efficient than interpreted code. However, it is sometimes harder to debug because not as much information exists during the running of compiled code. Notice how symbols X and Y have completely disappeared from the assembly code and how calls to functions ZEROP and + have been optimized out. If TF causes a trap, we will not be able to examine the values of variables in the same way that we are able to in an error trap in interpreted code.

Compiled Lisp functions usually are loaded into the Lisp environment and treated like interpreted Lisp functions. Indeed, the Lisp system, and in particular EVAL and APPLY, are able to switch invisibly between compiled code and interpreted code.

Details of the best way to access the compiler vary among Common Lisp implementations. The standard interfaces that should be supported by all Common Lisps are the following three functions:

- (COMPILE-FILE *file name*) compiles the source code in the named file, producing a new file with a related name (usually with a different extension in systems where that makes sense) that contains compiled versions of all the functions defined in the source file.
- (COMPILE *symbol*) compiles the function associated with the named symbol and replaces its definition with the compiled version.
- (DISASSEMBLE *symbol*) displays the assembly code of a compiled function associated with the named symbol.

8.3 LISP STORAGE LAYOUT

A Lisp system divides an address space into three parts: a *stack* used for temporary variables and return addresses from function calls, *binary program space* for actual machine instructions, and a *heap* for Lisp data objects such as cons cells, strings, symbols, numbers and so on. Initially, a Lisp starts off with pieces of itself in all three of these parts. A user program provides additional objects to go into these parts that internally become indistinguishable from objects in the initial Lisp system itself.

A *pointer* is a unit of storage (e.g., an 18-bit half-word on a DEC-20, a 32-bit word on a VAX) that can contain the address of some other piece of storage (and perhaps have a few bits over). The stack and heap are made up of pointers.

A cons cell is simply a pair of pointers. A symbol is usually a collection of pointers, including one to point to the value, one to a string that is its print name, one to its functional definition,and one to a property list (we will talk about property lists in later chapters). Strings are stored in various ways, but usually as a sequence of 7- or 8-bit bytes. Numbers usually occupy a piece of storage that is the size of one or more pointers.

In some Lisps, all types of objects are stored throughout the heap. In others, the heap is segmented so that a segment contains items of only one size. This can make storage management easier (see the later section on garbage collection).

There are a number of ways in which the type of a Lisp object is stored.

In some Lisps, the location of the object within the address space is enough to deduce the type of the object. In these Lisps, each page of memory, or some bigger unit (usually its size is a power of 2), is dedicated to holding objects of a particular type. A page might contain only cons cells or it might contain only symbols, or perhaps only floating-point numbers. Thus, when a pointer is handed to a type predicate, such as CONSP, it picks up a few high-order bits to index into a page table in which the type of all the objects stored in that page is recorded. This scheme is known as BIBOP (BIg Bag Of Pages).[4]

Another scheme is to encode the type of the object in every pointer to it. This can be done when the size of pointers—for example, 32 bits—is bigger than the number of bits that are needed to specify the address of an object—for example, 24 or 28 bits. The remaining bits specify the type of the object pointed to (e.g., a symbol, a cons, or a string). This scheme is used in most micro-coded Lisp machines, and modern general-purpose architectures often include such "tag" bits.

A third scheme is to encode the type of an object in the storage representation of the object itself. One or more bits in each object in the same place, relative to the address specified for the object, specify its type. This means a type check has to access the object to find out its type. Sometimes this scheme is used in combination with tagged pointers when there are very few bits available to be used as tags. Suppose there is only one bit available—it might be used to signify whether the object being pointed to is a cons cell or an atom. Then all atoms (symbols, numbers, strings, etc.) would have embedded bits, identifying their particular type.

8.4 HOW SYMBOLS ARE IDENTIFIED

When Lisp reads an expression from the terminal or a file, it constructs a list that contains references to symbols. Somehow it must determine which symbol in storage is meant by a string of characters. It can't just make a new symbol for each symbol name typed in—it must get any existing symbol with the same

---

[4]This is the scheme used in Maclisp.

name. Thus, when (CDR X) is typed, the Lisp reader must find the original symbol called CDR in order to use its functional value in evaluating the expression.

Traditionally, the information necessary to find a symbol, given its name, is stored in something called the *obarray* (or *oblist*). This is a vector of lists of symbols. Typically, there might be a vector of 512 lists stored sequentially at a particular location in the heap.

An input string is "hashed." That is, a number from 0 to 511 is produced from it that looks somehow random, and, given any two strings that are not the same sequence of characters, the probability that the same number is produced should be extremely low. The same number should always be produced for two strings that are sequences of the same characters, and each of the 512 possible numbers should be produced with equal frequency. A simple (albeit not very good) hashing function would be to add all the character codes in the string and take the result modulo 512.

The hash number for a string is used to index into the obarray to retrieve one of the lists of symbols. This list is searched by comparing the input string to the print name of each symbol in the list. If a match on the strings is found, an existing symbol with the right name has been determined and it can be used in constructing the cons cells representation of the input expression. If no match is found, a new symbol must be created and then entered into the appropriate list (the one unsuccessfully searched) in the obarray so that future references will relocate it.

The vector of lists and the hashing scheme is only necessary for efficiency. In principle, one could construct a single enormous list, but the average number of string comparisons to locate a symbol would be large and time-consuming.

8.5 GARBAGE COLLECTION

Even with virtual memory, current computer architectures have limits on the size of an address space. Thus, there is an upper bound on the number of objects that can be created in a Lisp heap before it is full.[5] In most Lisp implementations, a program that is doing moderate amounts of consing, or that is producing strings or other data structures usually fills the heap in a few seconds, or at most in a few minutes of CPU time.

Fortunately, and usually, most of the objects, such as cons cells, that fill the heap are no longer needed by the time the heap is full. For instance, suppose that

---

[5]In Maclisp on a DEC-20, it is bounded by the address space that is 256K words. A cons cell in Maclisp takes one 36-bit word. The initial Lisp system and stack occupies about 50K words. Thus, even if cons cells were the only thing stored in the heap, space would run out after producing 200K of them. This number is extremely easy to achieve in running a program for just a few seconds. If you find this hard to believe, recall the number of CONS cells generated and discarded in our execution of OUR-EVAL on (TF 7).

we have a program that understands simple English stories. Each sentence might be parsed into a tree structure describing its syntax, and that structure would then be analyzed for semantic significance. Once that was done, the structure would no longer be needed. The next sentence would be parsed. So all the cons cells created to parse the first sentence still exist in the heap, but they will never be used again.

When the heap is full, the Lisp system invokes a procedure called the *garbage collector*. It looks at the whole heap carefully and tries to determine which cons cells, or other structures, are never going to be used again by the running program. If it finds any, it makes the storage they occupy available to future consing operations.

The only way a garbage collector can be sure that an object in the heap will never be used again is if there is no other object anywhere in the heap pointing to it, or if all objects that do point to it can be shown to be unusable in the future.

An example follows of how some list structure can be built and then later become inaccessible.

```
(DEFUN UNDERSTAND-A-STORY (STREAM DATABASE)
    (DO ((SENTENCE (READ-A-SENTENCE STREAM)
                   (READ-A-SENTENCE STREAM)))
        ;means at eof
        ((EQ SENTENCE STREAM)
         DATABASE)
        (COMPREHEND-AND-UPDATE-DATABASE
         (PARSE-SENTENCE SENTENCE)
         DATABASE)))
```

Each sentence that is read is formed into a list to which the symbol SENTENCE is bound. The next sentence that is read, however, replaces the value of SENTENCE, so unless PARSE-SENTENCE somehow saved a pointer to the sentence, under some globally accessible structure, during its execution (assume that PARSE-SENTENCE never returns its argument so COMPREHEND-AND-UPDATE-DATABASE will not see it), there will no longer be a pointer to the first sentence anywhere.

Let's suppose that there is a separate heap for cons cells. Any cons cell that can be reached must ultimately be reachable by following pointers from symbol values or from a temporary variable on the stack. One method of garbage collection is to have an extra bit associated with each cons cell, called the *mark bit*. Sometimes all these bits are grouped together in a big bit table with a simple linear relation between table position and cons cell address. In other Lisps, a spare bit right in the cons cell is used. At the start of a garbage collection, we assume that all of these bits are set to off. Then all the symbols and the stack are checked for pointers to cons cells and any that are found are passed to a function that looks like this:[6]

```
(DEFUN MARK-CELL (CONS-CELL)
    (COND ((NOT (MARKEDP CONS-CELL))
            (SETMARK CONS-CELL)
            (IF (CONSP (CAR CONS-CELL))
                (MARK-CELL (CAR CONS-CELL)))
            (IF (CONSP (CDR CONS-CELL))
                (MARK-CELL (CDR CONS-CELL))))))
```

The predicate `MARKEDP` checks whether a cons cell's mark bit is on. If the cell is already marked, we do not do anything (this avoids infinite recursion). Otherwise, the function `SETMARK` turns on a cons cell's mark bit. At the end of this mark phase, every cons cell that is still accessible by the user's program has its mark bit set. Now the heap is *swept*. Each cons cell is examined with a linear sweep through the heap; this is easy to do because we have assumed that the heap contains only cons cells and that they all have the same size. Any unmarked cons cell has its `CDR` replaced so that it is included in a special list known as the *free list*. The function that checks each cons cell during sweeping looks something like this:

```
(DEFUN CHECK-CELL (CONS-CELL)
    (COND ((MARKEDP CONS-CELL)
            (UNSETMARK CONS-CELL))
          (T (RPLACD CONS-CELL *FREE-LIST*)
            (SETQ *FREE-LIST* CONS-CELL))))
```

Sweeping completes garbage collection. Notice that we unmark each cell for the benefit of the next time we do garbage collection. If `*FREE-LIST*` is `NIL`, the garbage collector failed to reclaim any storage and the Lisp system is in trouble; it really is full. Otherwise, Lisp can continue, and now function `CONS` will look something like

```
(DEFUN CONS (X Y)
    (IF (NULL *FREE-LIST*)
        (GARBAGE-COLLECT))
```

---

[6]We use Lisp code to demonstrate the operation of the garbage collector. Most Lisp garbage collectors have been written in assembler language and it is only recently that anyone has written them in Lisp. Only a subset of Lisp can be used; in particular, no consing can be done! This implies that the garbage collector functions must be compiled, not interpreted.

```
(LET ((CONS-CELL *FREE-LIST*))
     (SETQ *FREE-LIST* (CDR CONS-CELL))
     (RPLACA CONS-CELL X)
     (RPLACD CONS-CELL Y)
     CONS-CELL))
```

The problem with the garbage collection algorithm as we have described it is that it might use arbitrary amounts of stack when recursively tracing cons cells in the function MARK-CELL. There are complex algorithms that can do that recursive tracing with a fixed amount of stack by cleverly temporarily leaving back-pointers in cons cells as they trace.

Real garbage collectors must deal with complications if the heap allows a mixture of object types within single pages of memory. They also must garbage collect symbols, although they usually will be accessible via the obarray so they never get collected.[7]

Other garbage collectors, particularly in machines with large virtual address spaces, try to compact all the good cons cells into a contiguous part of memory to improve subsequent paging performance. This involves copying them all and updating all pointers that point to the original cons cells.

Another, usually less successful, method is to maintain reference counts on all cons cells and reuse cells whose count is zero. The amount of book-keeping necessary is usually prohibitive, and the collector never reclaims unused circular structures.

SUMMARY

There are three major components to a Lisp system: a compiler, a set of functions for use at run time (including an interpreter), and a storage management system. The compiler takes Lisp programs and transforms them to equivalent programs in machine language, typically gaining a speed factor of 20. The interpreter walks over the list structure of a Lisp program calling named functions on the arguments that follow them. Common Lisp is lexically scoped, and every time a function is entered, the name space of known variables is reset to include only globals and the arguments to the function. The storage management system is able to detect when data structures are no longer accesible to the user and automatically reclaims the storage space they occupy for reuse.

---

[7]Maclisp allows, by user request, the garbage collection of *truly worthless symbols* by finding those that are referred to *only* by the obarray.

The functions covered in this chapter all pertain to using the compiler. They are shown in Table 8-1.

Table 8-1

Function	Args	Description
COMPILE-FILE	1	compile a file
COMPILE	1	compile a function
DISASSEMBLE	1	disassemble a compiled function

9

MACROS

We have observed throughout the previous eight chapters that the form of Lisp programs is the same as the form of Lisp data structures. We have made very little use of that fact. In general, it is a very powerful idea. We can manipulate programs just as we can manipulate data.

In this chapter, we introduce a convenient tool for manipulating programs to achieve data abstraction and control abstraction. The tool is the *macro facility* of Common Lisp. Macros let us efficiently introduce new data structures, hiding the details of representation from any functions that use them. Macros also let us introduce new control structures that look like special forms (such as IF and DO) in that they don't follow the usual evaluation rule for s-expressions.

With macros, explicit manipulations of Lisp program structures only have to occur in the definition of macros, not at the points at which they are used, as would be the case in trying to use list structure transformations for data and control abstractions without the help of macros.

9.1 ABSTRACT DATA STRUCTURES

We have occasionally used lists as data structures, where each position within a list is used to store some field of the data structure. For example, suppose we are writing a program that is to reason about stacking blocks on a table. We might have a situation like

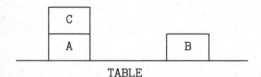

We might represent each block by a list that records its properties:

(name color is-on is-under)

Suppose further that we keep a list of all the block records in the global variable *BLOCKS*. Then we might write some functions to display the state of our blocks world. For example,

```
(DEFUN PRINT-WORLD ()
    (MAPC #'PRINT-BLOCK *BLOCKS*)
    (FORMAT T "~%")
    'T)
```

```
(DEFUN PRINT-BLOCK (BLOCK)
   (FORMAT T
           "~%Block ~S (~S) is "
           (CAR BLOCK)
           (CADR BLOCK))
   (COND ((NULL (CADDR BLOCK))
          (FORMAT T "unsupported "))
         ((EQ 'TABLE (CADDR BLOCK))
          (FORMAT T "on the table "))
         (T (FORMAT T
                    "on block ~S "
                    (CAADDR BLOCK))))
   (IF (NULL (CADDDR BLOCK))
       (FORMAT T
               "and supports nothing.")
       (FORMAT T
               "and supports block ~S."
               (CAR (CADDDR BLOCK)))))
```

Given the foregoing and these two functions, we would get the following output:

```
eval> (PRINT-WORLD)

Block C (GREEN) is on block A and supports nothing.
Block B (BLUE) is on the table and supports nothing.
Block A (RED) is on the table and supports block C.
T
```

Although it is not clear from the code, PRINT-BLOCK assumes that the third and fourth elements of the list are either NIL or another of the block records (and in the case of the third element, *is-on*, it can also be the symbol TABLE). There are two things to note from this:

- The data structures are circular, as the list for block A contains the list for block C, which contains the list for block A, and so on. Thus, if we want to print the lists themselves, we ought to set *PRINT-LEVEL* to something small.

- Function PRINT-BLOCK is difficult to understand because it is too cluttered with details of the structure of our representation for blocks (e.g., CADDR and CADDDR, etc.), rather than with some indication of what those data field accesses represent.

To solve the second problem, we need to abstract out of PRINT-BLOCK any references to the structure of block records. We could do this by defining a number of functions to access parts of a block record. For example,

```
(DEFUN BLOCK-NAME (X) (CAR X))


(DEFUN BLOCK-COLOR (X) (CADR X))


(DEFUN BLOCK-SUPPORT (X) (CADDR X))


(DEFUN BLOCK-TOP (X) (CADDDR X))
```

Now we can modify PRINT-BLOCK to refer to the components of a block record by name. It becomes much more readable.

```
(DEFUN PRINT-BLOCK (BLOCK)
    (FORMAT T
            "~%Block ~S (~S) is "
            (BLOCK-NAME BLOCK)
            (BLOCK-COLOR BLOCK))
    (COND ((NULL (BLOCK-SUPPORT BLOCK))
            (FORMAT T "unsupported "))
          ((EQ 'TABLE (BLOCK-SUPPORT BLOCK))
            (FORMAT T "on the table "))
          (T (FORMAT T
                    "on block ~S "
                    (BLOCK-NAME (BLOCK-SUPPORT BLOCK)))))
    (IF (NULL (BLOCK-TOP BLOCK))
        (FORMAT T
                "and supports nothing.")
        (FORMAT T
                "and supports block ~S."
                (BLOCK-NAME (BLOCK-TOP BLOCK)))))
```

Because we have made a block into an abstract data type relative to the function PRINT-BLOCK, we now are free to change the representation of blocks without changing the function PRINT-BLOCK. We might decide that in our main computations we will rarely look at the color field of the record, so it makes more sense to position that last (since it takes longer to get to the fourth element of a list than it does to the second). All we have to do is change the access functions for block records.

```
(DEFUN BLOCK-NAME (X) (CAR X))

(DEFUN BLOCK-COLOR (X) (CADDDR X))

(DEFUN BLOCK-SUPPORT (X) (CADR X))

(DEFUN BLOCK-TOP (X) (CADDR X))
```

It is not necessary to change PRINT-BLOCK at all, but we will need to change any other functions that manipulate block records directly. If we round out our access functions with one to create an instance of the record and ones to change the contents of any fields that might later be changed, we can eliminate all other functions from relying on the structure we choose for block records. Thus, we might add

```
(DEFUN MAKE-BLOCK (NAME COLOR)
     (LIST NAME NIL NIL COLOR))

(DEFUN CHANGE-SUPPORT (X Y) (RPLACA (CDR X) Y))

(DEFUN CHANGE-TOP (X Y) (RPLACA (CDDR X) Y))
```

giving a total of seven functions that define and operate on the representation of blocks. No other function need depend on the structure that we have chosen for our blocks. Our program source file should have all seven functions grouped together on a single page. Any and all changes to the representation of blocks can be isolated to that page.

Similarly, the world is represented in a particular way, as a list of block records bound to the global *BLOCKS*. Later we may wish to change this representation too, so we can plan ahead by abstracting out the operations we might wish to do on our world representation. For instance,

```
(DEFUN START-WORLD () (SETQ *BLOCKS* 'NIL))

(DEFUN ADD-BLOCK (BLOCK)
     (SETQ *BLOCKS*
          (CONS BLOCK *BLOCKS*)))
```

```
(DEFUN ALL-BLOCKS () *BLOCKS*)

;;; The following function relies on the CAR of each block
;;; being its name. Since ASSOC compares with EQL this means
;;; that we can use anything which tests which is EQL to things
;;; that print the same. Thus symbols and numbers can be block
;;; names, e.g. A, 3 and BIG-BLOCK.

(DEFUN GET-BLOCK (NAME) (ASSOC NAME *BLOCKS*))
```

So far, the only function we have that depends on the world representation is
PRINT-WORLD. We can change it to

```
(DEFUN PRINT-WORLD ()
    (MAPC #'PRINT-BLOCK (ALL-BLOCKS))
    (FORMAT T "~%")
    'T)
```

In summary, we have seven functions that provide an interface to our representation of individual blocks, and four functions that provide an interface to
our representation of the world. We do not need to know the internal details
of these representations or functions in order to write functions that manipulate
blocks and the world. Instead, we need only know the arguments expected by
these eleven functions and the results that they return. We have seen two such
functions thus far: PRINT-BLOCK and PRINT-WORLD.

9.2 LAYERS OF ABSTRACTION

Let's use the eleven data abstracting functions to build a higher-level interface
to our blocks world representation. The first few functions we will write are
useful for setting up a world model. The first one is used purely for internal
error checking:

```
(DEFUN ENSURE-BLOCK (NAME)
  (LET ((BLOCK (GET-BLOCK NAME)))
      (IF (NULL BLOCK)
          (FORMAT T
                  "~%Unknown block named: ~S"
                  NAME))
      BLOCK))
```

```
(DEFUN NEW-BLOCK (NAME COLOR)
  (LET ((NEW (MAKE-BLOCK NAME COLOR)))
       (ADD-BLOCK NEW)
       (CHANGE-SUPPORT NEW 'TABLE)
       NAME))

(DEFUN PUT-ON (A B)
  (LET ((BLOCKA (ENSURE-BLOCK A)))
     (IF (NULL BLOCKA)
         'NIL
         (COND ((EQ B 'TABLE)
                (CHANGE-SUPPORT BLOCKA 'TABLE)
                'T)
               (T (LET ((BLOCKB (ENSURE-BLOCK B)))
                    (COND ((NOT (NULL BLOCKB))
                           (CHANGE-SUPPORT BLOCKA BLOCKB)
                           (CHANGE-TOP BLOCKB BLOCKA)
                           'T)
                          (T 'NIL)))))))))
```

The function NEW-BLOCK sets up a block record, adds it to the world model, and makes sure that it starts out sitting on the table. With these, we can set up a model of our originally pictured world:

```
eval> (START-WORLD)
T


eval> (NEW-BLOCK 'A 'RED)
A


eval> (NEW-BLOCK 'B 'BLUE)
B


eval> (NEW-BLOCK 'C 'GREEN)
C


eval> (PUT-ON 'C 'A)
T
```

The four functions that someone using our blocks world modeler would need to know about are START-WORLD, NEW-BLOCK, PUT-ON, and PRINT-WORLD. We can write a few more functions, which we will define.

Function MOVE-BLOCK allows a user to change the world once it has been set up. It makes use of an auxiliary function LIFT-OFF and also subsumes PUT-ON. The function CLEARTOP? is used to check whether a block has nothing on top of it. The function SUPPORTS? returns any block that sits on top of another. These three functions all give error messages if the user refers to a nonexistent block. The fourth function lets the user check for nonexistence of a block without incurring the error message. This will be useful in distinguishing whether a block is sitting on another block or on a table.

```
(DEFUN LIFT-OFF (NAME)
    (LET ((BLOCK (ENSURE-BLOCK NAME)))
        (IF (NULL BLOCK)
            NIL
            (LET ((ON (BLOCK-SUPPORT BLOCK)))
                (CHANGE-SUPPORT BLOCK 'NIL)
                (IF (NOT (EQ ON 'TABLE))
                    (CHANGE-TOP ON 'NIL))
                'T))))

(DEFUN MOVE-BLOCK (NAME TO-NAME)
    (LIFT-OFF NAME)
    (PUT-ON NAME TO-NAME))

(DEFUN CLEARTOP? (NAME)
    (LET ((BLOCK (ENSURE-BLOCK NAME)))
        (IF (NULL BLOCK)
            NIL
            (NULL (BLOCK-TOP BLOCK)))))

(DEFUN SUPPORTS? (NAME)
    (LET ((BLOCK (ENSURE-BLOCK NAME)))
        (IF (NULL BLOCK)
            NIL
            (BLOCK-NAME (BLOCK-SUPPORTS BLOCK)))))

(DEFUN IS-BLOCK? (NAME)
    (IF (NULL (GET-BLOCK NAME))
        'NIL
        'T))
```

Now we have a new level of abstraction above the abstract interfaces to the data structures. Altogether there are seven functions that a user program might wish to manipulate: START-WORLD, NEW-BLOCK, MOVE-BLOCK, CLEARTOP? and PRINT-WORLD.

Our first round of abstraction in the previous section removed the details of how the components of a block representation were stored. Now we have even abstracted out what is stored for each block and how those representations are modified as the world is changed. We have seven functions that let us communicate a simple set of operations to our world model and simulation system.

We could set up the world model shown at the beginning of the chapter by using our newly abstracted primitives as follows:

```
eval> (START-WORLD)
T

eval> (NEW-BLOCK 'A 'RED)
A

eval> (NEW-BLOCK 'B 'BLUE)
B

eval> (NEW-BLOCK 'C 'GREEN)
C

eval> (MOVE-BLOCK 'C 'A)
T

eval> (PRINT-WORLD)

Block C (GREEN) is on block A and supports nothing.
Block B (BLUE) is on the table and supports nothing.
Block A (RED) is on the table and supports block C.
T
```

9.3 MACROS

Data abstraction has enabled us to write very clean functions, but at what cost? Every time we access a component of a block record, we now call a user defined function (e.g., BLOCK-NAME) that calls a predefined Lisp function (e.g., CAR) rather than only the predefined Lisp function itself. In both the interpreter and the compiled code, we have at least doubled the time to access a field (it is much worse than double in compiled code—CAR typically takes one instruction whereas a function call takes 5 or more).

We can eliminate this cost in compiled code using *macros*. Macros work in interpreted code also, but they save very little time. A macro is a function-like object that returns a Lisp expression to be evaluated in place of itself. An example will illustrate.

```
eval> (DEFMACRO BLOCK-NAME (X) (LIST 'CAR X))
BLOCK-NAME

eval> (BLOCK-NAME '(A NIL NIL RED))
A

eval> (MACROEXPAND '(BLOCK-NAME '(A NIL NIL RED)))
(CAR (QUOTE (A NIL NIL RED)))
```

The special form (actually its a macro!) DEFMACRO is used to define macros. It uses a similar syntax to DEFUN, and the argument list can contain &REST and &OPTIONAL, just as for DEFUN. When EVAL sees a macro in a functional position in an expression, it passes the rest of the elements of the expression to the macro, but *without evaluating them*. The macro is expected to return an *expression* to be *substituted* for the original, and then EVAL evaluates that instead. Thus, a macro provides a substitute expression for EVAL. The process of providing the substitution is called *macro expansion*. If the substitute expression is also headed by a macro, the process is repeated. The function MACROEXPAND, as shown in the example, is called internally by EVAL to manage the application of the macro. By using the function MACROEXPAND-1, which causes a single level of macro expansion, it iterates until a non-macro list is returned.

The compiler forces macro expansion before it compiles a Lisp function. Thus, for example, the function

```
(DEFUN PRINT-NAME (BLOCK) (PRINT (BLOCK-NAME BLOCK)))
```

will be compiled exactly as though it were

```
(DEFUN PRINT-NAME (BLOCK) (PRINT (CAR BLOCK)))
```

since (BLOCK-NAME BLOCK) macro expands to be (CAR BLOCK). Thus, macros buy back all the overhead spent in making our data types abstract. We get both the readability (and flexibility to change data representation) in a function such as our second version of PRINT-BLOCK while retaining the efficiency of the first.

```
(DEFMACRO BLOCK-NAME (X) (LIST 'CAR X))


(DEFMACRO BLOCK-COLOR (X) (LIST 'CADDDR X))


(DEFMACRO BLOCK-SUPPORT (X) (LIST 'CADR X))


(DEFMACRO BLOCK-TOP (X) (LIST 'CADDR X))


(DEFMACRO MAKE-BLOCK (NAME-EXP COLOR-EXP)
    (LIST 'LIST NAME-EXP NIL NIL COLOR-EXP))


(DEFMACRO CHANGE-SUPPORT (X Y)
    (LIST 'RPLACA
          (LIST 'CDR X)
          Y))


(DEFMACRO CHANGE-TOP (X Y)
    (LIST 'RPLACA
          (LIST 'CDDR X)
          Y))
```

Consider what happens during expansion of the form (MAKE-BLOCK NAME COLOR) in function NEW-BLOCK. Macro MAKE-BLOCK gets called with argument NAME-EXP bound to NAME and COLOR-EXP bound to COLOR. The macro then returns

```
                (LIST NAME NIL NIL COLOR)
```

which is the right piece of code, referring to the correct variables.

With the foregoing macro definitions, the clear and concise definition of PRINT-BLOCK as

```
(DEFUN PRINT-BLOCK (BLOCK)
    (FORMAT T
            "~%Block ~S (~S) is "
            (BLOCK-NAME BLOCK)
            (BLOCK-COLOR BLOCK))
    (COND ((NULL (BLOCK-SUPPORT BLOCK))
          (FORMAT T "unsupported "))
```

```
                ((EQ 'TABLE (BLOCK-SUPPORT BLOCK))
                 (FORMAT T "on the table "))
                (T (FORMAT T
                        "on block ~S "
                        (BLOCK-NAME (BLOCK-SUPPORT BLOCK)))))
        (IF (NULL (BLOCK-TOP BLOCK))
            (FORMAT T "and supports nothing.")
            (FORMAT T
                    "and supports block ~S."
                    (BLOCK-NAME (BLOCK-TOP BLOCK)))))
```

is compiled exactly as if it had been defined as

```
    (DEFUN PRINT-BLOCK (BLOCK)
        (FORMAT T
                "~%Block ~S (~S) is "
                (CAR BLOCK)
                (CADDDR BLOCK))
        (COND ((NULL (CADR BLOCK))
               (FORMAT T "unsupported "))
              ((EQ 'TABLE (CADR BLOCK))
               (FORMAT T "on the table "))
              (T (FORMAT T
                        "on block ~S "
                        (CAR (CADR BLOCK)))))
        (IF (NULL (CADDR BLOCK))
            (FORMAT T "and supports nothing.")
            (FORMAT T
                    "and supports block ~S."
                    (CAR (CADDR BLOCK)))))
```

The functions that specify interactions with the world model can also be made into macros for improved performance when compiled. For example,

```
    (DEFMACRO START-WORLD ()
        (LIST 'SETQ '*BLOCKS* ''NIL))

    (DEFMACRO ADD-BLOCK (BLOCK)
        (LIST 'SETQ
              '*BLOCKS*
              (LIST 'CONS BLOCK '*BLOCKS*)))
```

```
(DEFMACRO ALL-BLOCKS () '*BLOCKS*)

(DEFMACRO GET-BLOCK (NAME)
    (LIST 'ASSOC NAME '*BLOCKS*))
```

EXERCISES

E9.3.1 Given the macro

```
(DEFMACRO PERSON-FATHER (X)
    (LIST 'CAR (LIST 'CDR X)))
```

what do each of the following evaluate to?
a. (MACROEXPAND '(PERSON-FATHER X))
b. (MACROEXPAND '(PERSON-FATHER (BROTHER-OF X)))
c. (MACROEXPAND '(PERSON-FATHER '(FRED JOE MARY)))

E9.3.2 Suppose we represent a person by a list with the following form:

$$((first\text{-}name\ surname)\ (mother\ father)\ age)$$

Write macros called PERSON-NAME, PERSON-PARENTS, PERSON-MOTHER, PERSON-FATHER, and PERSON-AGE to retrieve the appropriate parts of a person record.

9.4 MACROS FOR CONTROL STRUCTURE

Macros let us do much more besides use efficient data abstractions. Because the "arguments" to a macro are not evaluated before being passed to the macro, we can write special forms that don't obey the usual evaluation rules. For instance, consider the problem of writing LET, in terms of the more primitive variable introduction mechanism LAMBDA. We have a form like

```
(LET ((BLOCK (GET-BLOCK NAME)))
    (IF (NULL BLOCK)
        (FORMAT T
                "~%Unknown block named: ~S"
                NAME))
    BLOCK)
```

Clearly, LET cannot be a function, because its first "argument" is a list but doesn't have a symbol or a LAMBDA in the functional position. In fact, we would like the foregoing to be treated identically to

```
((LAMBDA (BLOCK)
     (IF (NULL BLOCK)
         (FORMAT T
                 "~%Unknown block named: ~S"
                 NAME))
     BLOCK)
  (GET-BLOCK NAME))
```

We can define LET as a macro that expands exactly into that by

```
(DEFMACRO LET (ARGBINDS &REST BODY-EXPS)
     (LIST* (LIST* 'LAMBDA
                   (MAPCAR #'CAR ARGBINDS)
                   BODY-EXPS)
            (MAPCAR #'CADR ARGBINDS)))
```

As another example,

```
(LET ((A 3)
      (B '(C D)))
     (LIST A B B A))
==>
  ((LAMBDA (A B)
           (LIST A B B A))
     3
     (QUOTE (C D)))
```

where we use "==>" to show what the original code becomes when macros are expanded.

We can make use of a control structure macro to clean up some of our blocks world functions. We repeatedly have code that tries to ENSURE-BLOCK and returns NIL if that fails. For example,

```
(DEFUN CLEARTOP? (NAME)
     (LET ((BLOCK (ENSURE-BLOCK NAME)))
          (IF (NULL BLOCK)
              NIL
              (NULL (BLOCK-TOP BLOCK)))))
```

We could capture that idiom with a macro that provides a variable to be bound to the block instance named, then evaluates a code body on success. Thus, we would rewrite as

```
(DEFMACRO BIND-BLOCK (VARS &REST BODY)
    (LET ((INSTANCE-VAR (CAR VARS))
          (NAME-EXP (CADR VARS)))
        (LIST 'LET
              (LIST (LIST INSTANCE-VAR
                          (LIST 'ENSURE-BLOCK NAME-EXP)))
              (LIST 'COND
                    (LIST (LIST 'NULL INSTANCE-VAR)
                          NIL)
                    (LIST* T BODY)))))


(DEFUN CLEARTOP? (NAME)
    (BIND-BLOCK (BLOCK NAME)
        (NULL (BLOCK-TOP BLOCK))))
```

The function first is expanded to

```
(DEFUN CLEARTOP? (NAME)
    (LET ((BLOCK (ENSURE-BLOCK NAME)))
        (COND ((NULL BLOCK) NIL)
              (T (NULL (BLOCK-TOP BLOCK))))))
```

which then expands to

```
(DEFUN CLEARTOP? (NAME)
    ((LAMBDA (BLOCK)
            (COND ((NULL BLOCK) NIL)
                  (T (NULL (BLOCK-TOP BLOCK)))))
     (ENSURE-BLOCK NAME)))
```

We can rewrite other functions using this same macro. For example,

```
(DEFUN PUT-ON (A B)
    (BIND-BLOCK (BLOCKA A)
        (COND ((EQ B 'TABLE)
               (CHANGE-SUPPORT BLOCKA 'TABLE)
               'T)
              (T (BIND-BLOCK (BLOCKB B)
                    (CHANGE-SUPPORT BLOCKA BLOCKB)
                    (CHANGE-TOP BLOCKB BLOCKA)
                    'T)))))
```

```
(DEFUN LIFT-OFF (NAME)
   (BIND-BLOCK (BLOCK NAME)
      (LET ((ON (BLOCK-SUPPORT BLOCK)))
         (CHANGE-SUPPORT BLOCK 'NIL)
         (IF (NOT (EQ ON 'TABLE))
            (CHANGE-TOP ON 'NIL))
         'T)))
```

EXERCISES

E9.4.1 Write a macro OUR-IF that expands into COND and has the same effect as IF.

E9.4.2 Write a macro PRINT-BIND that binds a variable, prints its name and value, and then evaluates a body with the variable bound.

9.5 BACKQUOTE AND COMMA

Consider again our BIND-BLOCK example from the blocks world:

```
(DEFMACRO BIND-BLOCK (VARS &REST BODY)
   (LET ((INSTANCE-VAR (CAR VARS))
         (NAME-EXP (CADR VARS)))
      (LIST 'LET
         (LIST (LIST INSTANCE-VAR
                  (LIST 'ENSURE-BLOCK NAME-EXP)))
         (LIST 'COND
            (LIST (LIST 'NULL INSTANCE-VAR)
               NIL)
            (LIST* T BODY)))))
```

In looking at this code afresh, it is difficult to tell what is going on. There are two problems: (1) how the expression to be macro-expanded is parsed, or taken apart, and (2) what the form of the code is that is being produced. The first problem would be greatly alleviated if the second were solved. To get a feel for the code form that is returned, we can skim the body of the macro ignoring LISTs, LIST*s, and CONSes and trying to sieve out the rest of the key symbols (e.g., LET and COND) to get a broad perspective of what is being produced. The details of the produced code still require detailed examination.

To solve this problem, the characters backquote and comma have been given special meaning in Common Lisp. They provide a way of writing code templates into which variations are spliced. For example, we can write our BLOCK-NAME macro as

```
(DEFMACRO BLOCK-NAME (X)
    '(CAR ,X))
```

This is identical in behavior to our earlier definition:

```
(DEFMACRO BLOCK-NAME (X)
    (LIST 'CAR X))
```

The expression '(CAR ,X) gets read as though it were the expression (LIST 'CAR X).[1] One way of thinking about backquote and comma is that backquote quotes a list, except that comma can be used to "unquote" a portion of it anywhere inside. Thus, the s-expression following a comma is evaluated and put into the overall list structure. The resulting expression is put directly in the position at which the comma and its following expression occurred. For example,

```
eval> '(A B ,(+ 3 4) D)
(A B 7 D)

eval> (SETQ X '(C D))
(C D)

eval> '(A B ,X E)
(A B (C D) E)

eval> '(A B ,X (,(CADR X)) (E ,X))
(A B (C D) (D) (E (C D)))
```

---

[1] This is not completely true in all versions of Common Lisp. Sometimes '(CAR ,X) gets read as an expression that has the same effect as (LIST 'CAR ,X) but one that actually is different. The reason for this is that some Lisps have debuggers that wish to pretty print the internal LAMBDA expression of a function in the form in which the user would type it in. It cannot print all expressions involving LIST in backquote notation since perhaps the user really did type LIST there originally. Therefore, those Lisps might read the expression '(CAR ,X) as, say, (BACKQUOTE-LIST 'CAR X), where BACKQUOTE-LIST has the same functional definition as LIST. The pretty printer recognizes BACKQUOTE-LIST specially and prints it in backquote notation—it maps down all the arguments, printing without quotes those that are quoted, and printing those that aren't quoted with commas preceding them.

An additional wrinkle is that if a comma is followed by an atsign, the following expression is again evaluated, but this time it is *spread* or *spliced* into the list so that each element of the spliced subform becomes an element at the level at which the complete subform was specified. For example,

```
eval> '(A B ,@X E)
(A B C D E)

eval> '(A B ,@X (,(CADR X)) (E ,@X))
(A B C D (D) (E C D))
```

The last backquote expression was equivalent to

```
(LIST* 'A
       'B
       (APPEND X
               (LIST (LIST (CADR X))
                     (CONS 'E (APPEND X 'NIL)))))
```

EXERCISES

E9.5.1 Given

```
(SETQ A '(A LIST OF SYMBOLS))
(SETQ B 'ONE-SYMBOL)
(SETQ C '(ANOTHER LIST))
```

evaluate the following expressions:
a. '(,A ,B ,C)
b. '(THIS IS ,A)
c. '(THIS IS ,@A)
d. '(THIS IS ,B)
e. '(,@A AND ,C)
f. '(AND THIS IS . ,C)

E9.5.2 Given

```
(SETQ A '(X Y))
(SETQ B '(U V W))
(SETQ C 'Z)
```

write patterns using only backquote, comma, atsign, and the three variables A, B, and C to produce the following:

a. (X Y Z)
b. ((X Y) (Z))
c. (U V W X Y Z)
d. (((U V W) X Y) Z)

9.6 READABLE MACROS

Given the backquote tools, we can now rewrite our BIND-BLOCK macro in a slightly more readable fashion.

```
(DEFMACRO BIND-BLOCK (VARS &REST BODY)
    (LET ((INSTANCE-VAR (CAR VARS))
          (NAME-EXP (CADR VARS)))
        '(LET ((,INSTANCE-VAR (ENSURE-BLOCK ,NAME-EXP)))
            (COND ((NULL ,INSTANCE-VAR)
                   NIL)
                  (T ,@BODY)))))
```

The bulk of the macro body is a template for the code to be produced by the macro; the backquote gives us that hint, and the indenting shows the scope of the template. The first part of the macro is simply parsing the form that the BIND-BLOCK will head. The argument list does part of that parsing. VARS will get bound to the first element of the list following BIND-BLOCK, and BODY will be bound to a list of all the remaining elements. Recall that &REST is a special symbol in argument lists; it does not name a parameter itself, but says that all remaining supplied parameters should be bundled into a list and bound to the symbol that follows. The first part of the macro definition does a little more parsing, taking the two elements of VARS and binding them to variables. Now the expected structure of a BIND-BLOCK expressions should be clear:

$$(BIND\text{-}BLOCK \ (\ var\ name\text{-}exp)\ body\text{-}1 \ldots body\text{-}n)$$

We will reexamine some other macros, given the power of the backquote tools. First, recall our definition of LET, which transformed it into an embedded LAMBDA expression, and examine a companion definition using backquote:

```
(DEFMACRO LET (ARGBINDS &REST BODY-EXPS)
    (LIST* (LIST* 'LAMBDA (MAPCAR #'CAR ARGBINDS) BODY-EXPS)
        (MAPCAR #'CADR ARGBINDS)))
```

```
(DEFMACRO LET (ARGBINDS &REST BODY-EXPS)
  '((LAMBDA ,(MAPCAR #'CAR ARGBINDS)
            ,@BODY-EXPS)
    ,@(MAPCAR #'CADR ARGBINDS)))
```

The new definition clearly shows the template of the structure that it will produce. The depth of the symbol LAMBDA in the result is clear from this template, whereas it was somewhat buried in the first definition. Notice, too, how the natural indentation of the second definition shows the structure of the arguments that are to be suppled to the LAMBDA expression, making it obvious that these expressions are separate and not embedded in the body of the LAMBDA.

Now, as an additional example, consider the definition of IF as a macro that expands into a COND special form. Two definitions, without and with backquote, are shown:

```
(DEFMACRO IF (A B &OPTIONAL (C 'NIL))
    (LIST 'COND
          (LIST A B)
          (LIST 'T C)))

(DEFMACRO IF (A B &OPTIONAL (C 'NIL))
    '(COND (,A ,B)
           (T ,C)))
```

Again, the immediately apparent template in the second definition makes the intent of the macro clear.

Now let's consider the problem of writing a macro for LET* that turns it into a set of nested LETs. Thus, for instance, we would like the following to happen:

```
(LET* ((DESTINATION (END-POINT JOURNEY))
       (ORIGIN (START-POINT JOURNEY))
       (JOURNEY (DISTANCE ORIGIN DESTINATION)))
      ...)
==>
(LET ((DESTINATION (END-POINT JOURNEY)))
    (LET ((ORIGIN (START-POINT JOURNEY)))
        (LET ((JOURNEY (DISTANCE ORIGIN DESTINATION)))
            ...)))
```

There is no need to carry out the whole expansion in one step. A simple solution to writing LET* is that it should simply strip off the first argument and

its binding into an outer LET and leave the rest of the arguments and their bindings in an imbedded LET*. When the evaluator or compiler comes to evaluate
the new LET body, it will force expansion of the new LET* in a recursive manner. As long as the expansion eventually stops—for example, when there are no
arguments left—evaluation or compilation will proceed as if all the arguments
had been handled at once. Thus, we could write

```
(DEFMACRO LET* (BINDINGS &REST FORMS)
    (IF (NULL BINDINGS)
        '(PROGN ,@FORMS)
        '(LET (,(CAR BINDINGS))
             (LET* ,(CDR BINDINGS)
                 ,@FORMS))))
```

The expansion would proceed in a number of stages as

```
(LET* ((DESTINATION (END-POINT JOURNEY))
       (ORIGIN (START-POINT JOURNEY))
       (JOURNEY (DISTANCE ORIGIN DESTINATION)))
      ...)
==>
(LET ((DESTINATION (END-POINT JOURNEY)))
    (LET* ((ORIGIN (START-POINT JOURNEY))
           (JOURNEY (DISTANCE ORIGIN DESTINATION)))
          ...))
==>
(LET ((DESTINATION (END-POINT JOURNEY)))
    (LET ((ORIGIN (START-POINT JOURNEY)))
        (LET* ((JOURNEY (DISTANCE ORIGIN DESTINATION)))
              ...)))
==>
(LET ((DESTINATION (END-POINT JOURNEY)))
    (LET ((ORIGIN (START-POINT JOURNEY)))
        (LET ((JOURNEY (DISTANCE ORIGIN DESTINATION)))
            (LET* NIL ...))))
==>
(LET ((DESTINATION (END-POINT JOURNEY)))
    (LET ((ORIGIN (START-POINT JOURNEY)))
        (LET ((JOURNEY (DISTANCE ORIGIN DESTINATION)))
            (PROGN ...))))
```

Notice that the final PROGN is not strictly necessary, but it is easier to terminate the expansion when there are no bindings left, as we did in the example. In addition, it makes the macro work right in case we get (LET* NIL ...) from somewhere else (e.g., from some other macro!). The compiler should generate the same code, regardless of the presence or absence of the PROGN.

EXERCISES

E9.6.1 Using backquote and comma, rewrite the macros PERSON-NAME, PERSON-PARENTS, PERSON-MOTHER, PERSON-FATHER, and PERSON-AGE from exercise 9.3.2.

9.7 PITFALLS OF MACROLOGY

One must be careful when writing macros to avoid causing multiple evaluations of an expression at run time. For instance, suppose we decide to write SCALE-SQUARE, whose functional definition is

```
(DEFUN SCALE-SQUARE (SCALE EXP)
    (* SCALE EXP EXP))
```

as a macro instead, to avoid the overhead of a procedure call. For example,

```
(DEFMACRO SCALE-SQUARE (SCALE EXP)
    '(* ,SCALE ,EXP ,EXP))
```

Now suppose we want to scale square some quantity that either took a long time to compute, or whose computation has side effects. Two examples might be

```
(SCALE-SQUARE 3.0 (* X (+ Y Z)))
```

```
(SCALE-SQUARE
    2.0
    (COMPUTE-THE-GNP-AND-DELETE-SOURCE-FILE "govtrecords.txt"))
```

Consider what these two expand into:

```
(* 3.0
    (* X (+ Y Z))
    (* X (+ Y Z)))

(* 2.0
    (COMPUTE-THE-GNP-AND-DELETE-SOURCE-FILE "govtrecords.txt")
    (COMPUTE-THE-GNP-AND-DELETE-SOURCE-FILE "govtrecords.txt"))
```

The major computation is getting done twice in each case. We would have been better off having SCALE-SQUARE remain a function and pay the price of a function call. In these two cases, we should have generated code like

```
(LET ((TEMP (* X (+ Y Z))))
    (* 3.0 TEMP TEMP))

(LET ((TEMP (COMPUTE-THE-GNP-AND-DELETE-SOURCE-FILE
                "govtrecords.txt")))
    (* 2.0 TEMP TEMP))
```

This suggests that our definition of SCALE-SQUARE should be

```
(DEFMACRO SCALE-SQUARE (SCALE EXP)
    (IF (ATOM EXP)
        '(* ,SCALE ,EXP ,EXP)
        '(LET ((TEMP ,EXP))
            (* ,SCALE TEMP TEMP))))
```

Here we have done two things. We have first tested whether the expression we wish to square is an atom. In that case, there is no real overhead with having it evaluated twice. If the expression is not an atom, its value is bound to a temporary variable, named TEMP, and that is squared. The two foregoing examples are thus expanded correctly and the main expressions are only evaluated once.[2]

However, what if a variable already exists named TEMP—perhaps the user used that name, or perhaps it was generated by another macro. For example, consider how this code gets expanded:

---

[2]If your Lisp compiler is a good one, you could dispense with the (ATOM EXP) test and let the compiler notice when the LET was redundant.

```
(DEFUN SUM-SCALE-SQUARE (A B C D)
    (LET ((TEMP (+ A B)))
        (FORMAT T "~%Scaling factor is: ~S" TEMP)
        (SCALE-SQUARE TEMP (+ C D))))

 =>

(DEFUN SUM-SCALE-SQUARE (A B C D)
    (LET ((TEMP (+ A B)))
        (FORMAT T "~%Scaling factor is: ~S" TEMP)
        (LET ((TEMP (+ C D)))
            (* TEMP TEMP TEMP))))
```

It's wrong! For our macro to be 100 percent safe, we need to use a variable name that we know will not already be in use.

We can use the function GENSYM for this purpose. It takes no arguments and returns a fresh symbol. In most Common Lisps, the symbols will typically look like: G0027. Now we can rewrite our macro as

```
(DEFMACRO SCALE-SQUARE (SCALE EXP)
    (IF (ATOM EXP)
        `(* ,SCALE ,EXP ,EXP)
        (LET ((VAR (GENSYM)))
            `(LET ((,VAR ,EXP))
                (* ,SCALE ,VAR ,VAR)))))
```

and be sure there are no variable name conflicts.

Finally, notice that we really wrote the body of the macro twice. If we want to change the body details, we have to do it in two places. We can avoid that by making the macro definition recursive.

```
(DEFMACRO SCALE-SQUARE (SCALE EXP)
    (IF (ATOM EXP)
        `(* ,SCALE ,EXP ,EXP)
        (LET ((VAR (GENSYM)))
            `(LET ((,VAR ,EXP))
                (SCALE-SQUARE ,SCALE ,VAR)))))
```

This can result in a two-step expansion, but since the second time the EXP argument will already be an atom, it will stop at that point. For example,

```
(SCALE-SQUARE TEMP (+ C D))

==>

(LET ((G0078 (+ C D)))
     (SCALE-SQUARE TEMP G0078))

==>

(LET ((G0078 (+ C D)))
     (TIMES TEMP G0078 G0078))
```

SUMMARY

Macros can be viewed in a number of ways:

- Macros provide a mechanism for writing program-writing programs.
- Macros add an extra layer of interpretation to Lisp. In the interpreter, both layers get completed, one after the other. In the compiler, one layer gets done at compile time, and an assembly language program is produced to simulate the second layer at run time.
- Macros proved an efficient mechanism for abstracting the structure of data out of a program.
- Macros provide a mechanism for writing new special forms and control structures.

Macros can be defined with DEFMACRO. It takes a macro name, an argument list, and a body, and looks very similar to DEFUN. The difference is in how EVAL treats a macro.

When EVAL sees a list whose CAR is a macro, it hands the rest of the elements of the list, unevaluated, directly to the macro. The macro returns a result that EVAL then treats as an expression to be evaluated.

When the compiler sees a list whose CAR is a macro, it too hands the rest of the elements of the list, unevaluated, directly to the macro. The macro returns a result that the compiler then compiles, just as it would have compiled a list whose CAR was an ordinary function.

There are dangers in control structure macros. Sometimes a macro definition can unintentionally cause multiple evaluations of parts of a user's program. Generated temporary variables can be used to overcome this problem. The function GENSYM can be used for that purpose.

The functions introduced in this chapter are shown in Table 9-1.

In addition, we saw DEFMACRO, a macro-defining macro, and backquote and comma, two characters that make it easier to write macros.

Table 9-1

Function	Args	Description
GENSYM	0	generate a unique symbol
MACROEXPAND	1	expand macros until non-macro
MACROEXPAND-1	1	expand a single level

PROBLEMS

P9.1 Write part of a record structuring package for Common Lisp. We have seen the advantages of using abstract data structures with a few accessing macros, but it will get rather boring writing all those macros for every data structure that we use. Write two macros, DEFRECORD and ACCESS, that do the work for us. DEFRECORD is used to declare a record class and the fields it has. ACCESS is a generic field-accessing macro that given the record class and field name is able to generate code to access the field correctly. Your macros should behave as follows:

```
eval> (DEFRECORD DATE (YEAR MONTH DAY))
DATE

eval> (DEFRECORD EVENT (DATE PLACE EVENT-NAME SIGNIFICANCE))
EVENT

eval> (SETQ BIRTHDAY '(1983 10 5))
(1983 10 5)

eval> (ACCESS DATE MONTH BIRTHDAY) .
10

eval> (ACCESS DATE DAY '(1984 7 4))
4

eval> (MACROEXPAND '(ACCESS DATE MONTH BIRTHDAY))
(CAR (CDR BIRTHDAY))

eval> (MACROEXPAND '(ACCESS DATE DAY '(1984 7 4)))
(CAR (CDR (CDR (QUOTE (1984 7 4)))))

eval> (ACCESS EVENT SIGNIFICANCE
              '((1984 3 9)
                TERMAN-156
                CS-102-FINAL-DISTRIBUTION
                30.0))
30.0
```

Since multiple record classes (possibly with fields with the same names but in different positions in the lists) can be defined, you will need to store an association between record class name and field names. Signal errors when an unknown record class or unknown field is accessed.

P9.2   In Common Lisp, there is a macro somewhat simpler than DO for iteration over a list of elements. It has the form

(DOLIST (*var list return-form*) *body-1 ... body-n*)

Variable *var* takes on values from the list *list* and the *body-i* forms are evaluated at every iteration. When the end of the list is reached, the *return-form* is evaluated and returned. It can be omitted, in which case NIL is returned. An example of its use is

```
eval> (SETQ XX '(A B C))
(A B C)

eval> (DOLIST (V XX 'DONE) (TERPRI) (PRINC V))
A
B
C
DONE
```

Write the macro DOLIST.

P9.3   Another Common Lisp macro DOTIMES, which takes the form

(DOTIMES (*var count return-form*) *body-1 ... body-n*)

iterates the variable *var* over values 0 through *count* − 1, evaluating the body statements each time. It returns the value of *return-form* if it is supplied and NIL otherwise. Thus, it behaves like

```
eval> (DOTIMES (I 3 'DONE) (TERPRI) (PRINC I))
0
1
2
DONE
```

Write the macro DOTIMES.

10

EMBEDDING
LANGUAGES
IN
LISP

We have seen how easy it is to write an interpreter for one particular language in Lisp. In chapter 7, we wrote an interpreter (the function EVAL) for Lisp itself. In problem 7.1, we saw how easy it was to write an interpreter for a piece of a language with different semantics; in that case, it was for an infix language. That language, however, still used lists as the primary data structure for specifying language statements. These two tasks were easy for two reasons. First, in Lisp, procedures are data objects, just like any other data type, and can be passed around and finally applied to computed arguments using APPLY and FUNCALL. Second, language statements represented as lists are already in a form ideally suited for manipulation by Lisp.

In problem 7.4, we wrote an interpreter for a language with non-Lispish syntax, and with rather different semantics. In that case, it was necessary to write a parser for the language to turn it into a list data structure first. The actual interpretation was quite easy, again because Lisp procedures can be used as data objects and passed around before application.

In this chapter, we will work through an example of another way to embed a language in Lisp. In this case, we take language statements (whether or not the syntax is Lispish is not the issue since a parser can turn them into list data structures), translate them into Lisp expressions with equivalent semantics, and let the Lisp compiler compile them into machine language. Thus, we get the full power of a compiler producing efficient code, without the need to write a compiler for our new language. All we need to do is write a translator from the language to Lisp. We will use macros for that purpose. This is the only approach of the three described here that makes use of the fact that Lisp programs are represented as lists; lists are exactly the structures best manipulated by Lisp programs.

The language that we will build in this chapter is a rule-base language for planning tasks in a simple blocks world. The example is a little trivial in that it cannot produce workable plans in many situations, and the number of interesting rules expressable in the language is low. However, the semantics of the world, the description and implementation of the rule language, and the control structure are all simple enough to be demonstrated and explained in a few pages. A more complete planning or rule system would be a major undertaking.

10.1 BLOCKS WORLD REVISITED

Recall our blocks world from chapter 9. We set up a representation for two-dimensional blocks that could be stacked on a table. Blocks were named by atoms. The following functions provided an abstract interface to the blocks world, freeing the user from any need to know the details of the Lisp representation used.

■ (START-WORLD) initializes the world to be an empty table.

- (PRINT-WORLD) prints a description of the world.
- (NEW-BLOCK *name color*) declares the existence of a block and initializes it to sit on the table.
- (MOVE-BLOCK *name to-name*) moves a block named *name* to be on top of one named *to-name*. Both blocks should have clear tops for this to be legal. The latter argument also can be TABLE.
- (CLEARTOP? *block-name*) is a predicate that says whether the named block has a clear top.
- (IS-BLOCK? *name*) is a predicate that says whether there is a block named *name*.
- (SUPPORTS? *block-name*) returns the name of a block supported by the block named *block-name*.

Recall the world situation from chapter 9:

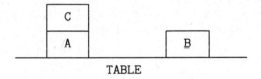

We could set up this world model using our primitives as follows:

```
eval> (START-WORLD)
T


eval> (NEW-BLOCK 'A 'RED)
A


eval> (NEW-BLOCK 'B 'BLUE)
B


eval> (NEW-BLOCK 'C 'GREEN)
C


eval> (MOVE-BLOCK 'C 'A)
T


eval> (PRINT-WORLD)

Block C (GREEN) is on block A and supports nothing.
```

```
Block B (BLUE) is on the table and supports nothing.
Block A (RED) is on the table and supports block C.
T
```

10.2 SPECIFYING A RULE LANGUAGE

It is not always legal to call MOVE-BLOCK in our world. If a block to be moved has something on top of it, we say it is illegal to move it (the robot hand is shaky and the upper block might tumble). If the place we are moving to already has a block on top of it, it is illegal to move there too—in fact, our world updating functions will cause an inconsistent set of relations to be true in our model in that case.

Suppose we wanted to build a program that understands these things and is able to carry out simple building tasks in our blocks world. Let's make it a rule-based system as is the current vogue in artificial intelligence. We will use a collection of simple rules that each embody a little piece of knowledge about the world.

Such a rule set is

```
(RULE R1
      TO-PROVE (CLEARTOP? X)
      PROVE (IS-BLOCK? X)
            (MOVABLE? (SUPPORTS? X) 'TABLE)
      DO (FORMAT T
                 "Moved ~S to the table~%"
                 (SUPPORTS? X))
         (MOVE-BLOCK (SUPPORTS? X) 'TABLE))

(RULE R2
      TO-PROVE (MOVABLE? X Y)
      PROVE (EQ Y 'TABLE)
            (IS-BLOCK? X)
            (CLEARTOP? X))

(RULE R3
      TO-PROVE (MOVABLE? X Y)
      PROVE (IS-BLOCK? X)
            (IS-BLOCK? Y)
            (CLEARTOP? X)
            (CLEARTOP? Y))
```

```
(RULE R4
      TO-PROVE (ON? X Y)
      PROVE (MOVABLE? X Y)
      DO (MOVE-BLOCK X Y)
         (FORMAT T "Moved ~S to ~S~%" X Y))
```

Each rule has a name (e.g., R2) and two to three clauses. The TO-PROVE clause says what statement will be true about the world after it is finished. For instance, rule R1 says that it will make sure that (CLEARTOP? X) returns T for whatever X gets bound to. The PROVE clause lists a number of things that this rule wants to be true first. These can either be things that are directly computable using existing functions—for example, (IS-BLOCK? X)—or things that need to be established by invoking other rules—for example, (MOVABLE? Y X). Notice that this is not an exclusive disjunction. CLEARTOP? is both directly computable and provable by a rule. The idea is that if something is not already true in the database, a rule should be used that knows how to make it true. Rules can change what is true in the database by applying some action to it—for example, moving a block. Rule R1 specifies such an action in its DO clause. (It also tells the user what it is doing.)

Thus, a rule system should do the following when confronted with the task of achieving some goal—for example, (ACHIEVE '(ON? 'A 'B)) (which says that block A should be stacked on top of block B).

- If there is a functional definition of the goal predicate, invoke it and see if the goal is already satisfied.
- If not, find a rule that claims to be able to prove such a goal and pass control to it.
- The rule should ask the rule system to prove all of its prerequisites (in its PROVE clause). If one or more of these fails, give up. Notice that this may leave the world in a different state than when it started.
- If they all succeed, carry out any operations in the DO clause and then declare that the goal has been accomplished.

A rule system that works this way is said to use *backward chaining* as it starts with a goal and tries to work backwards finding subgoals that achieve the desired goal when they are combined.

10.3 DEFINING A RULE LANGUAGE WITH MACROS

We will start with the following assumption: Each rule will be turned into a Lisp function. This saves us having to write an interpreter. Instead, we will write a translator from rule language to Lisp. Suppose that rule functions are stored in an association list, *RULE-MATCHES*, indexed by the predicate that they prove. Then we could have the following rule coordinator:

```
(DEFUN TRY-PROVE (PREDICATE &REST ARGS)
    (IF (AND (FBOUNDP PREDICATE)
             (APPLY (SYMBOL-FUNCTION PREDICATE)
                    ARGS))
        'T
        (LET ((FUNS (CDR (ASSOC PREDICATE *RULE-MATCHES*))))
            (DO ((FUNLIST FUNS (REST FUNLIST)))
                ((NULL FUNLIST)
                 'NIL)
                (IF (APPLY (SYMBOL-FUNCTION (CAR FUNLIST))
                           ARGS)
                    (RETURN 'T))))))
```

Thus, given

```
eval> (TRY-PROVE 'ON? 'A 'B)
```

the function TRY-PROVE will first see if ON? is a defined function and apply it to the given arguments. If the result is true, the goal is achieved. Otherwise the list of functions that can achieve goals of ON? is extracted, and each function is tried in turn until one succeeds. This suggests, for example, that rule R4 should turn into the following function definition:

```
(DEFUN R4 (X Y)
    (COND ((TRY-PROVE 'MOVABLE? X Y)
           (MOVE-BLOCK X Y)
           (FORMAT T "Moved ~S to ~S~%" X Y)
           'T)
          (T NIL)))
```

Thus, we should define RULE as a macro that returns a DEFUN expression. In addition, it should make sure that the rule gets properly inserted into the *RULE-MATCHES* association list. The actual input form of the rule needs some parsing, given the foregoing example rules. Assume for now the existence of a function PARSE-RULE-FORMS that returns a list of three things: the s-expression to be proved, a list of all the precondition s-expressions that must first be proved, and a list of actions. The definition of RULE then becomes

```
(DEFMACRO RULE (NAME &REST FORMS)
  (LET ((PARSED (PARSE-RULE-FORMS FORMS)))
    (LET ((TO-PROVE (CAR PARSED))
          (PROVE-LIST (CADR PARSED))
          (ACTION-LIST (CADDR PARSED)))
      '(PROGN
         (MERGE-RULE ',(CAR TO-PROVE) ',NAME)
         (DEFUN ,NAME ,(CDR TO-PROVE)
                (COND (,(IF (NULL (CDR PROVE-LIST))
                            (MAKE-TRY-PROVE (CAR PROVE-LIST))
                            '(AND ,@(MAPCAR #'MAKE-TRY-PROVE
                                            PROVE-LIST)))
                        ,@ACTION-LIST
                        'T)
                      (T NIL)))))))

(DEFUN MAKE-TRY-PROVE (FORM)
  '(TRY-PROVE ',(CAR FORM) ,@(CDR FORM)))
```

The two cases of exactly one or more things to be proved are taken care of
with the conditional use of an AND clause. If all are successful, the actions are
done and T is returned from the function written by this macro.

The code returned by the macroexpansion of a rule definition includes the
definition of the function and a call to MERGE-RULE to enter the name of the
rule into the association list, to be associated with the name of the predicate
it establishes. MERGE-RULE must see whether an entry already exists for the
predicate and create one if it does not exist. Thus, it could be defined as

```
(SETQ *RULE-MATCHES* NIL)

(DEFUN MERGE-RULE (TO-PROVE NAME)
  (LET ((ENTRY (ASSOC TO-PROVE *RULE-MATCHES*)))
    (IF (NULL ENTRY)
        (SETQ *RULE-MATCHES*
              (CONS (LIST TO-PROVE NAME)
                    *RULE-MATCHES*))
        (RPLACD ENTRY (CONS NAME (CDR ENTRY))))))
```

We need to fill in the definition of PARSE-RULE-FORMS, which can do some
error checking while it is splitting out the components of the rule description.
Notice the use of the result returned by MEMBER.

```
(DEFUN PARSE-RULE-FORMS (FORMS)
  (IF (NOT (EQ (CAR FORMS) 'TO-PROVE))
```

```
        (ERROR "Nothing proved in rule body: ~S"
                FORMS))
    (LET ((KEYWORD (CADDR FORMS)))
     (IF (NOT (OR (EQ KEYWORDS 'PROVE)
                  (EQ KEYWORDS 'DO)))
         (ERROR
          "Expected goal then something to prove or do, got: ~S"
          FORMS))
     (LIST (CADR FORMS)
           (IF (EQ KEYWORDS 'PROVE)
               (DO ((POSSIBS (CDDDR FORMS) (CDR POSSIBS))
                    (GOOD-ONES NIL
                               (CONS (CAR POSSIBS)
                                     GOOD-ONES)))
                   ((OR (NULL POSSIBS)
                        (EQ (CAR POSSIBS) 'DO))
                    (NREVERSE GOOD-ONES)))
               'NIL)
           (CDR (MEMBER 'DO FORMS)))))
```

Finally, we need to provide a user-level interface to the rule system. We showed an example of ACHIEVE earlier.

```
(DEFUN ACHIEVE (FORM)
    (APPLY #'TRY-PROVE
           (CAR FORM)
           (MAPCAR #'EVAL (CDR FORM))))
```

Now the following will happen:

```
eval> (ACHIEVE '(ON? 'A 'B))
Moved C to the table
Moved A to B
T


eval> (PRINT-WORLD)

Block C (GREEN) is on the table and supports nothing.
Block B (BLUE) is on the table and supports block A.
Block A (RED) is on block B and supports nothing.
T
```

The rules that we have written really aren't very smart. Suppose we add another rule:

```
(RULE R5
      TO-PROVE (TOWER? X Y Z)
      PROVE (ON? Y Z)
            (ON? X Y))
```

This rule says that to make a tower with X stacked on top of Y which is on top of Z simply put Y on Z and then X on Y. However, consider the following, which occurs in this situation.

```
eval> (ACHIEVE '(TOWER? 'B 'C 'A))
Moved C to A
Moved C to table
Moved A to table
Moved B to C
T


eval> (PRINT-WORLD)

Block C (GREEN) is on the table and supports block B.
Block B (BLUE) is on block C and supports nothing.
Block A (RED) is on the table and supports nothing.
T
```

What happened was that C was first put on top of A, which was already on B. Then it came time to put B on C, which meant B needed a clear top before it could be moved. This meant that A had to be moved, but it did not have a clear top. So C first had to be moved off the top of it, then A could be moved off B, and now B could be put on top of C. The trouble was that in achieving the second subgoal of rule R5 the first was destroyed. This is known as a *brother-clobbers-brother's-subgoal*.

SUMMARY

In this chapter, we saw an example of how to build a macro-based translator from some other language into Lisp. This lets us compile a new language without having to write a compiler for it. Writing a translator is a much simpler task because we do not have to worry about variable binding mechanisms, procedure calling conventions, nonlocal control structures, and storage management. All those facilities are inherited directly from the underlying Lisp implementation.

Another popular way to embed new languages in Lisp is to write an interpreter for the language and perhaps a language parser as a front end of the system.

11

ADVANCED FEATURES

The Common Lisp language includes a number of advanced data representation features and control structures not found in earlier Lisps. In fact, many of these features have no counterparts at all in other computer languages. Most of these features require some degree of Lisp sophistication to understand and appreciate. For this reason they are grouped together here in a single chapter near the end of the book, rather than sprinkled throughout at the ends of chapters where they might functionally belong.

Once you are familiar with the features described in this chapter, you will probably find that you soon permeate your programs with one or more of them in almost every function you write. They greatly enhance the expressibility and elegance of the language.

11.1 SETF: A GENERALIZED SETTING FORM

We have seen several Lisp data types that have accessible components. Symbols, for instance, have a value cell and a function cell, places where their value and their functional value are stored. Cons cells have a CAR and a CDR. We have seen ways of accessing and changing some of these components:

Accessor	Setter
SYMBOL-VALUE	SET (SETQ)
SYMBOL-FUNCTION	???
CAR	RPLACA
CDR	RPLACD

Each component accessor has a corresponding function that lets us set the component to a new value, although we have not seen what the corresponding function is for SYMBOL-FUNCTION. The functions have a uniform argument order: the object whose component is to be changed and a new value for the component. Notice that, for historical reasons, the values returned by the setting functions are not always uniform:

```
eval> (SET 'X '(A B C))
(A B C)
```

```
eval> (RPLACA '(D E F) '(A B C))
((A B C) E F)
```

```
eval> (RPLACD '(D E F) '(A B C))
(D A B C)
```

Function SET returns the new value, whereas RPLACA and RPLACD return their first argument, the object whose component is to be changed. Later we will see some more component accessors for other parts of Lisp data structures. They too will have corresponding setting functions. For historical reasons, again, they will follow different conventions on what is to be returned and even different conventions on argument order.

In problem 9.1, we wrote a record structuring system that allowed us to give names to elements of a list and to access them with our own ACCESS macro. The behavior of that record structuring system is illustrated by the following:

```
eval> (DEFRECORD DATE (YEAR MONTH DAY))
DATE

eval> (SETQ BIRTHDAY '(1983 10 5))
(1983 10 5)

eval> (ACCESS DATE MONTH BIRTHDAY)
10

eval> (ACCESS DATE DAY '(1984 7 4))
4

eval> (MACROEXPAND '(ACCESS DATE MONTH BIRTHDAY))
(CAR (CDR BIRTHDAY))

eval> (MACROEXPAND '(ACCESS DATE DAY '(1984 7 4)))
(CAR (CDR (CDR (QUOTE (1984 7 4)))))
```

What if we want to change a component of a record instance, such as BIRTHDAY? We might be tempted to write another macro—CHANGE, say—which, like ACCESS, looks at the record class definition and generates some code to effect the changing of a named field value. We will have to modify CHANGE whenever we change the way ACCESS works, or when we extend the data representation that ACCESS can handle.

Fortunately, our litany of complaints comprise

■ remembering setter function names,

- different values returned by setters,
- different argument orders for setters,
- writing a setter for each type of accessor we write,

and all are answered in Common Lisp by a single marvelous macro called SETF. It is a universal setter, always takes its arguments in the same order, and returns a predictable result. It has the form

(SETF   place value)

It is a macro and so the code it produces does not necessarily evaluate its arguments in the normal manner. The first form, *place*, should be a piece of code that accesses some component of a data structure. The second is a form to be evaluated to a new value to replace what is already in the place accessed by the first. The value of the second form is always returned. Thus, SETF works like this:

```
eval> (SETF X '(A B C))
(A B C)

eval> X
(A B C)

eval> (SETF (CAR X) 'NEW)
NEW

eval> X
(NEW B C)

eval> (SETF (CADR X) (CAR '(ONE TWO)))
ONE

eval> X
(NEW ONE C)

eval> (SETF (CDR X) '(CDR HERE NOW))
(CDR HERE NOW)

eval> X
(NEW CDR HERE NOW)
```

```
eval> (SETF (ACCESS DATE DAY BIRTHDAY) 8)
8

eval> BIRTHDAY
(1983 10 8)

eval> (SETF (SYMBOL-FUNCTION 'BAZOLA) (SYMBOL-FUNCTION 'CAR))
#<unprintable-compiled-function> ;what is printed will vary

eval> (BAZOLA '(A B C))
A
```

Notice that the first "argument" does not get evaluated at all—it simply tells the SETF macro an accessible place that should be given a new value. SETF then writes code using the appropriate primitives to effect the change of value. The following are valid ways in which SETF might expand:

```
eval> (MACROEXPAND '(SETF X '(A B C)))
(SETQ X (QUOTE (A B C)))

eval> (MACROEXPAND '(SETF (CAR X) 'NEW))
(PROGN (RPLACA X (QUOTE NEW)) (QUOTE NEW))

eval> (MACROEXPAND '(SETF (CADR X) (CAR (BAZOLA X))))
((LAMBDA (G0534) (RPLACA (CDR X) G0534) G0534)
 (CAR (BAZOLA X)))

eval> (MACROEXPAND '(SETF (ACCESS DATE DAY BIRTHDAY) 8))
(PROGN (RPLACA (CDR (CDR BIRTHDAY)) 8) 8)
```

Notice that SETF even works for the record package written in problem 9.1.

The macro SETF hands its first argument to MACROEXPAND and examines the result returned. In the previous example,

$$(CAR \ (CDR \ (CDR \ BIRTHDAY)))$$

would be returned, which is easily handled as SETF knowns about CAR.

Full Common Lisp allows one to declare user-defined functions as setters in complex cases, and also to generalize the notion of SETF to read-modify-write macros (such as incrementing a number in an arbitrary place). We will not go into those details here—see the Common Lisp manual if you are interested.

EXERCISES

E11.1.1   What is the value of the variable X after each of the following statements is evaluated in order?
a. (SETF X '(A B C))
b. (SETF (CAR X) 'B)
c. (SETF (CDDR X) 'D)
d. (SETF (CDR (CDR X)) '(C C))
e. (SETF (CDR X) NIL)
f. (SETF (CAR X) '(C C))

E11.1.2   Write an expression using SETF to effect the following transformations on the value of a variable X, assuming maximal shared structure between initial and final values each time:
a. (A B C) ==> NIL
b. (A B C) ==> (A B C D)
c. ((A B) (C D)) ==> ((A B) (D D))
d. ((A B) (C D)) ==> ((A B) (C D E))

11.2 DEFSTRUCT: **A RECORD PACKAGE**

There is a built-in data abstraction facility in Common Lisp. It is somewhat more comprehensive that the one we developed in problem 9.1. It enables the user to define record classes, with named fields (or slots), default values, and even to control the underlying representation to be used. The facility is known as the DEFSTRUCT facility, because that is the name of the declaration macro. As with most facilities in Common Lisp, there are many arcane and complex features of DEFSTRUCT that you will probably never need to know. We will examine only the features needed to use DEFSTRUCT effectively in all but the most exceptional circumstances.

Record structures are declared using the DEFSTRUCT macro. Its most straightforward form is

(DEFSTRUCT   *class* . *fields*)

where *class* is the name of the record class being declared and *fields* is a list of field names. Thus, for instance, we could declare a record class describing dates with

```
eval> (DEFSTRUCT DATE YEAR MONTH DAY)
DATE
```

which declares a record class called DATE with three fields YEAR, DATE, and MONTH. When this expression is evaluated, a *constructor* function MAKE-DATE is defined for creating instances of DATE records and three *accessor* functions DATE-YEAR, DATE-MONTH, and DATE-DAY for accessing fields of instances of DATE records.

Examples of the use of the functions produced by DEFSTRUCT follow:

```
eval> (SETQ BIRTHDAY (MAKE-DATE :MONTH 10 :DAY 5 :YEAR 1983)
#S(DATE YEAR 1983 MONTH 10 DAY 5)


eval> (DATE-MONTH BIRTHDAY)
10


eval> (SETF (DATE-DAY BIRTHDAY) 8)
8


eval> (DATE-DAY BRITHDAY)
8


eval> BIRTHDAY
#S(DATE YEAR 1983 MONTH 10 DAY 8)
```

Notice that the record instances are not represented as lists. Their standard Common Lisp printed representation is shown, although details may vary between Common Lisp implementations[1]. Record instances are internally represented by some type of vector structure, making access to all fields of the record equally cheap in terms of computation time. If lists were used, later fields would take much longer to access because the list would have to be traced down each time.

The constructor function, whose name is formed by appending "MAKE-" to the record class name, takes keyword arguments (recall section 7.3) to specify fields and their values. The keywords are formed by preceding field names with ":". It does not matter in which order the fields are specified in the arguments to the constructor. If a field is not specified at all, its value defaults to NIL.

The accessor functions have names formed by appending the class name and a hyphen to the field names. Each accessor function takes a record instance as

---

[1]In particular, when one record instance refers to another that refers back to the original, it is necessary that the printer be rather smart to avoid printing forever. Observed behaviors of Common Lisp implementations include printing forever and computing forever without printing anything, trying to figure out ahead of time how many characters should be printed. This behavior can always be controlled with *PRINT-LEVEL*, or with more specialized switches in some Common Lisp implementations. Fortunately, it usually is not necessary to print record instances in working programs.

an argument and returns the value of the appropriate field.

The foregoing example also shows that SETF works on DEFSTRUCT field accessors. In fact, SETF is the only defined way to alter the contents of a field of a record instance.

It is possible to declare that the default for a field be other than NIL. Instead of listing just a symbol as the name of a field in a DEFSTRUCT declaration, it is permissible to list a field name and a default form. This form is evaluated to provide a default value for a field if none is provided in the call to the constructor function. Thus, for example,

```
eval> (DEFSTRUCT DATE
         (YEAR '1984)
         MONTH
         DAY)
DATE

eval> (MAKE-DATE :DAY 4 :MONTH 7)
#S(DATE YEAR 1984 MONTH 7 DAY 4)
```

Notice that the accessors created by DEFSTRUCT are *functions*, not *macros*. This is so that they can be passed as arguments to functions such as MAPCAR. However, this would seem to mean that using DEFSTRUCT as a data abstraction mechanism will be costly in terms of efficiency (see chapter 9). Some Common Lisp compilers interact with DEFSTRUCT, however, and are able to determine a macro expansion of accessor functions and regain the lost efficiency. This is not true of all Common Lisp compilers, however; it is not a requirement of the Common Lisp language definition. Before you buy a Common Lisp, be sure to ask the salesperson whether their product has this capability.

EXERCISES

E11.2.1 Given the definitions

```
(DEFVAR *LOAN-TERM* 25)

(DEFSTRUCT LOAN
    PRINCIPAL
    RATE
    (TERM *LOAN-TERM*))
```

what will the value of the TERM field be in each of the following cases:
a. (MAKE-LOAN :PRINCIPAL 100000.00 :RATE 0.15)
b. (MAKE-LOAN :RATE 0.13 :TERM 10 :PRINCIPAL 45000.00)

c. (SETQ *LOAN-TERM* 30)
    (MAKE-LOAN :RATE 0.14 :PRINCIPAL 60000.00)

E11.2.2 Declare a record structure to represent vectors in three-space, such that
it is only necessary to specify explicitly the value of nonzero components.

11.3 BLOCK: **STRUCTURED UNITS WITHIN FUNCTIONS**

In section 3.6, we examined the DO construct for structured iteration. We
also saw the RETURN special form, which allowed us to exit a DO-loop at
any time without having to continue evaluation of Lisp forms according to the
ordinary Lisp evaluation rules. This capabaility is an instance of a more general
control structure in Common Lisp that allows nonlocal exits from within the
textual body of a block of code (i.e., it does not include nonlocal exits from
within the definitions of called functions—see section 11.4 for a less efficient
means of achieving this).

There are two special forms that give this capability: BLOCK and RETURN-
FROM. The first has the form

(BLOCK *name* *form-1* *form-2* ... *form-n*)

where *name* is a symbol, which does not get evaluated. Under normal circumstances BLOCK acts just like a PROGN, evaluating each of *form-1*, *form-2*, through
form-n in turn. If, however, there is a RETURN-FROM, which takes the form

(RETURN-FROM *name* *value*)

anywhere in the text of one of the BLOCK forms, whose *name* is the same symbol
as that for the BLOCK, then if it is evaluated the BLOCK will be exited immediately
and will return the value of the form *value* as its value. If no RETURN-FROM is
encountered, BLOCK returns the value of its last form—namely, *form-n*—as its
value.

Consider the following example:

```
(DEFUN PARTY (GUESTS)
    (BLOCK THE-PARTY
        (IF (NULL GUESTS)
            (RETURN-FROM THE-PARTY 'NO-GOOD))
        (FORMAT T "~%Guests included: ")
        (DOLIST (PERSON GUESTS)
            (FORMAT T "~S, " PERSON))
```

```
(FORMAT T "and probably more...")
(IF (> (LENGTH GUESTS) 30)
        'CROWDED
        'GREAT)))
```

This example could be written without the BLOCK construct, but sometimes, especially when testing for a very rare, or error, condition, the foregoing style may be clearer.

In Common Lisp, every function has an *implicit* BLOCK wrapped around its body with the same name as the function. This makes it possible always to exit a function from anywhere within it using RETURN-FROM. Thus, the previous function could be rewritten as

```
(DEFUN PARTY (GUESTS)
    (IF (NULL GUESTS)
        (RETURN-FROM PARTY 'NO-GOOD))
    (FORMAT T "~%Guests included: ")
    (DOLIST (PERSON GUESTS)
            (FORMAT T "~S, " PERSON))
    (FORMAT T "and probably more...")
    (IF (> (LENGTH GUESTS) 30)
        'CROWDED
        'GREAT))
```

and it would retain its original behavior.

If BLOCKs are nested with the same name, a RETURN-FROM refers to leaving the innermost block that the RETURN-FROM statement is within and that has the same name.

How does this relate to RETURN and DO? It turns out the RETURN is simply the macro:

```
(DEFMACRO RETURN (VALUE) '(RETURN-FROM NIL ,VALUE))
```

Furthermore, every DO acts as though it is a BLOCK whose name is NIL. Thus, a RETURN in the body of a DO says to exit a BLOCK named NIL, which always turns out to be the encompassing DO. We can effectively change the name of a DO by writing a macro DO-NAMED as

```
(DEFMACRO DO-NAMED (NAME &REST DOFORM)
    '(BLOCK ,NAME
            (DO ,@DOFORM)))
```

It is just like DO, except that immediately preceding all the variable forms is a *name* of the DO-loop. Thus, it is possible to exit from an outer DO-NAMED while in the body of an inner DO-NAMED. This macro is not part of the official Common Lisp language definition, but it is a common macro that people write and use.

We will now give an example function in which DO-NAMED and RETURN-FROM combine to make a simpler program than might be needed with unnamed DOs and plain RETURN. The function takes a list of clauses that form an implicit conjunction. Each clause may be a symbol or a list of terms that form an implicit disjunction. Each term must be a symbol. The symbols NIL and T stand for "false" and "true", respectively, while all other symbols stand for free variables. The function simplifies input expressions by propagating the effects of the presence of symbols NIL and T being present in conjunctions and disjunctions. In addition, it checks for invalid elements in the expressions; non-symbol atoms in the conjunction, and non-symbols in the disjunction. In each case, the entire expression is simplified to MALFORMED. Some examples follow:

```
eval> (SIMPLIFY-LOGICAL-EXP '((A B C) (D E T F) X (G NIL H)))
((H G) X (C B A))

eval> (SIMPLIFY-LOGICAL-EXP '((A B C) (D E 3 F) (C NIL H)))
MALFORMED

eval> (SIMPLIFY-LOGICAL-EXP '((A B C) (D E F) NIL (G H T)))
NIL
```

By naming the DO-loops, it is possible to exit entirely when a malformed expression is discovered while processing an inner disjunction. Consider the definition

```
(DEFUN SIMPLIFY-LOGICAL-EXP (EXP)
  (DO-NAMED AND-LOOP
    ((CLAUSE-LIST EXP (CDR CLAUSE-LIST))
     (SIMPCLAUSE-LIST
       NIL
       (LET* ((CLAUSE (CAR CLAUSE-LIST))
              (SIMPCLAUSE
                (IF (ATOM CLAUSE)
                    CLAUSE
                    (DO-NAMED OR-LOOP
```

```
                        ((TERM-LIST CLAUSE (CDR TERM-LIST))
                         (SIMPTERM-LIST
                          NIL
                           (COND ((EQ (CAR TERM-LIST) 'T)
                                  (RETURN-FROM OR-LOOP 'T))
                                 ((EQ (CAR TERM-LIST) 'NIL)
                                  SIMPTERM-LIST)
                                 ((SYMBOLP (CAR TERM-LIST))
                                  (CONS (CAR TERM-LIST)
                                        SIMPTERM-LIST))
                                 (T (RETURN-FROM
                                        AND-LOOP
                                        'MALFORMED)))))
                          ((NULL TERM-LIST)
                           SIMPTERM-LIST)))))
                  (COND ((NULL SIMPCLAUSE)
                         (RETURN-FROM AND-LOOP 'NIL))
                        ((EQ SIMPCLAUSE 'T)
                         SIMPCLAUSE-LIST)
                        ((AND (ATOM SIMPCLAUSE)
                              (NOT (SYMBOLP SIMPCLAUSE)))
                         (RETURN-FROM AND-LOOP 'MALFORMED))
                        (T (CONS SIMPCLAUSE
                                 SIMPCLAUSE-LIST))))))
            ((NULL CLAUSE-LIST)
             SIMPCLAUSE-LIST)))
```

Strictly speaking, we did not need to name the inner DO loop because a plain RETURN from within it would have the same effect as a RETURN-FROM a block named OR-LOOP.

EXERCISES

E11.3.1 Given the definition

```
(DEFUN T1 (X)
    (IF (EQL X 3)
        23
        (BLOCK T2
            (IF (EQL X 7)
                (RETURN-FROM T2 7))
```

```
(BLOCK T2
        (IF (EQL X 9)
            (RETURN-FROM T2 9))
        (IF (EQL X 11)
            (RETURN-FROM T1 11))
        (* 2 X))
(IF (< X 0)
    (RETURN-FROM T2 (- 0 X)))
(* 3 X))))
```

what will the following expressions return?

a. (T1 3)
b. (T1 4)
c. (T1 7)
d. (T1 8)
e. (T1 9)
f. (T1 10)
g. (T1 11)
h. (T1 -3)

11.4 CATCH AND THROW: NONLOCAL EXITS

Programs written in Lisp tend to use very deeply nested functions. Sometimes something that happens way down deep in a function provides a critical piece of information that should be used to change the whole processing strategy at a much higher level. Let's look at an example of this. The example is somewhat long, but it should provide a realistic understanding of the problem.

Suppose that we are writing a program that understands short stories written in very simple English. Each story is contained in a separate file, and each sentence has a simple structure. We want our system to be tolerant of format errors in the story file, bad syntax, and incomprehensible sentences. Rather than signalling an error and stopping processing on such conditions, the program might simply print a warning message and try to pick up processing at the next reasonable place in the input file or files.

Our first function UNDERSTAND-A-STORY takes an open input stream and reads sentences from it, using a function READ-A-SENTENCE. The latter function returns a valid sentence or the STREAM itself if the end of file was next; otherwise, it returns NIL if the end of file or some other error occurs in midsentence. Our function checks for such an error signal, and if there is none it sends the sentence off to be parsed by PARSE-SENTENCE. A parsed structure is returned on success and NIL is returned on failure. Once that has been checked for, the parsed structure is handed to a comprehending function. Thus, we have

```
(DEFUN UNDERSTAND-A-STORY (STREAM DATABASE)
    (DO ((SENTENCE (READ-A-SENTENCE STREAM)
                   (READ-A-SENTENCE STREAM)))
        ((EQ SENTENCE STREAM)
         ;; means we had already got to the eof
         DATABASE)
        (IF (NULL SENTENCE)
             ;; something illegal happened during READ,
             ;; like the end of file in mid sentence.
             (RETURN 'NIL)
             (LET ((PARSING (PARSE-SENTENCE SENTENCE)))
                  (IF (NOT (NULL PARSING))
                      (COMPREHEND-AND-UPDATE-DATABASE
                          PARSING
                          DATABASE)))))))
```

Following problem 5.4, we parse the sentences with procedures corresponding to word groupings. We look at the first word of the sentence and determine its type (e.g., *noun*, *verb*, *q-word*, etc.). The function that does this, CHECK-LEXICON, returns NIL if the word is unknown. This error condition is checked by PARSE-SENTENCE and it then tries either to parse a query or an assertion.

```
(DEFUN PARSE-SENTENCE (SENTENCE)
    (LET ((WORDTYPE (CHECK-LEXICON (CAR SENTENCE))))
         (COND ((NULL WORDTYPE)
                'NIL)
               ((EQ WORDTYPE 'Q-WORD)
                (PARSE-QUERY (CDR SENTENCE)))
               (T (PARSE ASSERTION SENTENCE)))))
```

Now we look at the function to parse an assertion. It successively calls functions to parse a noun phrase, parse a verb, and then again to parse a noun phrase. Each of these functions returns NIL if the head of the sentence does not contain an instance of the type of phrase for which it is looking. If the sentence is headed by such a phrase, a CONS of the parsed phrase and the remainder of the sentence is returned. In each case, the function PARSE-ASSERTION first checks for the error condition before proceeding.

```
(DEFUN PARSE-ASSERTION (SENTENCE)
   (LET ((NOUN-PHRASE (PARSE-NOUN-PHRASE SENTENCE)))
```

```
(IF (NULL NOUN-PHRASE)
    'NIL
    (LET ((VERB (PARSE-VERB (CDR NOUN-PHRASE))))
      (IF (NULL VERB)
          'NIL
          (LET ((NP2 (PARSE-NOUN-PHRASE (CDR VERB))))
            (COND ((NULL NP2)
                   'NIL)
                  ((NOT (NULL (CDR NP2)))
                   (FORMAT
                     T
                     "~%Dangling words ~S at end of ~S."
                     (CDR NP2)
                     SENTENCE)
                   'NIL)
                  (T (LIST (CAR NOUN-PHRASE)
                           (CAR VERB)
                           (CAR NP2)))))))))
```

In reviewing these three functions, we notice that a lot of the code is devoted to checking for a null result from a called function and to passing NIL back up the line on detection of this. Function PARSE-ASSERTION, for example, has four error checks in it—three of them are simply to pass back errors that have occurred in a lower level of processing.

There are two special forms that make writing such programs much cleaner. They allow nonlocal exits from a function, passing through many nested calling functions to some desired trap point. When an error condition is first detected— for example, such as in CHECK-LEXICON—they allow control to revert back to the best place to continue: the DO loop of UNDERSTAND-A-STORY. This is a much stronger form of nonlocal transfer of control because it can cross function boundaries.

The two forms are

(CATCH *tag form-1 ... form-n*)

and

(THROW *tag form*)

The CATCH form evaluates *tag*, which should evaluate to any Lisp object,[2] and

---

[2] Usually people use symbols as tags for readability of their code.

remembers that as its identity. Then it evaluates each of the argument forms in turn—that is, *form-1* through *form-n*—and returns the value of the last form as its result. A THROW evaluates its *tag* and then evaluates the following *form*. It immediately starts searching backwards through enclosing forms and function calls until it reaches a CATCH from which it was called in one of its forms and whose saved *tag* matches, using EQ,[3] the tag of the THROW. The CATCH is then exited normally with the value of the THROW's form as its result.

The idea is very similar to the use of BLOCK and RETURN-FROM, but with CATCH and THROW we can completely exit a function, indeed pass through many functions, before reaching the appropriate CATCH. RETURN-FROM and BLOCK are restricted to cooperating within a single function, and they must use fixed names for BLOCKs rather than the dynamic values used for tags in CATCH and THROW. All possibilities of transfer of control within a BLOCK can be determined by the compiler, whereas the possibilities for CATCH and THROW are determined only when the code is running and functions call other functions that were not even written when the first one was compiled. Thus, a compiler knows more about the situation in BLOCKs and can produce much more efficient code than for CATCHes and THROWs.

An example of THROW and CATCH follows. Given the function definitions

```
(DEFUN SUM-POLY (LST)
    (CATCH 'FOUND-INFINITY
           (APPLY #'+
                  (CATCH 'DIFFERENT-TAG
                         (MAPCAR #'EVAL-POLY LST)))))

(DEFUN EVAL-POLY (X)
    (IF (EQ 'INFINITY X)
        (THROW 'FOUND-INFINITY 'INFINITY)
        (+ 3.0 (* X (+ -2.0 (* X 1.3)))))))
```

the following will occur:

```
(SUM-POLY '(3.0 2.2 3.3))
24.149

eval> (SUM-POLY '(3.0 INFINITY 3.3))
INFINITY
```

---

[3]This provides another good reason to use symbols as tags.

In the first example, EVAL-POLY is only passed numbers as its argument, never the symbol INFINITY. Therefore, it simply evaluates the arithmetic expression and returns the result, which gets consed into the list constructed by MAPCAR and is eventually handed to +, whose result is the result of the function SUM-POLY. In the second example, the second time EVAL-POLY is called it is with the symbol INFINITY as its argument. In that case, the THROW is called and the symbol INIFINTY is thrown right through the MAPCAR and APPLY and caught by the CATCH whose tag is FOUND-INFINITY matching the tag of the THROW. Notice that the THROW was not caught by the inner CATCH that had a different tag, namely DIFFERENT-TAG.

The foregoing examples are only illustrative. Let's see how we can modify our earlier story understanding system. If we make every error detected during the parsing of a sentence THROW to some tag outside the scope of the the the thing which uses the result of parsing, then we do not need to worry about propagating errors during parsing. Let's suppose that they throw to a tag BAD-SYNTAX. Function CHECK-LEXICON, for instance, throws to such a tag if it cannot determine the part of speech of a word. We also assume that the READ-A-SENTENCE function throws to a tag ABORT-STORY when it reads an end of file within an sentence. Thus, our three previous functions become

```
(DEFUN UNDERSTAND-A-STORY (STREAM DATABASE)
    (DO ((SENTENCE (READ-A-SENTENCE STREAM)
                   (READ-A-SENTENCE STREAM)))
        ((EQ SENTENCE STREAM)
         ;; means we had already got to the eof
         DATABASE)
        (CATCH 'BAD-SYNTAX
                (COMPREHEND-AND-UPDATE-DATABASE
                    (PARSE-SENTENCE SENTENCE)
                    DATABASE))))

(DEFUN PARSE-SENTENCE (SENTENCE)
  (IF (EQ 'Q-WORD (CHECK-LEXICON (CAR SENTENCE)))
      (PARSE-QUERY (CDR SENTENCE))
      (PARSE ASSERTION SENTENCE)))

(DEFUN PARSE-ASSERTION (SENTENCE)
  (LET* ((NOUN-PHRASE (PARSE-NOUN-PHRASE SENTENCE))
         (VERB (PARSE-VERB (CDR NOUN-PHRASE)))
         (NP2 (PARSE-NOUN-PHRASE (CDR VERB))))
        (COND ((NULL (CDR NP2))
               (LIST (CAR NOUN-PHRASE)
                     (CAR VERB)
                     (CAR NP2)))
```

```
                        (T (FORMAT
                            T
                            "~%Dangling words ~S at end of ~S."
                            (CDR NP2)
                            SENTENCE)
                        (THROW 'BAD-SYNTAX NIL)))))
```

Notice how much cleaner these definitions are. They can all be written with the assumption that no errors that occur below then can affect them. In particular, the third of the three functions only checks for one error condition now (rather than four previously) and that is an error that it detects directly.

It is assumed that the first function is called as

```
(CATCH 'ABORT-STORY
    (UNDERSTAND-A-STORY
        STREAM
        DATABASE))
```

so that a THROW caused by READ-A-SENTENCE will be caught.

EXERCISES

E11.4.1 Given the function definitions

```
(DEFUN T1 (X)
    (CATCH 'BAZOLA
        (CONS X (T2 X))))

(DEFUN T2 (X)
    (IF (ZEROP X)
        (THROW 'BAZOLA 'ZERO)
        (CATCH 'ZTESCH
            (T3 X)
            X)))

(DEFUN T3 (X)
    (COND ((< X 0)
        (THROW 'BAZOLA (- 0 X)))
        ((< X 5)
        (THROW 'ZTESCH (* 2 X)))
        (T (* 4 X))))
```

evaluate the following s-expression:

a. (T1 0)

b. (T1 3)

c. (T1 7)

d. (T1 -3)

e. (T1 -7)

E11.4.2   For what values of X will changing the 4 to an 8 in the definition of T3 affect the value of (T1 X)?

11.5 UNWIND-PROTECT: **EXITING NONLOCALLY, BUT CLEANLY**

Now suppose that we wish to read many stories from a list of files. Further suppose that it is possible that some stories contain untruths, making it possible for our database, into which everything is being entered, to become inconsistent. In this case we might want to give up processing the list of files. Suppose that the inconsistency is detected in the function COMPREHEND-AND-UPDATE-DATABASE and it causes a throw to a tag INCONSISTENT-DATABASE. Then we might write our top-level function as

```
(DEFUN PROCESS-STORIES (FILELIST)
   (CATCH 'INCONSISTENT-DATABASE
        (LET ((DATABASE (INIT-DATABASE)))
          (DOLIST (FILENAME FILELIST)
               (LET ((STREAM (OPEN FILENAME
                                    :DIRECTION :INPUT)))
                   (CATCH 'ABORT-STORY
                        (UNDERSTAND-A-STORY
                            STREAM
                            DATABASE))
                   (CLOSE STREAM)))
          DATABASE)))
```

The problem here is that an error results in a file being left open. We can get around this by using UNWIND-PROTECT. It takes the form

(UNWIND-PROTECT *protected-form cleanup-1 ... cleanup-n*)

The argument forms are evaluated left to right. The value of the *protected-form* is returned. It is guaranteed that the *cleanup-i* forms will always be evaluated even if a THROW occurs within the *protected-form*. In such a case, the search for a matching tag is suspended while the clean-up operations are done, then resumed. Thus, we can modify our top-level function to be

```
(DEFUN PROCESS-STORIES (FILELIST)
   (CATCH 'INCONSISTENT-DATABASE
          (LET ((DATABASE (INIT-DATABASE)))
               (DOLIST (FILENAME FILELIST)
                       (LET ((STREAM (OPEN FILENAME
                                          :DIRECTION :INPUT)))
                            (UNWIND-PROTECT
                                (CATCH 'ABORT-STORY
                                       (UNDERSTAND-A-STORY
                                         STREAM
                                         DATABASE))
                                (CLOSE STREAM))))
               DATABASE)))
```

Now no file will be left open, but we can still throw from way down deep up to the INCONSISTENT-DATABASE tag.

EXERCISES

E11.5.1 Given the function definitions

```
(DEFUN F1 (X)
    (CATCH 'BAZ
           (PRINT (F2 X))
           7))

(DEFUN F2 (X)
    (UNWIND-PROTECT (PROGN (PRINT (F3 X))
                           (PRINT 'EXITING)
                           23)
                    (PRINT 'PROTECTING)))

(DEFUN F3 (X)
     (IF (EQL X 3)
         (THROW 'BAZ 'THROWN)
         (* 3 X)))
```

what will each of the following expressions cause to be printed?
a. (F1 5)
b. (F1 3)
c. (F1 23)

11.6 MULTIPLE VALUES

Sometimes we have wanted to return more than one thing from a function. For instance, in parsing English sentences in section 11.4 we had functions that needed to tell a calling function what structure had been parsed and what remained of the sentence. We consed the two results together and passed back the cons cell. The cons cell was discarded by the calling function. The effect of using a cons cell for passing back multiple values is to increase markedly the overall cost of a function call as it moves the need for garbage collection ever closer. Another approach might have been to store the rest of the sentence to be parsed in a global variable and to have every parsing routine look there for its argument. This would not have worked in our examples, however because sometimes the parsing process needed to be backtracked to an earlier version of how much of the sentence remained to be parsed.

In Common Lisp, functions can return more than one value in a way that does not require consing of a list or some other data structure to bundle them into a single object.

Any expression that calls the function VALUES as the last thing it does returns multiple values rather than a single value. Multiple values can be used within a function or can be the result of a function. VALUES takes zero or more arguments and makes them its values. It has the form

$$\text{(VALUES } val\text{-}1 \ldots val\text{-}n)$$

Thus, the function

```
(DEFUN SUM-DIFF-SQUARE (X Y)
    (LET ((XSQ (* X X))
          (YSQ (* Y Y)))
        (VALUES (+ XSQ YSQ) (- XSQ YSQ))))
```

returns two values; both the sum and difference of the squares of its two arguments.

Although a function might return multiple values, a calling function can remain unaware of it and can treat the called function as one that returns a single value. If the called function returns no values (e.g., it calls VALUES with zero arguments), any caller expecting precisely one argument will think it was given NIL. Otherwise, it takes the first of the multiple values. For example,

```
eval> (FORMAT
          T
          "Here are none: ~S, and one ~S, not two. And next: ~S."
```

```
(VALUES)
(VALUES 'JUST-ONE 'ANOTHER)
'THIS)
```
Here are none: NIL, and one JUST-ONE, not two. And next: THIS.
NIL

A caller must explicitly ask for multiple values to get them. One way to do this is with the special form MULTIPLE-VALUE-BIND. It takes the form

(MULTIPLE-VALUE-BIND *varlist form body-1 ... body-n*)

MULTIPLE-VALUE-BIND is a *variable introducing* form, much in the manner of LET. The difference is that all the new variables get their values from evaluating a single form. The *varlist* is a list of variable names. The form *form* is evaluated and the multiple values it returns are bound to variables in the argument list. If there are too few values, the remaining arguments get bound to NIL. If there are too many, the extra values are ignored. Given the foregoing function definition, the following would happen:

```
eval> (MULTIPLE-VALUE-BIND (SUM DIFF EXTRA)
          (SUM-DIFF-SQUARE 5 4)
          (LIST SUM DIFF EXTRA))
(41 9 NIL)

eval> (MULTIPLE-VALUE-BIND (JUST-ONE)
          (SUM-DIFF-SQUARE 5 4)
          (LIST JUST-ONE))
(41)
```

Of course, forming all the values into a list entirely defeats the purpose of using the multiple value facility in the first place!

With this, we might rewrite some of our parsing functions as

```
(DEFUN PARSE-ASSERTION (SENTENCE)
    (MULTIPLE-VALUE-BIND (NP1 MORE1)
        (PARSE-NOUN-PHRASE SENTENCE)
      (MULTIPLE-VALUE-BIND (VERB MORE2)
          (PARSE-VERB MORE1)
```

```
        (MULTIPLE-VALUE-BIND (NP2 EXTRA)
            (PARSE-NOUN-PHRASE MORE2)
          (COND ((NULL EXTRA)
                 (LIST NP1 VERB NP2))
                (T (FORMAT T
                           "~%Dangling words ~S at end of ~S."
                           EXTRA
                           SENTENCE)
                   (THROW 'BAD-SYNTAX NIL)))))))

(DEFUN PARSE-VERB (MORE-SENTENCE)
    (LET ((WORD (CAR MORE-SENTENCE)))
        (COND ((EQ 'VERB (CHECK-LEXICON WORD))
               (VALUES (LIST 'VERB WORD)
                       (CDR MORE-SENTENCE)))
              (T (FORMAT T
                         "~%Expected a verb, not ~S."
                         WORD)
                 (THROW 'BAD-SYNTAX NIL)))))
```

Multiple values often are useful when a function must return a result as well as an indication of success or failure. A single value can be returned and NIL can mean failure, but this scheme doesn't work if NIL is a valid successful result. A second value to indicate success or failure explicitly saves the day.

There is only one restriction on where multiple values can be returned. The function VALUES may not be called in a place at which the flow of control is dependent on the value returned by VALUES. For example, the following is illegal:

```
(DEFUN MVF (X Y)
    (OR (VALUES (SOME Y) (OTHER X))
        (FINAL-CALL X Y)))
```

because the OR terminates conditionally on the result of evaluating its first (and similarly for subsequent) argument.

EXERCISES

E11.6.1 Given the definitions

```
(DEFUN T1 (X)
    (MULTIPLE-VALUE-BIND (A B C)
        (T2 X)
      (LIST A B C)))
```

```
(DEFUN T2 (X)
    (COND ((< X 0) (VALUES X (- 0 X)))
          ((> X 0) (VALUES X (* X X) (* X X X) (* X X X X)))
          (T (VALUES 'IT 'WAS 'ZERO)))))
```

what be will the values of each of the following expressions?
a. (T1 0)
b. (T1 3)
c. (T1 -5)

E11.6.2 Evaluate the following expression:

```
(MULTIPLE-VALUE-BIND (A B)
    (VALUES)
  (MULTIPLE-VALUE-BIND (A B)
      (IF (NULL A)
          1
          (VALUES 2 3))
    (MULTIPLE-VALUE-BIND (A B)
        (IF (NULL A)
            4
            (VALUES 5 6))
      (AND A B))))
```

SUMMARY

This chapter examined a number of advanced control and representation features of Common Lisp. All are used via special forms. Those seen in this chapter are shown in Table 11-1.

Special form SETF is a generalized *setter*. It can be used to change the value of an "place" in a Lisp data structure. Its first argument, if evaluated, would access some "place" in a data structure. SETF arranges that the value stored in that place is replaced by the value of the second argument given to SETF. The new value is always returned by SETF.

A data abstraction facility is used via the DEFSTRUCT declaration macro. It causes a *constructor* function for instances of a declared record class and *accessor* functions for each field of a record class to be defined. SETF is used as the setter on each of these fields. Smart compilers compile the calls to the access functions as though they were appropriate macros.

Structured, named blocks are declared with BLOCK. They can be exited from any piece of code within their textual scope with a RETURN-FROM using the matching block name.

Special forms CATCH and THROW allow for nonlocal exits through many levels of function calls. UNWIND-PROTECT allows the programmer to guarantee that

Table 11-1

Special Form	Subforms	Description
SETF	2	set value of arbitrary place
DEFSTRUCT	$1 \Rightarrow \infty$	define a record class
BLOCK	$2 \Rightarrow \infty$	named block of statements
RETURN-FROM	2	return from named block
CATCH	$2 \Rightarrow \infty$	receive a tagged thrown value
THROW	2	throw a tagged value
UNWIND-PROTECT	$2 \Rightarrow \infty$	force evaluation despite a throw
VALUES	$0 \Rightarrow \infty$	produce multiple values
MULTIPLE-VALUE-BIND	$2 \Rightarrow \infty$	receive multiple values

some action will be taken, no matter what nonlocal transfers of control are happening.

Functions can return multiple values without having to cons them into a list. Special form VALUES produces multiple values and MULTIPLE-VALUE-BIND can be used to receive them. If one function calls another expecting only a single value to be returned, that is what it sees no matter how many values the called function tries to return. The caller must explicitly ask for multiple values (with MULTIPLE-VALUE-BIND) in order to see them, although multiple values will pass right through a function if the last thing it does is call a multiple-value-producing function.

All of these advanced features of Common Lisp have considerably more layers of complexity available to the brave and restless programmer. The details can be found in the Common Lisp manual.

PROBLEMS

P11.1 Write a macro MY-SETF that takes two arguments. The first is a place that must have its value changed and the second is a new value. The code produced by MY-SETF always returns the new value as its result. The places to be handled include anything that macro-expands to a symbol, a CAR or a CDR. After doing a MY-SETF, the place always evaluates to the new value. For example,

```
eval> (MY-SETF X '(A B C))
(A B C)
```

```
eval> X
(A B C)

eval> (MY-SETF (CAR X) 'D)
D

eval> X
(D B C)

eval> (DEFMACRO MY-CAR (Y) '(CAR ,Y))
MY-CAR

eval> (MY-SETF (MY-CAR X) 'B)
B

eval> X
(B B C)

eval> (DEFUN ADD-ONE (X)
         (LET ((NEW (PLUS X 1)))
            (FORMAT "~%Adding 1 to ~S gives ~S." X NEW)))
ADD-ONE

eval> (MY-SETF (CDR X) (ADD-ONE 3))
Adding 1 to 3 gives 4.
4

eval> X
(B . 4)

eval> (MACROEXPAND '(MY-SETF (CAR X) Y))
(PROGN (RPLACA X Y) Y)
```

Notice that the last two examples indicated that different code templates will be necessary under different circumstances. Implement a "reasonable" test of circumstances and justify it.

P11.2 Write a pattern matcher that matches pattern expressions of variables to data expressions. It should return an association list of variables and values on success (perhaps NIL) or the symbol LOSER on failure. The idea is that if you substituted in the values for the variables at the places they occur in the pattern, the pattern would be EQUAL to the data. Thus, the following should happen:

```
eval> (MATCH '(A B C) '(A B C))
NIL

eval> (MATCH '(A B D) '(A B C))
LOSER
```

```
eval> (MATCH '(A (? B) C) '(A E C))
((B . E))

eval> (MATCH '(WHO IS THE (? RELATION) OF (? PERSON))
             '(WHO IS THE MOTHER OF JOE))
((PERSON . JOE) (RELATION . MOTHER))

eval> (MATCH '((? A) B (? A) . (? C))
             '((D E) B (D E) F))
((C F) (A D E))

eval> (MATCH '((? A) B (? A) . (? C))
             '((D E) B (D F) E))
LOSER
```

Variables are specified with (? *var*). If a variable occurs more than once, it should match EQUAL pieces of data. Variable A in the last example was matched against two different things and the complete match failed. Use CATCH and THROW.

P11.3 Write the DOLIST macro again. This time, use your function MATCH to check its syntax and extract the necessary fields. Then use the resulting a-list and SUBLIS to produce the result of the macro without resorting to backquote and commas. Recall the form of the macro is

(DOLIST (*var list return-form*) *body-1* ... *body-n*)

Your definition should start off with:

(DEFMACRO DOLIST (&REST FORMS)

P11.4 Rewrite MATCH so that it returns two values. The first is the association list (perhaps NIL) of variables and values for a succesful match, and NIL for a failed match, while the second value is a flag indicating success (with T) or failure (with NIL).

12

OTHER
FEATURES
OF
COMMON
LISP

There are a number of aspects of Common Lisp that have not been covered in the first eleven chapters of this book. Descriptions of their main features are included here for completeness, although chances are that you often would not need them if you were only writing new programs for symbolic computations. Some aspects in this chapter are inherited from earlier versions of Lisp and you will only need to know about them if you are working on old programs or code written by old programmers. The other aspects covered here concern arithmetic and arrays. Simple uses of arrays are quite straightforward. You will need to worry about advanced features of arrays only if you are writing programs with a heavy numerical component and very large sets of data (e.g., images from a camera).

12.1 USING PROPERTY LISTS

Most Lisps provide a way of associating *values* of *properties* with symbols, via *property lists.* Property values can be accessed with GET and set with SETF. A property name is any Lisp object, but EQ is used internally to identify it, so it is safest to stay with symbols as property names. In a sense, this gives a mechanism for providing an arbitrary set of named values for a symbol.[1] Thus, for instance,

```
eval> (SETF (GET 'BLOCK-A 'COLOR) 'RED)
RED

eval> (SETF (GET 'BLOCK-B 'SIZE) 'BIG)
BIG

eval> (MAPCAR #'(LAMBDA (BLOCK) (GET BLOCK 'COLOR))
              '(BLOCK-A BLOCK-B))
(RED NIL)

eval> (SETF (GET 'BLOCK-B 'COLOR) 'BLUE)
BLUE
```

---

[1] In early versions of Maclisp a symbol's *value* was stored on its property list under the property name VALUE, a symbol's print name was stored under another property name, and any functional definition was stored under a third. This made for easy implementation of Lisp, but it was not very efficient. Most Common Lisp's will have space inside symbols to store such information.

```
eval> (MAPCAR #'(LAMBDA (BLOCK) (GET BLOCK 'COLOR))
              '(BLOCK-A BLOCK-B))
(RED BLUE)

eval> (SETF (GET 'BLOCK-A 'SIZE) '(VERY SMALL))
(VERY SMALL)

eval> (MAPCAR #'(LAMBDA (BLOCK) (GET BLOCK 'SIZE))
              '(BLOCK-A BLOCK-B))
((VERY SMALL) BIG)
```

Notice that if a symbol doesn't have a certain property, NIL is returned—this is indistinguishable from the case of the symbol having the property with value NIL. To get around this problem in Common Lisp, GET takes an optional third argument that is returned if the desired property is not found.

Property lists often are used as a data structuring mechanism, employing the built-in Lisp mechanism for resolving symbol reference via the *obarray* as a way of providing a simple way of naming record instances. For instance, a family relationship database might be constructed by associating relationships as properties with the symbols representing the names of people. For example,

```
eval> (SETF (GET 'JOHN 'FATHER) 'FRED)
FRED

eval> (SETF (GET 'FRED 'SONS) (LIST 'JOHN))
(JOHN)
```

Now we can redefine some of our earlier family relationship functions from problem 4.3.

```
(DEFUN FATHER-OF? (PERSON) (GET PERSON 'FATHER))

(DEFUN MOTHER-OF? (PERSON) (GET PERSON 'MOTHER))
```

Properties have the following good properties:

- They have always been in Lisps.
- They provide access to a built-in association mechanism for fast look up.
- Only "fields" of a "record class" that are instantiated for a particular instance take up storage.

■ There is no need to predeclare field names because storage of fields is completely dynamic.

12.2 REPRESENTING PROPERTY LISTS

Properties are stored in a list. Each symbol includes space to point to such a list. The property list can be examined using SYMBOL-PLIST. Given the examples of the previous section, we would get

```
eval> (SYMBOL-PLIST 'BLOCK-A)
(SIZE (VERY SMALL) COLOR RED)

eval> (SYMBOL-PLIST 'BLOCK-B)
(COLOR BLUE SIZE BIG)
```

The property name and the value of that property are stored as successive elements on the list. A property name can appear only once in a property list. Notice that the function GET is equivalent to

```
(DEFUN GET (SYMBOL PROPERTY)
    (DO ((PLIST (SYMBOL-PLIST SYMBOL) (CDDR PLIST)))
        ((NULL PLIST)
         NIL)
        (IF (EQ (CAR PLIST) PROPERTY)
            (RETURN (CADR PLIST)))))
```

When property values are overwritten, the list structure of the property list is destructively changed. Some Lisps move a newly changed property to the front of the property list to make subsequent accesses quicker. There is neither a generally accepted convention on this nor on where a new property should be stored on the list—at the head, or at the tail.

A property can be removed completely from a property list using REMPROP, which has the form

```
eval> (REMPROP 'BLOCK-B 'SIZE)
T

eval> (REMPROP 'BLOCK-B 'SIZE)
NIL
```

```
eval> (SYMBOL-PLIST 'BLOCK-B)
(COLOR BLUE)
```

Function `REMPROP` returns `NIL` if it couldn't find the property and non-`NIL` if it could.

Properties have the following bad properties:

- They have always been in Lisps.
- Each access to a property requires a search of a linear list, and the average time is thus dependent on the total number of properties stored on a particular symbol's property list. A vector-like representation for a record makes access a constant time operation.
- Each "field" of a "record" represented on a property list takes four pointers' worth of storage rather than the one that would be needed in a vector-like representation.
- It is easy to misspell a property name in one place in a large program and then it is almost impossible to realize that it is the source of a buggy program, because there are no checks that a given property name matches some predeclared expectation.

12.3 ARITHMETIC

We have done very little arithmetic in Lisp.

Many applications of artificial intelligence have large arithmetical components—for example, vision and robotics. Other application areas that are made more tractable by programming in Lisp also have heavy arithmetical needs—for example VLSI design systems.

There is a general misconception that arithmetic is necessarily slow in Lisp. This view has a basis in that it was true in the early days of Lisp implementations and remains true in some new implementations. It is possible, however, to write compilers that produce extremely efficient code for arithmetic from within Lisp. In fact, in experiments done during the early 1970s it was shown that MIT's Maclisp compiler produced faster arithmetic code than did DEC's Fortran compiler for the same machine.

One problem with Lisp arithmetic is that operations are *generic* over number type. Recall the discussion of section 2.6 about the difference between `FIXNUM`s and `SINGLE-FLOAT`s. Thus, `+` can be given floating- or fixed-point numbers and it handles them all in a "sensible" way, using type coercion.[2] Thus, for instance,

---

[2] It is *traditional* that Lisps handle arbitrary-sized integers within their generic arithmetic operations. Try `(EXPT 23 100)` in your Common Lisp.

```
eval> (+ 2 3)
5

eval> (+ 2.1 3.6)
5.7

eval> (+ 2.1 3)
5.1
```

Often one uses integer arithmetic rather than floating arithmetic in the hope of gaining execution speed by making direct use of a machine's inherently faster integer arithmetic capabilities. Clearly, a compiled generic + must lose any such efficiency gain in the overhead of deciding whether the arguments given to it are integers or floating-point numbers, and then in dispatching to the appropriate "addition" instruction, perhaps after doing some type coercion.

Unlike Pascal, say, Lisp is not strongly typed, so the compiler cannot deduce in advance that arguments to + will always be integers. A couple of mechanisms are available to the user to *tell* the compiler that it is intended that arguments to a particular instance of + will in fact always be integers or floating-point numbers. Such declarations of intention do not guarantee their run-time maintenance. In fact, if the intentions are not met, the results can be unpredictable and produce incredibly mysterious and buggy behavior by the program.

 The two mechanisms are

- The user can explicitly declare particular variables to be of a particular type, and can declare arbitrary expressions to return a particular type. For example,

```
(DEFUN FOO (X)
    (DECLARE (TYPE FIXNUM X))
    (+ X (THE FIXNUM (ZTESCH 3 2 X))))
```

says first that variable X will always be bound to a fixed-size integer and second that the expression (ZTESCH 3 2 5) will return a fixed-size integer. Therefore, the compiler can deduce that this particular + can be open coded as a single machine instruction. The DECLARE special form can only be used to declare the type of a variable. The THE form can declare the type of any expression. Thus, we could provide the same information about the specificity of types supplied to the + with

```
(DEFUN FOO (X)
    (+ (THE FIXNUM X) (THE FIXNUM (ZTESCH 3 2 X))))
```

■ There can be multiple versions of each arithmetic function, each of which expects particular types of arguments. The names of these multiple versions are not specified in the Common Lisp language definition and may vary. In all Common Lisps, the addition function + expects arguments of any type. Some Common Lisps have a function +&, which expects integer arguments, and +$F, which expects single precision floating point numbers. For the latter two functions, a compiler can generate a single instruction to use the hardware arithmetic unit directly to carry out the operation.

12.4 KEYWORD ARGUMENTS TO STANDARD FUNCTIONS

We saw keywords in chapter 7. They provide a way of naming arguments to be handed to functions that expect a large number of optional arguments. It turns out that very many of the Common Lisp functions that we have seen throughout the book accept additional keyword arguments that can modify their behavior. We will review some of the most useful cases, using the MEMBER function as an example of one of the many functions that take keyword arguments.

Recall the MEMBER function from chapter 4. It takes two arguments, *item* and *list*, say, and compares *item* to each element in *list* using EQL to return the rest of the list on success and using NIL to return the rest of the list on failure. Thus, it works as

```
eval> (MEMBER 'B '(A B C D))
(B C D)

eval> (MEMBER (+ 1 2) '(A B 3 D))
(3 D)

eval> (MEMBER '(C D) '((A B) (C D) (E F)))
NIL
```

The last example returned NIL because the test for equality was EQL and in this case (C D) is not EQL to (C D). Using a :TEST keyword argument, it is possible to change the test to anything else. For example,

```
eval> (MEMBER '(C D) '((A B) (C D) (E F)) :TEST #'EQUAL)
((C D) (E F))

eval> (MEMBER 3 '(1 2 0 4 2 0 3) :TEST #'<)
(4 2 0 3)
```

The value of the :TEST argument should be a function that can be applied to two arguments. The item being tested for membership is paired with each element of the list in succession and passed to the :TEST function. When non-NIL is returned, the membership test is passed and the rest of the list is returned. Thus, in our second example it turned out that for the fourth element of the list the membership test was equivalent to evaluating (< 3 4), which returns T, and thus the rest of the tested list, starting with the successfully tested element, was returned.

A very common way to use MEMBER is with the :TEST function EQUAL.

The :TEST keyword argument can be used in a number of other functions that we have seen throughout the book. They include ASSOC, SUBST, SUBLIS, UNION, and so on. There are thirty such functions listed in the Common Lisp manual.

In addition to a :TEST functionm it also is possible to supply a :TEST-NOT function, which causes the test to be considered to pass when it returns NIL. Thus, the following would happen:

```
eval> (MEMBER 3 '(1 2 0 4 2 0 3) :TEST-NOT #'>)
(4 2 0 3)
```

It is not permitted to supply both a :TEST function and a :TEST-NOT function.

In addition, it is possible to select a subcomponent (or in fact any function of) elements of the list being searched. This is done with the :KEY keyword argument. For instance, suppose we wish to find which element of a list has a certain CADR. The following could be done:

```
eval> (MEMBER 'D '((A B) (C D) (E F)) :KEY #'CADR)
((C D) (E F))
```

A :KEY argument can be used in conjunction with either a :TEST or a :TEST-NOT argument.

We have almost finished with MEMBER. There are two more variations on it: MEMBER-IF and MEMBER-IF-NOT (and similarly for all those other functions like those listed above). Each takes a predicate, a list, and an optional :KEY keyword argument. The predicate is applied to elements of the list until it returns true for MEMBER-IF or false for MEMBER-IF-NOT. Thus, for instance,

```
eval> (MEMBER-IF #'NUMBERP '(A B 3 D E))
(3 D E)
```

```
eval> (MEMBER-IF-NOT #'NUMBERP
                     '((2 BAD) (B 4) (4 ALL))
                     :KEY #'CAR)
((B 4) (4 ALL))
```

12.5 ARRAYS

Arrays are fully supported objects that can have large rank and that can have typed elements for storage efficiencies. There are many details to the story on the uses and pitfalls of arrays in Common Lisp. There are many keywords that can be supplied to array creating functions, and there is a type hierarchy of arrays. The details become messy very quickly. Fortunately, there is a very simple subset of array lore that will satisfy all the needs of the vast majority of Common Lisp programmers.

There are two functions that need be considered. The function

$$(\text{MAKE-ARRAY } \textit{dim-1 dim-2} \ldots \textit{dim-n})$$

makes an n dimensional array with each the ith index ranging from 0 to $\textit{dim-i}-1$. Components of an array can be accessed with the function

$$(\text{AREF } \textit{array index-1 index-2} \ldots \textit{index-n})$$

where $\textit{array}$ was constructed as shown.

Elements of an array can be changed with SETF.

12.6 ANCIENT LISP

We will describe some aspects of ancient Lisp that are still in everyday use by some people, mainly due to inertia rather than superiority or elegance. Compare the following primitives to those you have seen in this book. The modern primitives are evidence of a trend toward structured code that is easily understood and debugged.

There are two special forms, PROG and GO, that allow unstructured iteration. The latter can be used only within the former. The two take the general forms

$$(\text{PROG } \textit{varlist body-1} \ldots \textit{body-n})$$

and

$$(GO \ tag).$$

A PROG, known as the *program feature*, introduces a set of new variable instances. It is like LET in the sense of introducing variables. Today's Lisps usually bind these variables to NIL, but originally Lisps left them unbound. Common Lisp goes a step further and allows these so-called *prog-variables* to be initialized as in LET. If no initialization value is provided, the variable can simply appear at the top level of the variable list. Thus, it might look like

```
(PROG (V W (X (FOO B)) Y) ...
```

Each of the *body-i* statements is evaluated in turn. If a RETURN is evaluated within one of these statements, the PROG is immediately exited with the value of the RETURN form as its value. If the last statement in the PROG-body is reached, the PROG is exited with value NIL.

In addition, the flow of control can be altered within a PROG by the use of GO. This helps in writing completely nonunderstandable programs. Body statements of the PROG that are symbols are treated not as expressions to be evaluated but as *labels*. Notice that there is no point to evaluating such symbols anyway, because evaluating them has no side effects and the value of a body expression of a PROG can never be returned from it. When a statement of the form (GO *label*) is evaluated within the PROG, control immediately transfers to the body statement following a matching label. Notice that GO does not evaluate its argument. For example,

```
(DEFUN MEMBER (ITEM LIST)
    (PROG (MORE)
          (SETQ MORE LIST)
          LOOP
          (COND ((NULL MORE)
                    (RETURN NIL))
                 ((EQL ITEM (CAR MORE))
                    (RETURN MORE)))
          (SETQ MORE (CDR MORE))
          (GO LOOP)))
```

There are various complicated rules that vary between Lisps on how deeply a GO can be nested and on what happens when one PROG is embedded in another.

In Common Lisp, the body of a DO is allowed to be just like the body of a PROG with GOs and labels. We already knew it could contain RETURNs. Actually in Common Lisp both PROG and DO are usually implemented in terms of BLOCKs and TAGBODYs. The latter is the Common Lisp primitive allowing the use of GO.

Consider a second example of iteration using PROG and GO. The standard way to use them to compute m^n is

```
(DEFUN POWER (M N)
      (PROG (RESULT EXPONENT)
            (SETQ RESULT 1)
            (SETQ EXPONENT N)
            LOOP
            (COND ((ZEROP EXPONENT) (RETURN RESULT)))
            (SETQ RESULT (* M RESULT))
            (SETQ EXPONENT (- EXPONENT 1))
            (GO LOOP)))
```

Compare this unstructured list of statements to the richly structured version that we know how to write:

```
(DEFUN POWER (M N)
      (DO ((RESULT 1 (* M RESULT))
            (EXPONENT N (- EXPONENT 1)))
          ((ZEROP EXPONENT)
           RESULT)))
```

SUMMARY

In this chapter, we saw a mixture of traditional Lisp features that the modern programmer has little call for and some advanced features of Common Lisp that the beginner need not encounter.

The functions covered included three for manipulating property lists that are a mechanism for associating arbitrarily many named values with a symbol, and two for making and using arrays. They are shown in Table 12-1. Array elements are altered by using the ubiquitous SETF macro.

Arithmetic code can be speeded by telling the compiler known facts about the number types of variables and expressions. The THE special form is used for this purpose.

The original form of iteration in Lisp used go-to statements using the special form GO within the body of a PROG special form. The latter introduces variables and provides a list of statements that are executed sequentially unless a GO is encountered. The special forms can be summarized in Table 12-2.

Now you know Common Lisp.

Table 12-1

Function	Args	Description
GET	$2 \Rightarrow 3$	get a named property
SYMBOL-PLIST	1	property list of a symbol
REMPROP	2	remove a property
MAKE-ARRAY	$1 \Rightarrow \infty$	create a new array instance
AREF	$2 \Rightarrow \infty$	access an array element

Table 12-2

Special Form	Subforms	Description
DECLARE	1	declare information to compiler
THE	2	make in-line type declaration
GO	1	transfer control to a label
PROG	$2 \Rightarrow \infty$	execute block of statements

APPENDIX

1

OTHER LISPS

The Common Lisp language is largely compatible with a number of dialects of Lisp. It was designed to be as compatible as possible with all the descendants of Maclisp. These include Spice Lisp, Zetalisp, Standard Lisp, Nil, and Scheme. In this appendix, we will follow up on the forked road signs throughout the book to point out the major differences between Maclisp, Franz Lisp, and Common Lisp. We give particular attention to Franz Lisp, which is a somewhat similar dialect of Lisp and very popular because of its price and the fact that it runs on VAXen under Berkeley Unix. The companies that market versions of Zetalisp provide compatability packages for Common Lisp. The base Zetalisp is already almost a superset of Common Lisp. The definitions of Spice Lisp and Nil have changed over time to keep in synchronization with the definition of Common Lisp, and so there should be no differences.

The other major dialect of Lisp is Interlisp. It diverged from Maclisp too long ago to make it plausible for Common Lisp to be designed in such a way that it too was compatible. The differences between Common Lisp and Interlisp are large and numerous, with many different concepts, and so we will not try to cover them here.

A1.1 ESSENTIAL LISP

A1.1.1 WHAT DOES LISP LOOK LIKE?

We have used "`eval>` " throughout this book to indicate when Lisp is ready to accept an expression to evaluate. Very few Lisps, Common Lisp, or others use this prompt as yet. Every Lisp seems to have its own convention. Maclisp has no prompt at all; the user must keep track of whether a value already has been printed for the last expression to know whether it is worth typing a new one. Franz Lisp starts by prompting the user with "`->` " but changes when an error has occurred. It is possible for the user to alter the prompting behavior in both Maclisp and Franz Lisp, so even seeing the prompt is not a sure way of identifying the underlying Lisp.

A more pervasive incompatibility occurs with Franz Lisp. Common Lisp, Maclisp, and all of their close relatives accept input in any case and convert it to uppercase. Thus, both "`car`" and "`CaR`" get read as though they were "`CAR`". Franz Lisp, however, is case sensitive, and the three examples would all be treated as different symbols. The Lisp function to find the first part of a cons cell is actually "`car`" while the others will start off undefined and remain that way unless the user defines them. All functions in Franz Lisp have lowercase names.

A1.1.4 THE LISP EVALUATION RULE

In Common Lisp, the function + can add numbers of any type; for example, two integers, or an integer and a floating-point number, or two floating-point numbers. In both Maclisp and Franz Lisp the + function only can be used when all arguments are integers below a certain size (in the former, they must be representable by 36 bits and in the latter by 32). The generic addition function is "PLUS" in Maclisp and Franz Lisp.

A1.1.8 VARIABLES AND REFERENCE

Both Maclisp and Franz Lisp allow functions to refer to variables in any function that called them. This only works efficiently in interpreted Lisp, however, and by default the compilers for each of the two languages do not allow it, although declarations for individual variables can circumvent the restriction.

Following Scheme, Common Lisp insists that compiled and interpreted functions have the same semantics. Therefore, variable references are resticted to be within functions or to global variables.

A1.1.9 PREDICATES

Neither Maclisp nor Franz Lisp have the predicate CONSP pre-defined. Both have LISTP, although in Maclisp it is not present at first but is automatically loaded when called.

In Maclisp the predicates "<" and ">" can be used only to compare two fixed-precision integers or two floating-point numbers. It is illegal to mix types in the two arguments. The same is true in Franz Lisp in compiled code, but it seems not to be an error in interpreted code. In most dialects of Lisp, including these two, the generic functions that compare any types of numbers are LESSP and GREATERP.

A1.1.10 IF: A CONDITIONAL FORM

The primitive conditional form in both Maclisp and Franz Lisp is COND. Franz Lisp knows nothing of IF, but Maclisp automatically loads a macro definition of it if it is used.

A1.2 STANDARD LIST OPERATIONS

A1.2.3 RECURSIVE FUNCTIONS AND DEBUGGING

The semantics of TRACE and UNTRACE are fairly standard among Lisps, but what gets printed during tracing varies greatly even within Common Lisp implementations. The style used in this book is actually that of Maclisp. Some Common Lisp implementations use exactly the same format, but it is usually easy to figure out what is meant in other implementations. Function entry usually prints the name of the function and the arguments, and exit usually prints the returned value (along with the function name again).

A1.2.4 GLOBAL VARIABLES

The same remarks as applied to chapter 1, section 8, apply to this section. In Franz Lisp, `DEFVAR` is undefined. Instead, one must use

$$\texttt{(declare (special } \textit{variable}\texttt{))}$$

to make a variable global. `SETQ` must be used to initialize it.

A1.2.5 EQ: EQUALITY OF POINTERS

In Maclisp, integers in the range -372 to 776 inclusive are `EQ` to themselves, while in Franz Lisp the same is true for integers in the range -1024 to 1023. Neither language guarantees this to be true; it just happens to be so. Making programs depend on these quirks is risky business.

A1.2.6 EQL: AN INTERMEDIATE EQUALITY TESTER

No other Lisp has the rich set of numeric types defined in Common Lisp. In particular, Maclisp has only 36-bit precision floating-point numbers, and Franz Lisp has only 64-bit precision.

The function `TYPEP` usually only takes one argument in other Lisps and returns the type of an object. In order to remain compatible with a number of type hierarchies, the Common Lisp design was forced to make `TYPEP` into a "yes–no" predicate that can merely confirm or deny that an object has a certain type.

Functions `STRINGP` and `EQL` are unique to Common Lisp.

As is the case for "+", the function "−" is restricted in most Lisps to fixed-precision integer arguments. The generic function for mixed types of arguments is `DIFFERENCE`. In Common Lisp, the function "−" is generic. Likewise, `TIMES` and `QUOTIENT` are the generic functions in other Lisps, while Common Lisp uses `*` and `/`.

A1.2.8 LIST CREATION AND ACCESS FUNCTIONS

The functions `LIST*`, `NTH`, and `NTHCDR` do not appear in Franz Lisp.

A1.3 CONTROL STRUCTURES

Surprisingly, Maclisp, Franz Lisp, and Common Lisp agree completely in their definitions of these control structures. Between implementations of Common Lisp, which is the *primitive* conditional of IF and COND and which is a macro that expands to the other, may vary (note, of course, that Franz Lisp does not include IF at all).

A1.4 MORE LIST OPERATIONS

A1.4.1 LISTS AS SETS

In Common Lisp, the default test used in determining membership among the top-level elements of a list is EQL. This function does not exist in either Maclisp or Franz Lisp. In both of those dialects, EQUAL is used in MEMBER. They also include a function MEMQ that uses EQ for a test. Chapter 12 showed how the test function used by MEMBER could be changed in Common Lisp. This is not possible in the other Lisps. However, in Common Lisp we can define the MEMQ function as

```
(DEFUN MEMQ (EL LST) (MEMBER EL LST :TEST #'EQ))
```

The functions UNION, NUNION, INTERSECTION, and NINTERSECTION are not defined as parts of either Maclisp or Franz Lisp but are likely to be available in libraries.

A1.4.2 LISTS AS DATABASES

Similarly to MEMBER, Common Lisp ASSOC uses EQL as a test, whereas Maclisp and Franz Lisp use EQUAL. Again they both have a specialization of the Common Lisp function called ASSQ, which uses EQ as a test.

A1.4.3 LIST COPYING FUNCTIONS

None of the functions COPY-LIST, COPY-ALIST, or COPY-TREE is defined in Maclisp or Franz Lisp, although Franz Lisp includes COPY, which is the same as COPY-TREE. A common way to get the effect of COPY-LIST in these two dialects is illustrated by the easiest way to define that function:

```
(DEFUN COPY-LIST (LST) (APPEND LST NIL))
```

The functions SUBST and SUBLIS appear in both Maclisp and Franz Lisp, but their definitions are different to both Common Lisp definitions and to each other.

In Maclisp, the function SUBST uses EQ to check for substitutions (rather than the default EQL in Common Lisp) and copies the whole list structure of its third argument. Common Lisp, on the other hand, tries to share as much list structure as possible between the old and new. Maclisp's SUBLIS, however, tries to share structure just as does Common Lisp's SUBLIS, the only difference being that Maclisp again uses EQ rather than EQL. The fact that SUBST copies all of the list structure leads to the following commonly used idiom in Maclisp:

```
(DEFUN COPY-TREE (TREE) (SUBST NIL NIL TREE))
```

There are no destructive versions, NSUBST and NSUBLIS, of these functions in Maclisp.

In Franz Lisp, the function SUBST (which of course must be typed "subst" because of case sensitivity) uses EQUAL as the test function. The Franz Lisp manual does not say how much structure is copied, but experimentation shows that it follows the Maclisp definition. Franz Lisp has a destructive version called DSUBST. Franz Lisp has a SUBLIS but no corresponding destructive version. The manual implies indirectly that EQUAL is used for the comparison (and that would be campatible with Franz Lisp's definition of SUBST), but experimentation shows that EQ is used. The manual is mute on the issue of shared structure in SUBLIS, but it does follow the Maclisp and Common Lisp definition.

A1.5 PROGRAMMING STYLE

All the issues of good programming style are equally applicable to Maclisp, Franz Lisp, and any other Lisp.

A1.6 INPUT AND OUTPUT

A1.6.1 FORMAT: AN INTRODUCTION

The function FORMAT is not included in Franz Lisp, but does exist as an automatically loadable library in Maclisp. The full definition of Common Lisp FORMAT includes much more than was included in this book. The Maclisp version diverges from the complete Common Lisp definition, but is mostly consistent with the features we have described here. The only variations are in some fencepost behaviors with the T directive in which one less space is sometimes printed.

A1.6.2 OPENING AND CLOSING A FILE

The Maclisp version of OPEN takes precisely two arguments. The first is a file name and the second is a list of options about how the file should be opened. For normal output, this list would be (OUT ASCII). For input, it would be (IN ASCII) (the order of elements of the list is not important). In general, Maclisp does not support keyword arguments.

In Franz Lisp, different functions must be used for opening input and output files. For output, the equivalent is OUTFILE, which takes a single argument that is the file name.

Both Maclisp and Franz Lisp have a CLOSE function that should be applied to the objects returned by their OPEN functions in order to close and release the file.

A1.6.3 THE STANDARD PRINT FUNCTIONS

The printing functions are very similar between Maclisp and Common Lisp, although there is a somewhat annoying incompatibility. Maclisp is the historical villain. All four of these printing functions return T in Maclisp,[1] while in Common Lisp function TERPRI returns NIL, and the others return their first argument.[2]

There are more significant differences in Franz Lisp. The function PRIN1 does not exist, while TERPRI is called TERPR (which returns NIL). The PRINT function does not start things off with a new line, so it is more similar to PRIN1. Function PRINC always returns T, while PRINT always returns NIL!

The names of the symbols that control printing length and depth are different in Lisp's other than Common Lisp, although their effects are the same. PRINLEVEL is used instead of *PRINT-LEVEL* and PRINLENGTH instead of *PRINT-LENGTH* in both Maclisp and Franz Lisp.

The symbol *PRINT-BASE*, which controls the base in which numbers are printed, is replaced in Maclisp by BASE. There is no such control in Franz Lisp. In Maclisp, in addition to different radices for printing numbers, it is also possible to grossly change their printed notation by setting the value of BASE to be the symbol ROMAN. Try it!

When BASE is 10 in Maclisp, all integers are followed by a decimal point. This can be suppressed by setting the symbol *NOPOINT to T.

---

[1]The rationale for this was to allow the bad programming practice of including a PRINT statement in the middle of an AND clause without any possibility of it affecting the logical result of the AND.

[2]The rationale for the latter is that one can wrap a PRINT function around an expression, for debugging purposes, without affecting the passing on of the value of the expression.

A1.6.5 SIGNALLING ERRORS

The function ERROR appears in both Maclisp and Franz Lisp although the arguments it takes vary. In both dialects, ERROR can take zero, one, or two arguments. The arguments are printed as the "error message." Neither resembles a FORMAT control string.

A1.6.6 READ: AN INPUT FUNCTION

Neither Maclisp nor Franz Lisp allow the *eof-errorp* argument to READ. Thus, their second optional argument is *eof-value*, the third optional argument in Common Lisp. Both Maclisp and Franz Lisp cause errors at the end of a file if and only if they are reading part of a list and expecting to see more right parentheses.

The symbol *READ-BASE* is used only in Common Lisp. In the other dialects, its place is taken by IBASE. In Maclisp, it is permissible for IBASE to have value ROMAN.

A1.7 FUNCTIONS

A1.7.3 KEYWORD ARGUMENTS

Neither Maclisp nor Franz Lisp support keyword arguments or keywords as self-evaluating symbols.

A1.7.5 APPLY: FOR LISTS OF ARGUMENTS

The definition of APPLY has been generalized in Common Lisp over that in earlier Lisps. Early versions of APPLY took only two arguments: the function to be applied and a list of arguments to apply it to. Common Lisp allows single arguments to be inserted ahead of the list of arguments. In both Maclisp and Franz Lisp, a Common Lisp APPLY could be defined with the following macro:

```
(DEFMACRO CL-APPLY (FUNCTION &REST ARG-SPECS)
   '(APPLY ,FUNCTION (LIST* ,@ARG-SPECS)))
```

(except that LIST* is not defined in Franz Lisp).

A1.7.6 THE VALUE AND FUNCTIONAL VALUE OF A SYMBOL

The value of a symbol is found with SYMEVAL in both Maclisp and Franz Lisp, rather than the Common Lisp function SYMBOL-VALUE.

Function BOUNDP works the same in all three Lisps, but FBOUNDP is not found in Franz Lisp. There it is called GETD. The function SYMBOL-FUNCTION does not exist in either Maclisp or Franz Lisp. In the former, it can be defined as

```
(DEFUN SYMBOL-FUNCTION (SYM) (CADR (FBOUNDP SYM)))
```

and in the latter it is equivalent to GETD again.

Whether something is a true function rather than a macro or special form can be found using FUNCTIONP in Common Lisp. In Maclisp, it can be found by understanding the obscure possible values for the CAR of what is returned by FBOUNDP, and in Franz Lisp by understanding a different set of obscure possible values returned by the function GETDISC.

A1.7.8 MAPPING FUNCTIONS

The Common Lisp function MAPL is known as MAP in both Maclisp and Franz Lisp.

A1.9 MACROS

A1.9.3 MACROS

The function MACROEXPAND-1 does not exist in Franz Lisp.

A1.11 ADVANCED FEATURES

A1.11.1 SETF: A GENERALIZED SETTING FORM

Both Maclisp and Franz Lisp have versions of SETF available. The Franz Lisp SETF does not necessarily expand to code that returns the second argument to SETF as its value. For instance, the following expansion happens:

```
(SETF (CAR X) Y)  ==>  (RPLACA X Y)
```

A1.11.2 DEFSTRUCT: A RECORD PACKAGE

There are versions of DEFSTRUCT that run in Franz Lisp, but it is not part of the language definition. A version of DEFSTRUCT is automatically loaded into

Maclisp if the user tries to use it. It has almost the same characteristics as the DEFSTRUCT subset described in this book, but it diverges from the full Common Lisp definition. The major difference is that field names do not become keywords for the creation function, and the field accessors are macros rather than functions.

A1.11.3 BLOCK: STRUCTURED UNITS WITHIN FUNCTIONS

Special forms BLOCK, RETURN-FROM and DO-NAMED do not exist in either Maclisp or Franz Lisp.

A1.11.4 CATCH AND THROW: NONLOCAL EXITS

These are called *CATCH and *THROW in both Maclisp and Franz Lisp.

In Franz Lisp, the *CATCH form takes only two subforms: the tag and a form to evaluate. It does not include the implicit PROGN of Common Lisp and Maclisp. Unfortunately, the Franz Lisp compiler does not mention that it is throwing away any extra code that you included in the hope of making use of the non-existent PROGN feature. This can be the source of much frustration in transporting programs written for Common Lisp or Maclisp to Franz Lisp, as programs suddenly and unexpectedly start exhibiting bizarre behavior that is not always obviously due to the major lobotomy they have suffered.

A1.11.6 MULTIPLE VALUES

Multiple values do not exist at all in Franz Lisp, and are faked using global variables in Maclisp. The result is that they are not so efficient, and there are some subtle differences in the semantics of multiple values and how long they are accessible.

A1.12 OTHER FEATURES OF COMMON LISP

A1.12.1 USING PROPERTY LISTS

Neither Maclisp nor Franz Lisp allow the third argument to GET allowed by Common Lisp to be returned in the case that the property is not found.

A1.12.2 REPRESENTING PROPERTY LISTS

The function PLIST is used instead of SYMBOL-PLIST in both Maclisp and Franz Lisp.

A1.12.3 ARITHMETIC

Declarations are handled by DECLARE in Maclisp and Franz Lisp. The details on the effects of declarations in these languages are often left fuzzy.

In Maclisp and Franz Lisp, the generic arithmetic operators are PLUS, DIFFERENCE, TIMES, QUOTIENT, and so on. The fixed-precision integer arithmetic functions are +, -, *, / (// in Maclisp), and so on. The single-precision floating-point operations are +$, -$, *$, /$ (//$ in Maclisp), and so on.

A1.12.4 KEYWORD ARGUMENTS TO STANDARD FUNCTIONS

Neither Maclisp nor Franz Lisp support keyword arguments.

A1.12.5 ARRAYS

Arrays are handled differently in both Maclisp and Franz Lisp; each has its own mechanisms driven by hardware considerations rather than language semantics.

APPENDIX

2

SOLUTIONS

SOLUTIONS TO CHAPTER 1

EXERCISES

E1.2.1

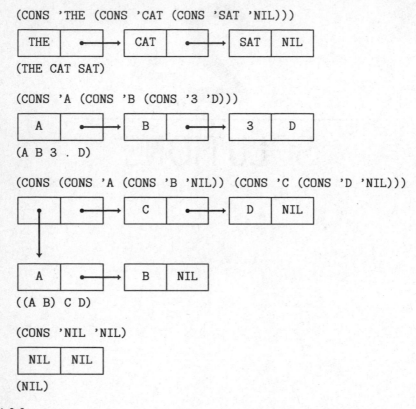

```
(CONS 'THE (CONS 'CAT (CONS 'SAT 'NIL)))
```

```
┌─────┬───┐    ┌─────┬───┐    ┌─────┬─────┐
│ THE │ ●─┼───▶│ CAT │ ●─┼───▶│ SAT │ NIL │
└─────┴───┘    └─────┴───┘    └─────┴─────┘
```

(THE CAT SAT)

```
(CONS 'A (CONS 'B (CONS '3 'D)))
```

```
┌───┬───┐    ┌───┬───┐    ┌───┬───┐
│ A │ ●─┼───▶│ B │ ●─┼───▶│ 3 │ D │
└───┴───┘    └───┴───┘    └───┴───┘
```

(A B 3 . D)

```
(CONS (CONS 'A (CONS 'B 'NIL)) (CONS 'C (CONS 'D 'NIL)))
```

```
┌───┬───┐    ┌───┬───┐    ┌───┬─────┐
│ ● │ ●─┼───▶│ C │ ●─┼───▶│ D │ NIL │
└─┼─┴───┘    └───┴───┘    └───┴─────┘
  │
  ▼
┌───┬───┐    ┌───┬─────┐
│ A │ ●─┼───▶│ B │ NIL │
└───┴───┘    └───┴─────┘
```

((A B) C D)

```
(CONS 'NIL 'NIL)
```

```
┌─────┬─────┐
│ NIL │ NIL │
└─────┴─────┘
```

(NIL)

E1.2.2

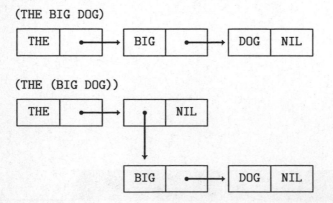

(THE BIG DOG)

```
┌─────┬───┐    ┌─────┬───┐    ┌─────┬─────┐
│ THE │ ●─┼───▶│ BIG │ ●─┼───▶│ DOG │ NIL │
└─────┴───┘    └─────┴───┘    └─────┴─────┘
```

(THE (BIG DOG))

```
┌─────┬───┐    ┌───┬─────┐
│ THE │ ●─┼───▶│ ● │ NIL │
└─────┴───┘    └─┼─┴─────┘
                 │
                 ▼
           ┌─────┬───┐    ┌─────┬─────┐
           │ BIG │ ●─┼───▶│ DOG │ NIL │
           └─────┴───┘    └─────┴─────┘
```

((THE (BIG DOG)) BIT HIM)

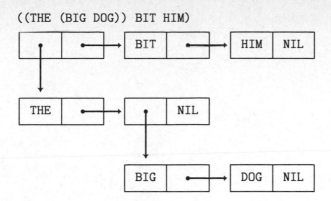

E1.3.1

```
eval> (LIST 'BIG 'CAT 'SAT)
(BIG CAT SAT)

eval> (CONS 'THE (LIST 'BIG 'CAT 'SAT))
(THE BIG CAT SAT)

eval> (LIST 'ALL (LIST 'GOOD 'PEOPLE)
            'SHOULD (LIST 'GO 'AHEAD))
(ALL (GOOD PEOPLE) SHOULD (GO AHEAD))
```

E1.3.2

```
eval> (CAR (CDR '(A B C D))
B

eval> (CAR (CDR (CAR '((A B) C D))))
B

eval> (CDR (CAR (CDR '(A (B C) D))))
(C)
```

E1.5.1

```
(B U V W)
```

E1.5.2

```
(U V W)
```

E1.5.3

```
(A A B)
```

E1.5.4

```
((A B) (LIST (QUOTE A) (QUOTE B)))
```

E1.7.1 4.6

E1.7.2 36

E1.7.3 54

E1.9.1 a. NIL, b. NIL, c. T, d. NIL, e. NIL, f. T, g. T, h. NIL

E1.9.2 a. NIL, b. T, c. T, d. NIL, e. T, f. T, g. NIL, h. T

PROBLEMS

P1.1

```
(DEFUN DOT-PRODUCT (VECTOR1 VECTOR2)
    (+ (* (CAR VECTOR1) (CAR VECTOR2))
       (* (CAR (CDR VECTOR1)) (CAR (CDR VECTOR2)))
       (* (CAR (CDR (CDR VECTOR1)))
          (CAR (CDR (CDR VECTOR2))))))
```

P1.2

```
(DEFUN COUNT-NUMBERS (LIST)
    (IF (NULL LIST)
        0
        (+ (IF (NUMBERP (CAR LIST))
               1
               0)
           (COUNT-NUMBERS (CDR LIST)))))
```

P1.3

```
(DEFUN LONGER-LISTP (LIST1 LIST2)
    (IF (NULL LIST1)
        'NIL
        (IF (NULL LIST2)
            'T
            (LONGER-LISTP (CDR LIST1) (CDR LIST2)))))
```

P1.4

```
(DEFUN SAME-LENGTH (LIST)
    (IF (NULL LIST)
        'NIL
        (CONS 'T (SAME-LENGTH (CDR LIST)))))
```

P1.5

```
(DEFUN NEW-LIST (N)
    (IF (ZEROP N)
        'NIL
        (CONS 'T (NEW-LIST (+ N -1)))))
```

SOLUTIONS TO CHAPTER 2

EXERCISES

E2.1.1
a. (A A A A A)
b. (A A A)
c. (A (B C) B C)
d. (ADDS NOTHING)

E2.1.2

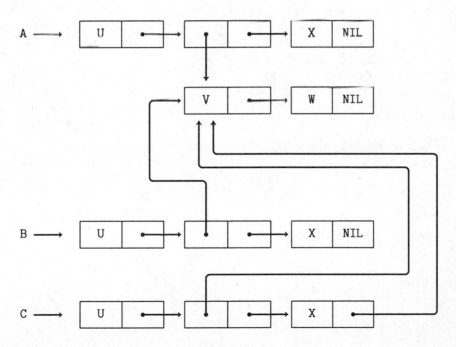

E2.2.2 The Lisp system may use APPEND for its ordinary operations—as part of the trace facility, for instance. If the user supplies a new buggy version of APPEND, Lisp may degenerate into unusability.

E2.3.1
a. (D C B A)
b. ((D E) (B C) A)
c. (((E F G) H) D (A (B C)))

E2.4.1

```
(DEFUN REPORT-APPEND (X Y)
    (PROGN (SETQ *COUNT* 0)
           (COUNT-APPEND X Y)
           *COUNT*))
```

E2.5.1   a. T, b. NIL, c. NIL, d. undefined, e. T, f. undefined, g. NIL, h. NIL

E2.6.1   a. T, b. NIL, c. NIL, d. T, e. T, f. T, g. NIL, h. NIL

E2.7.1   a. T, b. T, c. NIL, d. T, e. T, f. T, g. T, h. NIL

E2.8.1   a. B, b. B, c. C, d. E, e. E, f. (F), g. ((G H I)), h. (H I)

E2.8.2
a. (CADDR '(A B C D E))
   (THIRD '(A B C D E))
b. (CADDAR '((A B C) (D E F)))
   (THIRD (FIRST '((A B C) (D E F))))
c. (CAADR '((A B) (C D) (E F)))
   (FIRST (SECOND '((A B) (C D) (E F))))
d. (CADADR '(A (B C D) E F))
   (SECOND (SECOND '(A (B C D) E F))))

E2.9.1

```
eval> (SETQ X '(A B C))
(A B C)

eval> (SETQ Y (APPEND '(1 2 3) X))
(1 2 3 A B C)

eval> (RPLACA X '4)
(4 B C)

eval> Y
(1 2 3 4 B C)

eval> (RPLACD X 'NIL)
(4)

eval> Y
(1 2 3 4)
```

E2.9.2
a. (RPLACA (CDDR '(A B C D E)) 'SEE)
b. (RPLACA (CDDAR '((A B C) (D E F))) 'SEE)
c. (RPLACA (CADR '((A B) (C D) (E F))) 'SEE)
d. (RPLACA (CDADR '(A (B C D) E F)) 'SEE)

PROBLEMS

P2.1

```
(DEFUN ALL-LENGTH (LIST)
    (IF (NULL LIST)
        0
        (+ (IF (ATOM (CAR LIST))
               1
               (ALL-LENGTH (CAR LIST))
          (ALL-LENGTH (CDR LIST)))))
```

Note that a NIL that occurs as an element of a list must be counted as one, whereas one that occurs as the last CDR of a list counts as zero. That is why ATOM, rather than LISTP, was used as the test on the CAR of the list.

P2.2

```
(DEFUN ALL-REVERSE (LST)
    (ALL-REVERSE-AUX LST 'NIL))

(DEFUN ALL-REVERSE-AUX (REM SOFAR)
    (IF (NULL REM)
        SOFAR
        (REVERSE-AUX (CDR REM)
                     (CONS (IF (ATOM (CAR REM))
                               (CAR REM)
                               (ALL-REVERSE-AUX (CAR REM)
                                                'NIL))
                     SOFAR))))
```

P2.3

```
(DEFUN COUNT-REVERSE-1 (LST)
    (IF (NULL LST)
        'NIL
        (COUNT-APPEND (COUNT-REVERSE-A (CDR LST))
                      (COUNT-CONS (CAR LST) 'NIL))))
```

```
(DEFUN REPORT-REVERSE-1 (LST)
    (PROGN (SETQ *COUNT* 0)
           (COUNT-REVERSE-1 LST)
           *COUNT*))

(DEFUN COUNT-REVERSE-2 (LST)
    (COUNT-REVERSE-2-AUX LST 'NIL))

(DEFUN COUNT-REVERSE-2-AUX (REM SOFAR)
    (IF (NULL REM)
        SOFAR
        (COUNT-REVERSE-2-AUX (CDR REM)
                             (COUNT-CONS (CAR REM) SOFAR))))

(DEFUN COMPARE-REVERSES (LST)
    (- (REPORT-REVERSE-1 LST)
       (REPORT-REVERSE-2 LST)))
```

P2.4

```
(DEFUN EQUAL-SYMBOLS (X Y)
    (IF (ATOM X)
        (IF (NUMBERP X)
            (NUMBERP Y)
            (EQ X Y))
        (IF (ATOM Y)
            'NIL
            (IF (EQUAL-SYMBOLS (CAR X) (CAR Y))
                (EQUAL-SYMBOLS (CDR X) (CDR Y))
                'NIL))))
```

P2.5

```
(DEFUN TYPER (LIST)
    (IF (ATOM LIST)
        (IF (NUMBERP LIST)
            'NUMBER
            'SYMBOL)
        (CONS (TYPER (CAR LIST))
              (IF (NULL (CDR LIST))
                  'NIL
                  (TYPER (CDR LIST))))))
```

P2.6 Two solutions are below. The first RPLACs on all cons cells, even those that point to other cons cells—clearly, this is redundant but produces the correct result. The second version only RPLACs when it is necessary to replace an atom by its type symbol, but this version only will not work if its input is an atom—this could be fixed with auxiliary functions.

```
(DEFUN NTYPER (LIST)
    (IF (ATOM LIST)
        (IF (NUMBERP LIST)
            'NUMBER
            'SYMBOL)
        (PROGN (RPLACA LIST (NTYPER (CAR LIST)))
               (IF (NOT (NULL (CDR LIST)))
                   (RPLACD LIST (NTYPER (CDR LIST))))
               LIST)))

(DEFUN NTYPER (LIST)
    (PROGN (IF (ATOM (CAR LIST))
               (RPLACA LIST
                       (IF (NUMBERP (CAR LIST))
                           'NUMBER
                           'SYMBOL))
               (NTYPER (CAR LIST)))
           (IF (NOT (NULL (CDR LIST)))
               (IF (ATOM (CDR LIST))
                   (RPLACD LIST
                           (IF (NUMBERP (CDR LIST))
                               'NUMBER
                               'SYMBOL))
                   (NTYPER (CDR LIST))))
           LIST))
```

SOLUTIONS TO CHAPTER 3

EXERCISES

E3.1.1
a. NUMBERP, ATOM, NULL
b. NUMBERP, ATOM
c. NUMBERP
d. TOM, NUMBERP, CONSP

E3.1.2

```
(IF (EQ DAY 'SATURDAY)
    'FOOTBALL
    (IF (EQ DAY 'SUNDAY)
        'DIEM-SUM
        (IF (EQ DAY 'WEDNESDAY)
            'LAB
            'CLASS)))
```

E3.3.1
a. (3 . 4)
b. (4 . 3)
c. (4 . 4)

E3.6.1 a. 5, b. 6, c. 2

E3.6.2 The function ANON searches a list for two successive elements that are EQ. If it finds them it returns the rest of the list following them and otherwise NIL.

PROBLEMS

P3.1

```
;;; There are many possible variations of this function.
;;; This version first tests for EQ objects as that certainly
;;; suffices. That also takes care of all possibilities where
;;; either X or Y is an atom but not a number.

(DEFUN EQUAL-SYMBOLS (X Y)
    (COND ((EQ X Y)
           'T)
          ((NUMBERP X)
           (NUMBERP Y))
          ((OR (ATOM X) (ATOM Y))
           'NIL)
          (T (AND (EQUAL-SYMBOLS (CAR X) (CAR Y))
                  (EQUAL-SYMBOLS (CDR X) (CDR Y))))))
```

P3.2

```
;;; Make an empty tconc structure.

(DEFUN MAKE-TCONC ()
    (CONS 'NIL 'NIL))

;;; Add a single element to the end.

(DEFUN TCONC (TC NEW)
    ;; create the new last cons cell of the list
    (LET ((NEWL (CONS NEW 'NIL)))
         ;; this is only true if the tconc is empty
         ;; so then the last cons cell must also be the first
         ;; else tack it on to the previously last one
         (IF (NULL (CDR TC))
             (RPLACA TC NEWL)
             (RPLACD (CDR TC) NEWL))
```

```
      ;; in either case the CDR must be updated to
      ;; point to the last cons
      (RPLACD TC NEWL)
      TC))


;;; Add a list of elements to the end.


(DEFUN LCONC (TC LST)
      ;; if the list to be added is empty then nothing
      ;; need be done.
      (COND ((NOT (NULL LST))
             (IF (NULL (CDR TC))
                 (RPLACA TC LST)
                 (RPLACD (CDR TC) LST))
             (RPLACD TC (LAST LST))))
      ;; result in either case
      TC)


;;; Remove the first element fom the list.


(DEFUN REMOVE-HEAD (TC)
      (COND ((NULL (CAR TC))
             ;; empty tconc!
             'NIL)
            ((NULL (CDAR TC))
             ;; tconc with only one element so the
             ;; last cons cell of the list must be updated
             (LET ((ELEMENT (CAAR TC)))
                 (RPLACA TC 'NIL)
                 (RPLACD TC 'NIL)
                 ELEMENT))
            (T (LET ((ELEMENT (CAAR TC)))
                 (RPLACA TC (CDAR TC))
                 ELEMENT))))
```

P3.3   Appending something to the end of a list normally would require CDRing down to the end of it. Such an operation is dependent on the length of the list. By keeping an explicit pointer to the last cons cell in the list, we can attach an extra item to the end in constant time.

P3.4

```
      ;;; The initialization of MAX and MIN is correct because
      ;;; LIST is known to be at least one long.
```

```
(DEFUN RANGE (LIST)
    (DO ((ELS (CDR LIST) (CDR ELS))
        (MIN (CAR LIST)
            (IF (< (CAR ELS) MIN)
                (CAR ELS)
                MIN))
        (MAX (CAR LIST)
            (IF (> (CAR ELS) MAX)
                (CAR ELS)
                MAX)))
        ((NULL ELS)
        (LIST MIN MAX))))
```

P3.5

```
;;; The structure of the iteration must be changed greatly in
;;; order to pre-test each element making sure its a number
;;; before it gets fed to the comparison predicates. In order
;;; to get a good initialization for MAX and MIN we treat the
;;; first element of the list specially.

(DEFUN VALID-RANGE (LIST)
    (IF (NUMBERP (CAR LIST))
        (LET ((MIN (CAR LIST))  ;gets SETQed below
              (MAX (CAR LIST))) ;gets SETQed below
            (DO ((ELS (CDR LIST) (CDR ELS)))
                ((NULL ELS)
                (LIST MIN MAX))
                (LET ((CAND (CAR ELS)))
                    (COND ((NOT (NUMBERP CAND))
                          (RETURN 'INVALID))
                          ;; at most one of the next
                          ;; two cases can occur.
                          ((< CAND MIN)
                          (SETQ MIN CAND))
                          ((> CAND MAX)
                          (SETQ MAX CAND))))))
        'INVALID))
```

P3.6

```
;;; Not all functions are best written with iteration!

(DEFUN MAX-NO (OBJ)
    (MAX-NO-AUX OBJ 'NIL))
```

```
(DEFUN MAX-NO-AUX (OBJ BEST)
    (COND ((NUMBERP OBJ)
              (COND ((NULL BEST)
                      OBJ)
                    ((> BEST OBJ)
                     BEST)
                    (T OBJ)))
          ((ATOM OBJ)
           BEST)
          (T (MAX-NO-AUX (CAR OBJ)
                         (MAX-NO-AUX (CDR OBJ) BEST)))))
```

P3.7

```
;;; Recursive version of Fibonacci.

(DEFUN REC-FIBONACCI (N)
    (COND ((EQL N 0) 0)
          ((EQL N 1) 1)
          (T(+ (REC-FIBONACCI (- N 1))
               (REC-FIBONACCI (- N 2))))))

;;; Iterative version of Fibonacci.
;;; After each parallel binding in the DO the following
;;; is true:
;;;      FIB-I-1 = F(I - 1)
;;;      FIB-I   = F(I)

(DEFUN ITER-FIBONACCI (N)
    (DO ((I 1 (+ 1 I))
         (FIB-I-1 0 FIB-I)
         (FIB-I 1 (+ FIB-I FIB-I-1)))
        ((EQL I N)
         FIB-I)))
```

SOLUTIONS TO CHAPTER 4

EXERCISES

E4.1.1
a. (C D E)
b. NIL
c. (3 2 1)
d. NIL

E4.2.1
a. (SQUARE . 4)
b. NIL

E4.2.2 IS-BROTHER-OF-P

PROBLEMS

P4.1

```
(DEFUN MY-COPY-ALIST (ALIST)
    (IF (NULL ALIST)
        'NIL
        (CONS (IF (CONSP (CAR ALIST))
                  (CONS (CAAR ALIST) (CDAR ALIST))
                  (CAR ALIST))
              (MY-COPY-ALIST (CDR ALIST)))))
```

P4.2

```
(DEFUN INVERT-ALIST (ALIST)
  (LET ((NEWALIST 'NIL)) ;gets SETQed below
       (DO ((ENTRIES ALIST (CDR ENTRIES)))
           ((NULL ENTRIES)
            NEWALIST)
           (LET ((OLDKEY (CAAR ENTRIES))
                 (OLDVALUE (CDAR ENTRIES)))
                (LET ((NEWENTRY (ASSOC OLDVALUE
                                       NEWALIST)))
                    ;; if there is no entry for
                    ;; old value then add one,
                    ;; else put old key at head of
                    ;; new value list.
                    (IF (NULL NEWENTRY)
                        (SETQ NEWALIST
                              (CONS (LIST OLDVALUE
                                          OLDKEY)
                                    NEWALIST))
                        (RPLACD NEWENTRY
                                (CONS OLDKEY
                                      (CDR NEWENTRY)))))))))
```

P4.3

```
;;; Declare gobal variables which will hold the data
;;; structures.
```

```
(DEFVAR *MALES* 'NIL)     ;list of all males
(DEFVAR *FEMALES* 'NIL)   ;list of all females

(DEFVAR *MOTHERS* 'NIL)   ;associates a mother with a child
(DEFVAR *FATHERS* 'NIL)   ;associates a father with a child

;;; These two functions record that someone is a female or
;;; male if that is not already known.

(DEFUN IS-FEMALE (PERSON)
    (IF (NOT (MEMBER PERSON *FEMALES*))
        (SETQ *FEMALES* (CONS PERSON *FEMALES*)))
    'T)

(DEFUN IS-MALE (PERSON)
    (IF (NOT (MEMBER PERSON *MALES*))
        (SETQ *MALES* (CONS PERSON *MALES*)))
    'T)

;;; When it is stated that someone is a mother (father)
;;; then that is recorded and we also know the person
;;; is female (male).

(DEFUN IS-MOTHER-OF (MOTHER CHILD)
    (SETQ *MOTHERS*
          (CONS (CONS CHILD MOTHER) *MOTHERS*))
    (IS-FEMALE MOTHER)
    'T)

(DEFUN IS-FATHER-OF (FATHER CHILD)
    (SETQ *FATHERS*
          (CONS (CONS CHILD FATHER) *FATHERS*))
    (IS-MALE FATHER)
    'T)

;;; If a parent is declared then an entry can only be made in
;;; *MOTHERS* or *FATHERS* if the sex of the parent is already
;;; known?

(DEFUN IS-PARENT-OF (PARENT CHILD)
    (COND ((MEMBER PARENT *MALES*)
           (IS-FATHER-OF PARENT CHILD))
          ((MEMBER PARENT *FEMALES*)
           (IS-MOTHER-OF PARENT CHILD))
          (T 'NIL)))

;;; A query function to see if the sex of a person
;;; is known.
```

```
(DEFUN SEX-OF? (PARENT)
    (COND ((MEMBER PARENT *MALES*)
           'MALE)
          ((MEMBER PARENT *FEMALES*)
           'FEMALE)
          (T 'UNKNOWN)))

;;; Now we deal with grandmothers.

;;; Each person has a list of grandmothers associated.

(DEFVAR *GRANDMOTHERS* 'NIL)

;;; If we know two grandmothers of a person then we save
;;; them in the association list. If less than two
;;; granmothers are known, we should always recompute
;;; because additional facts might have been added.

(DEFUN GRANDMOTHERS-OF? (PERSON)
    (LET ((LOOKUP (CDR (ASSOC PERSON *GRANDMOTHERS*))))
        (IF (NULL LOOKUP)
            (LET ((POTENTIAL (COMPUTE-GRANDMOTHERS PERSON)))
                (IF (EQL 2 (LENGTH POTENTIAL))
                    (SETQ *GRANDMOTHERS*
                          (CONS (CONS PERSON POTENTIAL)
                                *GRANDMOTHERS*)))
                POTENTIAL)
            LOOKUP)))

;;; A grandmother is either a mother's mother or a
;;; father's mother.

(DEFUN COMPUTE-GRANDMOTHERS (PERSON)
    (NCONC (COMPUTE-GRANDMOTHER-THRU-PARENT PERSON *MOTHERS*)
           (COMPUTE-GRANDMOTHER-THRU-PARENT PERSON *FATHERS*)))

;;; Always returns a list of grandmothers, either 0 or 1 long.

(DEFUN COMPUTE-GRANDMOTHER-THRU-PARENT (PERSON RELATION)
    (LET ((PARENT-ENTRY (ASSOC PERSON RELATION)))
        (IF (NULL PARENT-ENTRY)
            'NIL
            (LET ((GM-ENTRY (ASSOC (CDR PARENT-ENTRY)
                                   *MOTHERS*)))
                (IF (NULL GM-ENTRY)
                    'NIL
                    (LIST (CDR GM-ENTRY))))))))
```

SOLUTIONS TO CHAPTER 5

PROBLEMS

P5.1

```
;;; A simplifier for expression involving operators +, * and
;;; POWER. The first function dispatches on operator, and for
;;; atomic terms simply returns them directly.

(DEFUN SIMPLIFY (EXP)
    (IF (CONSP EXP)
        (LET ((OP (CAR EXP)))
            (COND ((OR (EQ OP '+)
                       (EQ OP '*))
                   (SIMPLIFY-SUM-OR-PROD OP (CDR EXP)))
                  ((EQ OP 'POWER)
                   (SIMPLIFY-EXPONENT (CADR EXP) (CADDR EXP)))
                  ;; later we could make this an error. for
                  ;; now assume the expression is simplified.
                  (T EXP)))
        ;; atom terms are already simplified.
        EXP))

;;; OP must be one of + or *.
;;; ARGS is a list of terms to which OP is to be
;;; symbolically applied.
;;; There are four possibilities for the value of SIMPARG:
;;;  1. a numeric constant.
;;;  2. a single variable or a non-OP expression
;;;  3. an OP expression with no numeric terms.
;;;  4. an OP expression with a numeric term first.

(DEFUN SIMPLIFY-SUM-OR-PROD (OP ARGS)
  (LET* ((IDENTITY (COND ((EQ OP '+) 0)
                         ((EQ OP '*) 1)
                         ;; should catch errors here when
                         ;; we know how.
                         ))
         (CONSTANT IDENTITY) ; SETQed in the DO body
         (OTHERS 'NIL))      ; SETQed in the DO body
        (DO ((ARGLIST ARGS (CDR ARGLIST)))
            ((NULL ARGLIST)
             (COND ((NULL OTHERS)
                    CONSTANT)
                   ;; can drop an identity constant
```

```
                              ((ZEROP (- IDENTITY CONSTANT))
                               (IF (NULL (CDR OTHERS))
                                   (CAR OTHERS)
                                   (CONS OP OTHERS)))
                              ;; zero is a special case for *
                              ((AND (ZEROP CONSTANT)
                                    (EQ OP '*))
                               0)
                              (T (LIST* OP CONSTANT OTHERS)))))

                  ;; body of the DO
                  (LET ((SIMPARG (SIMPLIFY (CAR ARGLIST))))
                      (COND ((NUMBERP SIMPARG) ;case 1 above
                             (SETQ CONSTANT
                                  (COND ((EQ OP '+)
                                         (+ CONSTANT SIMPARG))
                                        ((EQ OP '*)
                                         (* CONSTANT SIMPARG))
                                        ;; signal an error here
                                        ;; when we know how.
                                        )))
                            ((AND (CONSP SIMPARG)
                                  (EQ OP (CAR SIMPARG)))
                             (LET ((FST (CADR SIMPARG)))
                                 (COND
                                   ((NUMBERP FST) ;case 4
                                    (SETQ CONSTANT
                                         (COND ((EQ OP '+)
                                                (+ CONSTANT
                                                   FST))
                                               ((EQ OP '*)
                                                (* CONSTANT
                                                   FST))))
                                    (SETQ OTHERS
                                         (APPEND (CDDR SIMPARG)
                                                 OTHERS)))
                                   (T (SETQ OTHERS ;case 3
                                            (APPEND (CDR SIMPARG)
                                                    OTHERS))))))
                            ;; case 2
                            (T (SETQ OTHERS
                                    (CONS SIMPARG OTHERS)))))))))

;;; This function takes a base and an exponent and simplifies
;;; them into a single exponent expression.
;;;
```

```
;;; Checks for a number of special cases after the base and
;;; exponent have both been simplified:
;;;   1. zero exponent
;;;   2. exponent of 1
;;;   3. base of 1
;;;   4. zero base and non-zero numeric exponent
;;;
;;; The idiom (AND (NUMBERP x) (ZEROP (- x 1))) is used to
;;; test for one, as it avoids the type problems of (EQL 1 x)
;;; or (EQL 1.0 x).

(DEFUN SIMPLIFY-EXPONENT (BASE EXPONENT)
    (LET ((SIMPBASE (SIMPLIFY BASE))
          (SIMPEXPONENT (SIMPLIFY EXPONENT)))
        (COND ((AND (NUMBERP SIMPEXPONENT)
                    (ZEROP SIMPEXPONENT))
               1)
              ((AND (NUMBERP SIMPEXPONENT)
                    (ZEROP (- SIMPEXPONENT 1)))
               SIMPBASE)
              ((AND (NUMDERP SIMPBASE)
                    (ZEROP (- SIMPBASE 1)))
               1)
              ((AND (NUMBERP SIMPBASE)
                    (ZEROP SIMPBASE)
                    (NUMBERP SIMPEXPONENT)) ;can't be zero
               0)
              (T (LIST 'POWER SIMPBASE SIMPEXPONENT)))))
```

P5.2

```
;;; Differentiator for sums, products and exponentials.
;;; Exponentials are assumed to be independent of the
;;; variable being differentiated with respect to.

(DEFUN DERIV (EXP VAR)
    (IF (ATOM EXP)
        (IF (EQ EXP VAR) 1 0)
        (LET ((OP (CAR EXP))
              (FIRSTARG (CADR EXP)))
            (LET ((SECONDARG (IF (NULL (CDDDR EXP))
                                 (CADDR EXP)
                                 (CONS OP (CDDR EXP)))))
                (COND ((EQ OP '+)
                       ;; (f+g)' = f' + g'
                       (LIST '+
                             (DERIV FIRSTARG VAR)
```

```
                          (DERIV SECONDARG VAR)))
                  ((EQ OP '*)
                  ;; (f*g)' = (f*g')+(f'*g)
                  (LIST '+
                        (LIST '*
                              FIRSTARG
                              (DERIV SECONDARG VAR))
                        (LIST '*
                              (DERIV FIRSTARG VAR)
                              SECONDARG)))
                  ((EQ OP 'POWER)
                  ;; (f↑g)' = g*(f↑(g-1))*f'

                  (LIST '*
                        SECONDARG
                        (LIST 'POWER
                              FIRSTARG
                              (LIST '+ SECONDARG -1))
                        (DERIV FIRSTARG VAR)))
                  ;; should signal an error here.
                  )))))
```

P5.3

```
;;; A differentiator with simplification.
;;; Simplifies both input and ouptut.

(DEFUN DIFF (EXP VAR)
     (SIMPLIFY (DERIV (SIMPLIFY EXP) VAR)))
```

P5.4 A few of the functions needed by PARSE follow. The rest are very similar in control structure, but vary according to the grammatical structures they are parsing. The global variables *WORDS* and *PLURALS* declared in the problem statement are assumed here.

```
;;; PARSE returns NIL if it can't parse the sentence, and a
;;; parse structure otherwise. It first tries to parse the
;;; sentence as a query, and if that doesn't work it tries it
;;; as an assertion.  Both PARSE-QUERY and PARSE-ASSERTION,
;;; and all parsers they in turn call, return NIL on failure,
;;; else a cons cell whose CAR is the parsed structure, and
;;; whose CDR is the as yet unparsed remainder of the
;;; sentence.
;;; If a query or assertion parse is successful, but there are
;;; unprocessed  words left then the parse is considered
;;; unsuccessful.
```

```
(DEFUN PARSE (SENTENCE)
    (LET ((QUESTION (PARSE-QUERY SENTENCE)))
        (COND ((NULL QUESTION)
                ;; didn't look like a query, how about
                ;; an assertion?
                (LET ((STATE (PARSE-ASSERTION SENTENCE)))
                    (COND ((NULL STATE)
                            'NIL)
                          ;; unparsed words remain, so fail.
                          ((NOT (NULL (CDR STATE)))
                            'NIL)
                          (T (CAR STATE)))))
              ;; unparsed words remain, so fail.
              ((NOT (NULL (CDR QUESTION)))
                'NIL)
              (T (CAR QUESTION)))))
```

```
;;; A query must look like: <q-word><verb><noun-phrase>.
;;; If they can't successively be found at the head of the
;;; sentence then fail.
```

```
(DEFUN PARSE-QUERY (SENTENCE)
    (LET ((Q-WORD (PARSE-Q-WORD SENTENCE)))
        (IF (NULL Q-WORD)
            'NIL
            (LET ((VERB (PARSE-VERB (CDR Q-WORD))))
                (IF (NULL VERB)
                    'NIL
                    (LET ((NOUN-PHRASE
                            (PARSE-NOUN-PHRASE (CDR VERB))))
                        (IF (NULL NOUN-PHRASE)
                            'NIL
                            ;; return the structure consed
                            ;; to what remains to be parsed.
                            (CONS (LIST 'QUERY
                                    (CAR NOUN-PHRASE))
                                  (CDR NOUN-PHRASE)))))))))
```

```
;;; Tries to find a noun at the head of a list of words. There
;;; are four possibilities for the first word.
;;;   1. It is a known noun.
;;;   2. It is a known plural of a known noun.
;;;   3. It is known to be another part of speech.
;;;   4. It is unknown and hence assumed to be a person's name.
;;;
;;; Like other parsers this function returns NIL on failure
```

```
;;; (case 3 above) or a cons of a structure and the remaining
;;; words to be parsed. There are two sorts of structures
;;; returned:
;;;   (NOUN <word>)   cases 1 and 2 (<word> is singular)
;;;   (NAME <word>)   case 4

(DEFUN PARSE-NOUN (WORD-STRING)
    (LET* ((WORD (CAR WORD-STRING))
           (PART (CDR (ASSOC WORD *WORDS*))))
        (COND ((NULL PART)
               (LET ((SINGULAR (CDR (ASSOC WORD
                                            *PLURALS*))))
                 ;; SINGULAR wil be NIL if the word
                 ;; wasn't a plural, so NOUN will not
                 ;; be found for it in *WORDS*.
                 (IF (EQ 'NOUN
                         (CDR (ASSOC SINGULAR
                                     *WORDS*)))
                     ;; case 2
                     (CONS (LIST 'NOUN SINGULAR)
                           (CDR WORD-STRING))
                     ;; case 4
                     (CONS (LIST 'NAME WORD)
                           (CDR WORD-STRING)))))
              ;; case 1
              ((EQ PART 'NOUN)
               (CONS (LIST 'NOUN WORD)
                     (CDR WORD-STRING)))
              ;; case 3
              (T 'NIL))))
```

P5.5 Function PROCESS needs to dispatch on the type of sentence structure.
The following function handles queries. It makes use of the function FIND-
RELATIVE defined in the problem description; function PROCESS-ASSERTION can
use the same function.

```
;;; Process a query which looks like (QUERY <noun-phrase>)
;;; <noun-phrase> can be either
;;;   1. (NOUN <noun>) which is handled for <noun>=MALE|FEMALE
;;;   2. (NAME <name>) which is not handled
;;;   3. (NOUN-PHRASE <noun> <name>) where <noun> is a
;;;        relationship.

(DEFUN PROCESS-QUERY (QUERY)
    (LET* ((NOUN-PHRASE (CADR QUERY))
           (NP-TYPE (CAR NOUN-PHRASE)))
        (COND ((EQ NP-TYPE 'NOUN)
```

```
;; case 1
(LET ((NOUN (CADR NOUN-PHRASE)))
     (COND ((EQ NOUN 'MALE)
            *MALES*)
           ((EQ NOUN 'FEMALE)
            *FEMALES*)
           (T 'SEMANTICALLY-CONFUSED)))))
((EQ NP-TYPE 'NOUN-PHRASE)
 ;; case 3
 (LET ((RELATIVE (FIND-RELATIVE
                   (CADR NOUN-PHRASE)
                   (CADDR NOUN-PHRASE))))
      (IF (NULL RELATIVE)
          'UNABLE-TO-ANSWER
          RELATIVE)))
;; case 2
(T 'SEMANTICALLY-CONFUSED)))))
```

P5.6

```
;;; This is the top level function called by the user, with
;;; a sentence, represented as a list, as an argument.
```

```
(DEFUN HEAR (SENTENCE)
    (LET ((PARSED (PARSE SENTENCE)))
         (COND ((NULL PARSED)
                'UNPARSABLE)
               ((OR (EQ 'QUERY (CAR PARSED))
                    (EQ 'ASSERTION (CAR PARSED)))
                (PROCESS PARSED))
               (T 'PARSER-ERROR))))
```

SOLUTIONS TO CHAPTER 6

EXERCISES

E6.1.1

```
(FORMAT T "~%Length: ~S~%Width:  ~S~%Height: ~S~%" L W H)
```

E6.1.2
a. The word is "bazola".
b. The symbol is 'BAZOLA'.
c. Using ~S makes a string print like: "this".
d. Using ~A will be different.

E6.3.1
a. 13
b. (34 ((B C # E F) A) G H ...)
c. ((A B C D ...) (F G H I ...) (K L M N) (O P Q R ...) ...)
d. (((A B) (C #) (F # I)) J K)

E6.3.2
a. "Hi there!"
b. Hi there!
c. HELLO
d. HELLO
e. (THIS IS A "string")
f. (THIS IS A string)

E6.4.1

```
(FORMAT T "~%Length  Width   Height~%------  -----   ------")
(FORMAT T "~% ~S~9T~S~17T~S" L W H)
```

E6.4.2

```
(FORMAT T
        "~%Dear ~A. ~A,~%You may already be a winner!"
        (IF (EQ SEX 'F)
            "Ms"
            "Mr")
        NAME)
```

PROBLEMS

P6.1

```
;;; Our BUFFER data structure consists of two cons
;;; cells and three items in the form:
;;;   (<stream> . (<flag> . <item>))
;;; where
;;;   <stream> is the input stream,
;;;   <flag>   is T if there is some thing already
;;;            read from the stream not yet gotten
;;;            with READ-NEXT, and NIL otherwise,
;;;   <item>   is an already read thing from the
;;;            stream--it is the buffered item.
;;; The functions of <flag> and <item> could not be
;;; combined into a single entry, because it is
;;; possible that NIL is an item in a file.
```

```
(DEFUN MAKE-BUFFER (STREAM)
    (CONS STREAM
          (CONS 'NIL 'NIL)))

(DEFUN PEEK-NEXT (BUFFER)
    (LET ((STREAM (CAR BUFFER))
          (FLAG (CADR BUFFER))
          (ITEM (CDDR BUFFER)))
         (IF (NULL FLAG)
             (LET ((NXT (READ STREAM NIL STREAM)))
                  (RPLACD (CDR BUFFER) NXT)
                  (RPLACA (CDR BUFFER) 'T)
                  NXT)
             ITEM)))

(DEFUN GET-NEXT (BUFFER)
    (LET ((NXT (PEEK-NEXT BUFFER)))
         (RPLACA (CDR BUFFER) 'NIL)
         NXT))
```

P6.2

```
;;; A simplifier for expression involving operators +, * and
;;; POWER. The first function dispatches on operator, and for
;;; atomic terms simply returns them directly.

(DEFUN SIMPLIFY (EXP)
    (IF (CONSP EXP)
        (LET ((OP (CAR EXP)))
             (COND ((OR (EQ OP '+)
                        (EQ OP '*))
                    (SIMPLIFY-SUM-OR-PROD OP (CDR EXP)))
                   ((EQ OP 'POWER)
                    (SIMPLIFY-EXPONENT (CADR EXP) (CADDR EXP)))
                   (T (ERROR "Unexpected operator '~S'." OP))))
        ;; atom terms are already simplified.
        EXP))
```

P6.3

```
;;; The first function manages the file, prints the
;;; output headers, then loops, calling PROCESS-PERSON,
;;; until the file is empty.

(DEFUN PROCESS (FILE)
    (LET ((STREAM (OPEN FILE :DIRECTION :INPUT)))
         (LET ((BUFFER (MAKE-BUFFER STREAM))
              (FORMAT T "~%Student    Score")
```

```
                (FORMAT T "~%-------    -----")
                (DO ()
                    ((EQ STREAM (PEEK-NEXT BUFFER)))
                    (PROCESS-PERSON BUFFER))
                (FORMAT T "~%~%")
                (CLOSE STREAM))))
```

```
;;; This function expects a buffered stream which is headed
;;; by a symbol, followed by some numbers and then either
;;; an end of file or data of the same form again.
;;; The symbol is taken as a person's name then the numbers
;;; are collected in reverse order into NUMS. The first
;;; number in the resulting list, must then be the score of
;;; on the final, between 0 and 30, and the rest of the
;;; numbers should be scores on up to seven homeworks, all
;;; between zero and 10. For simple errors, like incorrect
;;; numbers, the function is able to recover so that the
;;; rest of the file can be processed.
```

```
(DEFUN PROCESS-PERSON (BUFFER)
  (LET ((PERSON (GET-NEXT BUFFER)))
       (IF (NOT (SYMBOLP PERSON))
           (ERROR "File too weird at ~S" PERSON)
           (DO ((NUMS NIL (CONS (GET-NEXT BUFFER) NUMS)))
               ((NOT (NUMBERP (PEEK-NEXT BUFFER)))
                (LET ((SUM-HOMEWORKS
                          (DO ((HOMEWORKS (CDR NUMS)
                                          (CDR HOMEWORKS))
                               (SUM 0 (+ SUM (CAR HOMEWORKS))))
                              ((NULL HOMEWORKS)
                               SUM)
                              (LET ((HOMEW (CAR HOMEWORKS)))
                                   (IF (NOT (AND (NUMBERP HOMEW))
                                                 (< HOMEW 11)
                                                 (> HOMEW -1)))
                                       (RETURN NIL))))))
                     (IF (AND (NOT (NULL SUM-HOMEWORKS))
                              (< (LENGTH NUMS) 9)
                              (< (CAR NUMS) 31)
                              (> (CAR NUMS) -1))
                         (FORMAT T
                                 "~%~S~11T~S"
                                 PERSON
                                 (+ (CAR NUMS) SUM-HOMEWORKS))
                         (FORMAT T "~%~S~11Txx" PERSON)))))))))
```

P6.4

```
;;; Function START-DRIBBLE opens a file and then calls
;;; the function READ-EVAL-PRINT to continually read
;;; user input, evaluate it and print the result.

(DEFUN START-DRIBBLE (FILENAME)
    (LET ((OUT (OPEN FILENAME :DIRECTION :OUTPUT)))
         (READ-EVAL-PRINT OUT)
         (CLOSE OUT)
         'T))

;;; OUT is the output stream. This function loops, getting
;;; input from the user via function READ-INPUT, which
;;; is responsible for echoing it to the dribble file,
;;; and evaluating it and printing the result both on the
;;; the user terminal and into the output file.
;;; If the user wants to evaluate the s-expression
;;; (END-DRIBBLE) then this function intercepts it and
;;; exits, effectively ending the dribbling process.

(DEFUN READ-EVAL-PRINT (OUT)
    (DO ((INPUT (READ-INPUT OUT) (READ-INPUT OUT)))
        ((EQUAL INPUT '(END-DRIBBLE)))
        (LET ((VAL (EVAL INPUT)))
             (FORMAT T "~S~%" VAL)
             (FORMAT OUT "~S~%" VAL))))

;;; Prompts the user with a new prompt and reads what's
;;; typed by the user. The prompt and user input are
;;; also sent to the dribble file. It is not necessary
;;; to send the user input to the terminal as the user
;;; has already typed it there.

(DEFUN READ-INPUT (OUT)
    (FORMAT T "~%dribbler> ")
    (FORMAT OUT "~%dribbler> ")
    (LET ((INPUT (READ)))
         (FORMAT OUT "~S~%" INPUT)
         INPUT))
```

SOLUTIONS TO CHAPTER 7

EXERCISES

E7.1.1

```
(DEFUN PRINT (OBJECT &OPTIONAL (STREAM 'T))
   ...)
```

E7.1.2

```
A = FRED
B = (IS WELL)
C = (SUE KNOWS)
D = (EVERYTHING)
E = (SUE KNOWS EVERYTHING)
F = NIL
```

E7.2.1

```
(DEFUN ERROR (STRING &REST ARGLIST)
   ...)
```

E7.2.2

a. A = A
   B = B
   C = (C)
b. A = 1
   B = 2
   C = NIL
c. A = (A B)
   B = (C D)
   C = ((E F) (G H))
d. A = (A B)
   B = (C D)
   C = ((E F) (G H) (I J))

E7.4.1

a. (A B C D)
b. (C D)
c. ((A B) (C D) (E F) G H)
d. (A . B)

E7.5.1

a. (A B C D E)
b. (C D)
c. ((A (B)) (C (D)) (E (F)) G H)
d. (A . B)

E7.6.1   a. T, b. NIL, c. T, d. NIL, e. T, f. T, g. T, h. NIL, i. NIL

E7.6.2

a. (+ 1 2 3)
   1
   2
   3

b. (LIST (CONS (QUOTE A) (QUOTE B))
          (QUOTE C)
          (CAR (QUOTE (D E F))))
   (CONS (QUOTE A) (QUOTE B))
   (QUOTE A)
   (QUOTE B)
   (QUOTE C)
   (CAR (QUOTE (D E F)))
   (QUOTE (D E F))
c. (CONS (+ 2 3) (OUR-EVAL (QUOTE (QUOTE (4 U)))))
   (+ 2 3)
   2
   3
   (OUR-EVAL (QUOTE (QUOTE (4 U)))
   (QUOTE (QUOTE (4 U)))
   (QUOTE (4 U))

E7.7.1
a. (DO-BE DO-BE . DO)
b. (DO-BE DO-BE . DO)
c. (DO-BE DO DE DO)
d. 5.0
e. (X Y)

E7.8.1
a. ((A W) (B X) (C Y) (D Z))
b. (((A B C D) (W X Y Z))
   ((B C D) (X Y Z))
   ((C D) (Y Z))
   ((D) (Z)))
c. (A B C D)
d. (A B C D)
e. (A W B X C Y D Z)
f. ((A B C D) (W X Y Z) (B C D) (X Y Z) (C D) (Y Z) (D) (Z))

E7.8.2 a. MAPCAN, b. MAPC, c. MAPCAR, d. MAPCAN

PROBLEMS

P7.1

```
(DEFUN INFIX-EVAL (EXP)
    (IF (ATOM EXP)
        ;; assume it was a number if its and atom.
        EXP
        ;; for a list assume its (<exp> <op> <exp>).
```

```
            (FUNCALL (SYMBOL-FUNCTION (CADR EXP))
                     (INFIX-EVAL (CAR EXP))
                     (INFIX-EVAL (CADDR EXP)))))
```

P7.2

```
   (DEFUN INFIX-EVAL (EXP)
      (COND ((NUMBERP EXP)
             EXP)
            ((ATOM EXP)
             (ERROR "Non-numeric atom found: ~S" EXP))
            ((= 3 (LENGTH EXP))
             (LET ((OP (CADR EXP)))
                  (COND ((NOT (SYMBOLP OP))
                         (ERROR "Non-symbol operator: ~S" OP))
                        ((NOT (FBOUNDP OP))
                         (ERROR "Undefined operator: ~S" OP))
                        ((NOT (FUNCTIONP (SYMBOL-FUNCTION OP)))
                         (ERROR "Improperly defined operator: ~S"
                                OP))
                        (T (FUNCALL (SYMBOL-FUNCTION OP)
                                    (INFIX-EVAL (CAR EXP))
                                    (INFIX-EVAL (CADDR EXP)))))))
            (T (ERROR "Improperly formed expression: ~S"
                      EXP))))
```

P7.3

```
   (DEFUN MY-ERROR (CONTROL &REST PARAMETERS)
      (FORMAT 'T "~%~%>>ERROR: ")
      (APPLY #'FORMAT 'T CONTROL PARAMETERS)
      (PRIMITIVE-ERROR))
```

P7.4 The following might be a reasonable structure to parse the example program into:

```
   (PROGRAM
      ((L LISTP UNBOUND-VAR) (I FIXNUMP UNBOUND-VAR))
      (BLOCK
      (FUN-CALL PRINT-LIST ((CONSTANT "List? ")))
      (ASSIGN (L LISTP UNBOUND-VAR) (FUN-CALL READ NIL))
      (ASSIGN (I FIXNUMP UNBOUND-VAR) (CONSTANT O))
      (WHILE (FUN-CALL NEQL
                ((VAR-REF (L LISTP UNBOUND-VAR)) (CONSTANT NIL)))
             (BLOCK (ASSIGN (I FIXNUMP UNBOUND-VAR)
                    (FUN-CALL PLUS
                       ((VAR-REF (I FIXNUMP UNBOUND-VAR))
                        (CONSTANT 1))))
```

```
                     (ASSIGN (L LISTP UNBOUND-VAR)
                             (FUN-CALL CDR
                               ((VAR-REF (L LISTP
                                          UNBOUND-VAR)))))))
             (FUN-CALL PRINT-LIST
                       ((CONSTANT "Length is: ")
                        (VAR-REF (I FIXNUMP UNBOUND-VAR))))))
```

where there is one instance of each structure (L LISTP BOUND-VAR) and (I FIXNUMP UNBOUND-VAR). These are shared many times throughout the the parsed program. The idea is that the third item in each list will contain the current value of the variable when the foregoing program structure is interpreted. Below is the main function need to interpret expressions in the above structure. It could be called with the third item of the list—that is, the BLOCK statement—to run the entire program.

```
(DEFUN PROG-EVAL (EXP)
  (LET ((ID (CAR EXP)))
       (COND
         ((EQ ID 'BLOCK)
          ;; in a block just evaluate each statement
          (DO ((STATEMENTS (CDR EXP) (CDR STATEMENTS)))
              ((NULL STATEMENTS)
               'T)
              (PROG-EVAL (CAR STATEMENTS))))
         ((EQ ID 'ASSIGN)
          (LET* ((VAL (PROG-EVAL (CADDR EXP)))
                 (VAR (CADR EXP)))
                ;; check type of assigned value
                (IF (NOT (FUNCALL
                            (SYMBOL-FUNCTION (CADR VAR))
                            VAL))
                    (ERROR "Illegal value ~S for variable ~S"
                           VAL
                           (CAR VAR))
                    ;; it's ok so stash is as third element
                    (RPLACA (CDDR VAR) VAL))))
         ((EQ ID 'CONSTANT)
          (CADR EXP))
         ;; a variable's value is in the third element
         ((EQ ID 'VAR-REF)
          (CADDR (CADR EXP)))
         ;; for a function call evaluate all the
         ;; arguments then apply the right lisp function
```

```
          ((EQ ID 'FUN-CALL)
           (APPLY (SYMBOL-FUNCTION (CADR EXP))
                  (MAPCAR #'PROG-EVAL (CADDR EXP))))
          ;; for while iterate until the test fails
          ((EQ ID 'WHILE)
           (LET ((TST (CADR EXP))
                 (BODY (CADDR EXP)))
               (DO ()
                   ((NOT (PROG-EVAL TST)))
                   (PROG-EVAL BODY))))
          (T (ERROR "Unknown expression at runtime! ~S"
                    EXP)))))
```

SOLUTIONS TO CHAPTER 9

EXERCISES

E9.3.1
a. `(CAR (CDR X))`
b. `(CAR (CDR (BROTHER-OF X)))`
c. `(CAR (CDR '(FRED JOE MARY)))`

E9.3.2

```
   (DEFMACRO PERSON-NAME (PERSON)
       (LIST 'CAR PERSON))

   (DEFMACRO PERSON-PARENTS (PERSON)
       (LIST 'CADR PERSON))

   (DEFMACRO PERSON-MOTHER (PERSON)
       (LIST 'CAADR PERSON))

   (DEFMACRO PERSON-FATHER (PERSON)
       (LIST 'CADADR PERSON))

   (DEFMACRO PERSON-AGE (PERSON)
       (LIST 'CADDR PERSON))
```

E9.4.1

```
   (DEFMACRO OUR-IF (TEST THEN &OPTIONAL (ELSE 'NIL))
       (LIST 'COND
             (LIST TEST THEN)
             (LIST 'T ELSE)))
```

E9.4.2

```
(DEFMACRO PRINT-BIND (BINDER BODY)
    (LET ((VAR (CAR BINDER))
          (VALUE (CADR BINDER)))
        (LIST 'LET
              (LIST (LIST VAR VALUE))
              (LIST 'FORMAT
                    'T
                    '"~%Variable: ~S bound to: ~S."
                    VAR
                    VALUE)
              BODY)))
```

E9.5.1
a. ((A LIST OF SYMBOLS) ONE-SYMBOL (ANOTHER LIST))
b. (THIS IS (A LIST OF SYMBOLS))
c. (THIS IS A LIST OF SYMBOLS)
d. (THIS IS ONE-SYMBOL)
e. (A LIST OF SYMBOLS AND (ANOTHER LIST))
f. (AND THIS IS ANOTHER LIST)

E9.5.2
a. (,@A ,C)
b. (,A (,C))
c. (,@B ,@A ,C)
d. ((,B ,@A) ,C)

E9.6.1

```
(DEFMACRO PERSON-NAME (PERSON)
    '(CAR ,PERSON))

(DEFMACRO PERSON-PARENTS (PERSON)
    '(CADR ,PERSON))

(DEFMACRO PERSON-MOTHER (PERSON)
    '(CAADR ,PERSON))

(DEFMACRO PERSON-FATHER (PERSON)
    '(CADADR ,PERSON))

(DEFMACRO PERSON-AGE (PERSON)
    '(CADDR ,PERSON))
```

PROBLEMS

P9.1

```
;;; Global variable *RECDEFS* is an association
;;; list of known record classes and their fields.

(DEFVAR *RECDEFS* NIL)

(DEFMACRO DEFRECORD (CLASS FIELDS)
    (SETQ *RECDEFS*
          (CONS (CONS CLASS FIELDS)
                *RECDEFS*))
    '',CLASS)

(DEFMACRO ACCESS (CLASS FIELD INSTANCE)
    (LET ((FIELDS (CDR (ASSOC CLASS *RECDEFS*))))
        (IF (NULL FIELDS)
            (ERROR "Unknown record class: ~S" CLASS)
            (DO ((FIELDLIST FIELDS (CDR FIELDLIST))
                 (ACCESSFORM
                     INSTANCE
                     '(CDR ,ACCESSFORM)))
                ((NULL FIELDLIST)
                 (ERROR "Unknown field: ~S in class: ~S"
                        FIELD
                        CLASS))
                (IF (EQ FIELD (CAR FIELDLIST))
                    (RETURN '(CAR ,ACCESSFORM)))))))
```

P9.2

```
(DEFMACRO DOLIST (STEPPER &REST BODYFORMS)
    (LET ((VAR (CAR STEPPER))
          (LST (CADR STEPPER))
          (RETURN-VALUE (CADDR STEPPER))
          (STEPVAR (GENSYM)))
        '(DO ((,STEPVAR ,LST (CDR ,STEPVAR)))
             ((NULL ,STEPVAR)
              ;; because of the way this was extracted it
              ;; will default to NIL.
              ,RETURN-VALUE)
             (LET ((,VAR (CAR ,STEPVAR)))
                 ,@BODYFORMS))))
```

P9.3

```
(DEFMACRO DOTIMES (STEPPER &REST BODYFORMS)
    (LET ((VAR (CAR STEPPER))
          (COUNT (CADR STEPPER))
          (RETURN-VALUE (CADDR STEPPER))
          (MAXCOUNT (GENSYM)))
      '(LET ((,MAXCOUNT ,COUNT))
            (DO ((,VAR 0 (+ 1 ,VAR)))
                ((EQL ,VAR ,MAXCOUNT)
                 ;; because of the way this was extracted
                 ;; it will default to NIL.
                 ,RETURN-VALUE)
              ,@BODYFORMS))))
```

SOLUTIONS TO CHAPTER 11

EXERCISES

E11.1.1
a. (A B C)
b. (B B C)
c. (B B . D)
d. (B B C C)
c. (B)
f. ((C C))

E11.1.2
a. (SETF X NIL)
b. (SETF (CDDDR X) '(D))
c. (SETF (CAADR X) 'D)
d. (SETF (CDDADR X) '(E))

E11.2.1   a. 25, b. 10, c. 30

E11.2.2

```
(DEFSTRUCT VECTOR (X 0.0) (Y 0.0) (Z 0.0))
```

E11.3.1   a. 23, b. 12, c. 7, d. 24, e. 27, f. 30, g. 11, h. 3

E11.4.1
a. ZERO
b. (3 6)
c. (7 7)

d. 3
e. 7

E11.4.2 For no value of X does it matter, because the result of (* 4 X) will be returned as the value of T3, but that will be ignored by function T2 because there is an additional clause in the CATCH with tag ZTESCH that becomes its value and hence the value of function T2.

E11.5.1

```
eval> (F1 5)     ; a.

15
EXITING
PROTECTING
23 7


eval> (F1 3)     ; b.

PROTECTING THROWN

eval> (F1 23)    ; c.

69
EXITING
PROTECTING
23 7
```

E11.6.1
a. (IT WAS ZERO)
b. (3 9 27 81)
c. (-5 5)

E11.6.2

```
6
```

PROBLEMS

P11.1

```
;;; In general the generated code needs to refer to
;;; the VALUE twice.  Once to change the data
;;; structure and once to return it as the result.
;;; For expressions which are numbers or variables it
;;; costs nothing to evaluate them twice.  For more
;;; complex expression it may be costly to evaluate
```

```
;;; them twice, and in particular it will be incorrect
;;; if they have side effects such as the message
;;; printed by the ADD-ONE function.  Thus an extra
;;; variable is introduced to bind the result of VALUE
;;; when it is not an atom.

(DEFMACRO MY-SETF (PLACE VALUE)
    (LET ((EXPLACE (MACROEXPAND PLACE)))
        (COND ((SYMBOLP EXPLACE)
                '(SETQ ,EXPLACE ,VALUE))
              ((AND (CONSP EXPLACE)
                    (OR (EQ 'CAR (CAR EXPLACE))
                        (EQ 'CDR (CAR EXPLACE))))
               (MY-SETF-RPL (CAR EXPLACE)
                            (CADR EXPLACE)
                            VALUE))
              (T (ERROR "Can't handle place: ~S"
                        PLACE)))))

(DEFUN MY-SETF-RPL (ACCESS APLACE VALUE)
    (LET ((FUN (IF (EQ ACCESS 'CAR) 'RPLACA 'RPLACD)))
        (IF (ATOM VALUE)
            '(PROGN (,FUN ,APLACE ,VALUE)
                    ,VALUE)
            (LET ((VAR (GENSYM)))
                '(LET ((,VAR ,VALUE))
                     (,FUN ,APLACE ,VAR)
                     ,VAR)))))
```

P11.2

```
(DEFUN MATCH (PATTERN DATA)
    (CATCH 'NOMATCH
        (MATCH-AUX PATTERN DATA NIL)))

(DEFUN MATCH-AUX (PATTERN DATA ALIST)
    (COND ((ATOM PATTERN)
           (IF (EQ PATTERN DATA)
               ALIST
               (THROW 'NOMATCH 'LOSER)))
          ((EQ (CAR PATTERN) '?)
           (LET* ((VAR (CADR PATTERN))
                  (MATCH (ASSOC VAR ALIST)))
               (COND ((NULL MATCH)
                      (CONS (CONS VAR DATA) ALIST))
                     ((EQUAL (CDR MATCH) DATA)
                      ALIST)
                     (T (THROW 'NOMATCH 'LOSER)))))
```

```
                      ((ATOM DATA)
                       (THROW 'NOMATCH 'LOSER))
                      (T (MATCH-AUX (CDR PATTERN)
                                    (CDR DATA)
                                    (MATCH-AUX (CAR PATTERN)
                                               (CAR DATA)
                                               ALIST)))))
```

P11.3

```
    (DEFMACRO DOLIST (&REST BODY)
      (LET ((ALIST
              (MATCH
                '(((? VAR) (? LIST) . (? RETURN)) . (? BODY))
                BODY)))
           (IF (EQ ALIST 'LOSER)
               (ERROR "Malformed DOLIST form: ~S"
                      (CONS DOLIST BODY))
               (SUBLIS (CONS (CONS 'TEMP (GENSYM)) ALIST)
                       '(DO ((TEMP LIST (CDR TEMP)))
                            ((NULL TEMP)
                             . RETURN)
                            (LET ((VAR (CAR TEMP)))
                              . BODY))))))
```

P11.4

```
    (DEFUN MATCH (PATTERN DATA)
      (LET ((RESULT (CATCH 'NOMATCH
                           (MATCH-AUX PATTERN DATA NIL))))
           (IF (EQ RESULT 'LOSER)
               (VALUES NIL NIL)
               (VALUES RESULT 'T))))
```

APPENDIX
3

BIBLIOGRAPHY

Allen, John. *Anatomy of Lisp*. New York: McGraw-Hill, 1978.

McCarthy, John; Abrahams, P.W.; Edwards, D. J.; Hart, T. P.; and M. I. Levin. *Lisp 1.5 Programmer's Manual* 2nd ed. Cambridge, Mass.: MIT Press, 1965.

Moon, David. *Maclisp Reference Manual, Version 0*. Technical report, MIT Laboratory for Computer Science, 1978.

Moon, David, and Daniel Weinreb. *Lisp Machine Manual*. Technical report, MIT Artificial Intelligence Laboratory, 1981.

Pitman, Kent. *The Revised Maclisp Manual*. Technical report, MIT Laboratory for Computer Science, 1983.

Steele, Guy Lewis Jr. *Common Lisp: The Language*. Burlington, Mass.: Digital Press, 1984.

Teitelman, Warren. *Interlisp Reference Manual*. Technical report, Xerox Palo Alto Research Center, 1974.

INDEX